# More from Michael S. Heiser

*The Unseen Realm:*
*Recovering the Supernatural Worldview of the Bible*

*Supernatural:*
*What the Bible Teaches about the Unseen World—and Why It Matters*

*The Bible Unfiltered:*
*Approaching Scripture on Its Own Terms*

*I Dare You Not to Bore Me with the Bible*

*Reversing Hermon:*
*Enoch, the Watchers, & the Forgotten Mission of Jesus Christ*

*The Façade*

*The Portent*

# ANGELS

# ANGELS

WHAT THE BIBLE REALLY SAYS
ABOUT GOD'S HEAVENLY HOST

## MICHAEL S. HEISER

LEXHAM PRESS

*Angels: What the Bible Really Says about God's Heavenly Host*

Copyright 2018 Lexham Press

Lexham Press, 1313 Commercial St., Bellingham, WA 98225
LexhamPress.com

Print ISBN 9781683591047
Digital ISBN 9781683591054

Lexham Editorial: Douglas Mangum, Abigail Stocker
Cover Design: Brittany Schrock
Interior Design and Typesetting: Beth Shagene

# Contents

# Abbreviations

ABD      *Anchor Yale Bible Dictionary.* Edited by David Noel Freedman. 6 vols. New York: Doubleday, 1992

*Ant.*      Josephus, *Jewish Antiquities*

AYB      Anchor Yale Bible

*BAR*      *Biblical Archaeology Review*

BASOR      *Bulletin of the American Schools of Oriental Research*

BBR      *Bulletin for Biblical Research*

BCOT      Baker Commentary on the Old Testament

BECNT      Baker Exegetical Commentary on the New Testament

BNTC      Black's New Testament Commentaries

*BSac*      *Bibliotheca Sacra*

DDD      *Dictionary of Deities and Demons in the Bible.* Edited by Karel van der Toorn, Bob Becking, and Pieter W. van der Horst. Leiden: Brill, 1995. 2nd rev. ed. Grand Rapids: Eerdmans, 1999

DOTP      *Dictionary of the Old Testament: Pentateuch.* Edited by T. Desmond Alexander and David W. Baker. Downers Grove, IL: InterVarsity Press, 2003

DOTWPW      *Dictionary of the Old Testament: Wisdom, Poetry & Writings.* Edited by Tremper Longman III and Peter Enns. Downers Grove, IL: InterVarsity Press, 2008

DNTB      *Dictionary of New Testament Background.* Edited by Craig A. Evans and Stanley E. Porter. Downers Grove, IL: InterVarsity Press, 2000

| | |
|---|---|
| *DNWSI* | *Dictionary of the North-West Semitic Inscriptions.* Jacob Hoftijzer and Karel Jongeling. 2 vols. Leiden: Brill, 2003 |
| *DPL* | *Dictionary of Paul and His Letters.* Edited by Gerald F. Hawthorne and Ralph P. Martin. Downers Grove, IL: InterVarsity Press, 1993 |
| *DSD* | *Dead Sea Discoveries* |
| *DULAT* | *A Dictionary of the Ugaritic Language in the Alphabetic Tradition.* Gregorio Del Olmo Lete and Joaquín Sanmartín. 2 vols. Leiden: Brill, 2015 |
| *EHLL* | *Encyclopedia of Hebrew Language and Linguistics.* Edited by Geoffrey Khan. 4 vols. Leiden: Brill, 2013 |
| *ESV* | Holy Bible, English Standard Version |
| *GBH* | *A Grammar of Biblical Hebrew.* Paul Joüon and Takamitsu Muraoka. Rev. English ed. Roma: Pontificio istituto biblico, 2006 |
| *GKC* | *Gesenius' Hebrew Grammar.* Edited by Emil Kautzsch. Translated by Arthur E. Cowley. 2nd ed. Oxford: Clarendon, 1910 |
| *HALOT* | *The Hebrew and Aramaic Lexicon of the Old Testament.* Ludwig Koehler, Walter Baumgartner, and Johann J. Stamm. Translated and edited under the supervision of Mervyn E. J. Richardson. 5 vols. Leiden: Brill, 1994–2000 |
| *HUCA* | *Hebrew Union College Annual* |
| *HTR* | *Harvard Theological Review* |
| *ICC* | International Critical Commentary |
| *JBL* | *Journal of Biblical Literature* |
| *JESOT* | *Journal for the Evangelical Study of the Old Testament* |
| *JNES* | *Journal of Near Eastern Studies* |
| *JSOT* | *Journal for the Study of the Old Testament* |
| *JSP* | *Journal for the Study of the Pseudepigrapha* |
| *JTS* | *Journal of Theological Studies* |

| | |
|---|---|
| *KAI* | *Kanaanäische und aramäische Inschriften.* Herbert Donner and Wolfgang Röllig. 2nd ed. Wiesbaden: Harrassowitz, 1966–1969 |
| *KTU²* | *Die keilalphabetischen Texte aus Ugarit.* Edited by M. Dietrich, O. Loretz, and J. Sanmartín. Neukirchen-Vluyn, 1976. 2nd enlarged ed. of *KTU: The Cuneiform Alphabetic Texts from Ugarit, Ras Ibn Hani, and Other Places.* Edited by M. Dietrich, O. Loretz, and J. Sanmartín. Münster, 1995 (= CTU) |
| *LBD* | *The Lexham Bible Dictionary.* Edited by John D. Barry. Bellingham, WA: Lexham Press, 2016 |
| NAC | New American Commentary |
| NICOT | The New International Commentary on the Old Testament |
| *NIDNTTE* | *New International Dictionary of New Testament Theology and Exegesis.* Edited by Moisés Silva. 5 vols. Grand Rapids: Zondervan, 2014 |
| *NIDOTTE* | *New International Dictionary of Old Testament Theology and Exegesis.* Edited by Willem A. VanGemeren. 5 vols. Grand Rapids: Zondervan, 1997 |
| NIGTC | New International Greek Testament Commentary |
| *OTP* | *The Old Testament Pseudepigrapha.* Edited by James H. Charlesworth. 2 vols. New York: Doubleday, 1983, 1985 |
| *TLOT* | *Theological Lexicon of the Old Testament.* Edited by Ernst Jenni, with assistance from Claus Westermann. Translated by Mark E. Biddle. 3 vols. Peabody, MA: Hendrickson, 1997 |
| *TynBul* | *Tyndale Bulletin* |
| TNTC | Tyndale New Testament Commentaries |
| TOTC | Tyndale Old Testament Commentaries |
| *VT* | *Vetus Testamentum* |
| WBC | Word Biblical Commentary |
| *ZAW* | *Zeitschrift für die alttestamentliche Wissenschaft* |

# Introduction

THIS IS A BOOK ABOUT THE LOYAL MEMBERS OF GOD'S HEAVENLY HOST. Most Christians will refer to them as angels, but, as we'll learn, that's just one of many terms the Bible uses for supernatural beings who serve him.

To clarify, this is not a book about demons. While angels' failures are discussed here and there, fallen angels are nowhere the focus. In this book, I'm really only concerned with what the Bible says about the good guys.

What you'll read here isn't guided by Christian tradition, stories, speculations, or well-meaning myths about angels. Instead, our study is rooted in the biblical terminology for the members of God's heavenly host, informed by the wider context of the ancient Near Eastern world and close attention to the biblical text.

## WHY BOTHER?

But enough defending of our approach. We need to ask a more important question: Who cares? To be sure, popular interest in angels and angel stories is high, which is symptomatic of our culture's insatiable appetite for the supernatural. It seems every other movie or television show features a paranormal theme, alien superheroes, or some mischievous or malevolent deity. Bookstore shelves are well stocked with books about aliens, preternatural creatures, and, of course, angels and demons. That wouldn't be the case if they didn't sell, but sell they do.

Unfortunately, the content isn't very biblical, even when it tries. Hollywood does its best to mesmerize without informing, splattering CGI effects (and plenty of gore) over the screen as some unsuspecting human fights the forces of darkness in a reluctant-but-successful effort to save the world or win a heart.

Christian media contributes little that is innovative or even thoughtful in this arena. The Christian voice is usually divided between criticism of "demonic" media (a label that is occasionally accurate) and carefully mining Hollywood's creative output for Christian themes and images. That's a noble pursuit for sure, but such observations are only as useful as they are truly biblically informed. Unfortunately, they rarely are.

Much of what Christians think they know about angels is more informed by Christian tradition than Scripture. The angelology[1] of Christian tradition is, to say the least, quite incomplete and, in some ways, inaccurate.

But again, why should we care?

The simple answer is that, if God moved the biblical writers to take care when talking about the unseen realm, then it matters. But these days, that often doesn't satisfy, since rarely we are taught to think theologically in church. The Sunday experience of most of you reading these words is that the Bible is presented as though its content is little more than children's Sunday school stories with adult illustrations or perhaps pithy maxims about marriage, parenting, recovery, confession, and fortitude. Of course the Bible can, does, and should speak to these personal issues. Scripture is applicable to every season of life, with all of its joys, challenges, and failures. But there's more to the Bible than that—a lot more. To be blunt, Jesus is more than a cosmic life coach, and the God of the Bible had more in mind than a list of basic spiritual coping skills when he inspired its writers.

*But learning about angels isn't practical*—or so I've been told. I disagree, and I think that if you read this book you will as well. Think with me for a moment. A life well lived extends from wisdom. Biblical wisdom involves not only practical, principled, decision-making skills but eternal perspective. Eternal perspective requires understanding what makes God tick. That's only discoverable with a firm grasp of who God is, what he's

---

1. "Angelology" refers to theology related to angels and the rest of the heavenly host. It involves the development of ideas concerned with the heavenly host, such as their roles, hierarchy, names, and powers.

done, why he's done it, what else he intends to do, and why he doesn't want to do it alone. Grasping biblical theology is the means to these discoveries. And grasping biblical theology is impossible without knowing the Bible broadly and deeply.

Why should we care about angels? Because angelology helps us think more clearly about familiar points of biblical theology. God's supernatural family is a theological template for understanding God's relationship to his human family of believers—and our greater importance compared to them. Learning what the Bible says about angels ultimately is tied to thinking well about how God thinks about us. What God wants us to know about angels contributes to our eternal perspective. Several specifics come to mind.

## HOW GOD LOOKS AT US: Imagers of God

In our discussion of Old Testament angelology, I'll draw your attention to the plural language of Genesis 1:26 ("let *us* make humankind in *our* image," LEB). That language isn't a cryptic reference to the Trinity. God is speaking to his heavenly host. He is sharing a decision with them—decreeing his will, as it were. If he were speaking to the members of the Trinity, they would already know what's in God's mind, because they are coequal and coeternal with him. Instead, the plural language of Genesis 1:26 intentionally connects humanity, God, and the members of the heavenly host with respect to an important biblical concept: imaging God. Imaging God is about representation—acting on God's behalf at his behest. Humans image God on earth. The heavenly host images God in the spiritual, non-terrestrial world. The two are connected by design—and that has amazing ramifications.

The cliché concept of "being Jesus" to a lost person who needs Christ also captures this idea. Imagers function in God's place—not because God needs a break or is incapable, but because God has decreed that role. He has designed his supernatural creatures and humanity to fulfill that role. Humans were tasked to make the whole world like Eden: a place where God's goodness was known and his presence experienced; where humanity's needs were met and God's created world could be fully known and enjoyed; where imagers related to each other the way God related to them, with joy and love. God intended humanity to finish a task he had begun. He wanted participation—and that should sound familiar if one is familiar with the heavenly host, God's initial family.

Understanding this status provides an answer to questions like, "How should we then live?," "How do we image God?," and "How should we see and treat each other?" We image God by doing what he would do, when he would do it, and with the motivation he would have for doing it. Yes, we are lesser than God and will fail. But God forgives—another lesson on what imaging means. We image God when we imitate God, acting on his behalf. It's difficult to see how any facet of this could be deemed impractical for Christian living.

Many illustrations show that imaging theology is crucially needed. There would be no racism if we saw each other as imagers of the same God; imagers estranged from God are still imagers. Injustice and abuse of power would find no place if we valued the fact that we all image God equally. All our relationships—personal, home, business, work, church— would be different if we consciously remembered our equal status as imagers of God. Imaging God is not leashed to church ministry. It can and should occur wherever our lives intersect with others'.

You may not have realized it while you were reading, but we just thought theologically, by means of an insight about God's heavenly host. Believe it or not, the significant, practical idea of *imaging God* extended from a more insightful angelology—drawn from the plurals of Genesis 1:26, where God speaks to his heavenly host. That insight helped us think about practical holy living. Surprise!

## WHERE GOD WANTS US: At Home with God

The second way a biblical theology of the heavenly host helps mold eternal perspective is to remind us that the terrestrial world as we know it isn't our true home. We are children of God. They were children of God before us. Though there was no weakness or need in God (like loneliness) that our own creation was meant to fill, the Bible makes it clear that God wanted more children. Humans could not traverse to his home, but God could reside in their home. And so the presence of God descended to earth to take up residence.

The point is that God wants to be with his children. *He wants us where he is.* The plan was to blend his divine and human families on earth in deference to the limitations of human embodiment. Home is supposed to be where God is. But there's more to it than that.

The fall disrupted the home life God intended for his human children. Nevertheless, the intention stayed secure. God had anticipated the fall. In his foresight, God had already determined that he would become a man in Jesus Christ so that humankind could come home after the fall (1 Pet 1:19–20; compare Eph 1:4). The wonder of God's decision is amplified when we superimpose what we know of angels onto it. God did *not* create a plan with their rebellions in mind. Instead, God devised a plan of redemption focused on humanity. As we've seen, the writer of Hebrews explains this powerfully: "For it was not to angels that God subjected the world to come," but it was Jesus, who

> for a little while was made lower than the angels, namely Jesus, crowned with glory and honor because of the suffering of death, so that by the grace of God he might taste death for everyone. ... For surely it is not angels that he helps, but he helps the offspring of Abraham. Therefore he had to be made like his brothers in every respect, so that he might become a merciful and faithful high priest in the service of God, to make propitiation for the sins of the people. (Heb 2:9, 16–17)

Acknowledging that our supernatural siblings were part of God's original desire to have human children—so much so that he would act at the expense of the heavenly ones for our benefit—helps shape eternal perspective. If God wants us home to that degree, why would we fear departure from this terrestrial ball? As Psalm 116:15 puts it, "Precious in the sight of the LORD is the death of his faithful ones" (NRSV). It is incoherent to think that God is less interested in us now, after the cross, than he was before when our redemption is what the cross accomplished. We need not fear death, because we who believe have been granted eternal life—and we will still be in God's presence after supernatural rebels have long been judged.

If we should not fear death, we should not be so distracted by the affairs of a life that is not being lived in our real home. Do we really believe that life in this world, as wonderful as it can be, can compare to what is to come? Do we really believe that the pain and disappointment that are inevitably part of life in this world is where our story ends? We can mouth the right answers to both questions, but what we *really* believe about our future can be seen by how we live in the present.

## WHAT GOD HAS PLANNED FOR US:
Eternal Rule with Christ

I've met a number of Christians who will admit that, while they're glad to have eternal life, they find descriptions of heaven boring. I agree. The popular notion that heaven means floating around on clouds, gazing at God, and singing endless praise anthems is deeply flawed. The imagers of God, eternal members in his family, have a lot more to do than cloud-lounging and singing. But discerning that requires grasping heavenly host ("angelic") participation and reclaiming the nations currently under the dominion of evil, supernatural beings. A theology of the heavenly host is indispensable for conceiving our eternal destiny as co-rulers with Jesus.

First, "heaven" will be on earth. This is where Revelation 21–22 locates the eternal state, but that fact often is missed by Bible readers. Eternal life will be lived out in a new Eden—a global paradise that fulfills God's original intention. The presence of God and the glorified messianic king, Jesus, will be there. We're there, too, but we're not passive (or bored).

Having been transformed to be like the risen Christ (1 John 3:1–3; 1 Cor 15:35–49), believers in the new Eden inherit the rule of the nations. Jesus himself quotes a messianic psalm (Ps 2:9) and *applies it to us* (Rev 2:27). Jesus grants us the privilege (and duty) of sharing his throne with him to rule the earth (Rev 3:21).

How is it we have this authority? John tells us: "all who did receive him, who believed in his name, he gave the right to become children of God" (John 1:12). We are the children of God who rule the nations. Old Testament angelology makes the meaning of this clear—the nations are currently ruled by fallen sons of God, who oppress their populations (Deut 32:8; Ps 82:1–5). The psalmist recounts God's judgment in his heavenly assembly, that these sons of God will die like men (Ps 82:6–7)—they will be cast away and replaced when the Most High rises up and takes back the nations (Ps 82:8). Paul describes the eternal destiny of the believer in this light: we will judge angels (1 Cor 6:3), language that anticipates their removal and our installation as lords of all the earth with Jesus, who is not merely our king but our brother (Heb 2:11–13). I tried to capture the idea in my book *Supernatural*:

> The members of God's family have a mission: to be God's agents in restoring his good rule on earth and expanding the membership of his family. We are God's means to propel the great reversal begun in Acts 2, the birth of the church, the body of Christ, until the time when the Lord returns. As evil had spread like a contagion through humanity after the failure of the first Eden, so the gospel spreads like an antidote through the same infected host. We are *carriers* of the truth about the God of gods, his love for *all* nations, and his unchanging desire to dwell with his family in the earthly home he has wanted since its creation. Eden *will* live again.[2]

Why should we care about angels? Because knowledge of God's heavenly host helps us think more clearly about our status, our purpose, and our destiny. *That's* why.

## WHAT TO EXPECT

I've already shown my hand here: you won't get church tradition or talk about how angels got their wings (they don't have any). Instead, our focus will be the biblical text, and our doctrine will be informed by what we see in that text.

Our discussion naturally will begin with Old Testament terminology. That terminology then will serve as the basis for framing an Old Testament theology of the heavenly host. The Old Testament section of the book concludes with a chapter on important angels in the Old Testament.

Rather than jumping to the New Testament, the book will move from the Old Testament to Second Temple ("intertestamental") period literature.[3] During the years between the end of the Old Testament and Jesus'

---

2. Michael S. Heiser, *Supernatural: What the Bible Teaches about the Unseen World—And Why It Matters* (Bellingham, WA: Lexham Press, 2015), 163.

3. The Second Temple period gets its name from the time the temple was rebuilt (516 BC) after Jews returned from Babylonian exile to the destruction of that second temple (AD 70).

birth, Jewish scholars were thinking and writing a great deal about their Bible, the Old Testament. A lot of what they wrote influenced how the Jewish people—writers of the New Testament among them—thought about many things, including angels.

The third section of the book then turns to the New Testament. After surveying New Testament language for the heavenly host, noting its relationship to both the Old Testament and Second Temple period, we will devote a chapter to special topics in New Testament angelology. Finally, we will bring our study to a close with a fascinating (and hopefully fun) analysis of Christian myths about angels.

# CHAPTER 1

# Old Testament Terminology for the Heavenly Host

Nοτ surprisingly, understanding what the Hebrew Bible (Old Testament) says about the members of God's heavenly host must begin with the biblical text. It would be a mistake, however, to assume that merely detecting all the references in the Old Testament to angels accomplishes that task. As will become clear, there are a number of terms aside from "angel" that need discovery and consideration. But there is a preliminary step to casting that wider terminological net.

Before we encounter the range of terms for the beings who serve God in the spiritual world, we need to grasp the fact that a given word will not necessarily yield the same *kind* of information about those spirit beings. To illustrate: the label "spirit being" tells us only about the *nature* of a particular being (it is not embodied), not what that being *does* in God's service or its particular *status* in God's heavenly bureaucracy. This last sentence directs our attention to three kinds of information, all of which are relevant to the terms we'll consider in this chapter:[1]

- Terms that describe **nature** (what the members of the heavenly host *are* or *are like*)

- Terms that describe **status** (the hierarchical *rank* of the members of the heavenly host with respect to God and each other)

- Terms that describe **function** (what the members of the heavenly host *do*)

---

1. The terms we'll discuss in this chapter will also be relevant to rebellious spiritual beings (part 2, chapter 5), but there are additional terms for spiritual beings who are hostile to God.

Old Testament descriptions of the members of God's heavenly host typically fall into one of these categories, with occasional overlap. Our task in this chapter is to survey the terms in each category. We will reserve lengthy discussion of what these terms teach us about the heavenly to chapter 2.

## TERMS THAT DESCRIBE NATURE

### 1. "Spirit" (*rûaḥ*; plural: *rûaḥôṯ*)

The Old Testament makes it clear that the members of God's heavenly host are spirit beings—entities that, by nature, are not embodied, at least in the sense of our human experience of being physical in form.[2] This spiritual nature is indicated in several passages. The prophet Micaiah's vision of Yahweh, the God of Israel, reads as follows:

> I saw the LORD sitting on his throne, and all the host of heaven standing beside him on his right hand and on his left; and the LORD said, "Who will entice Ahab, that he may go up and fall at Ramoth-gilead?" And one said one thing, and another said another. Then a spirit [*rûaḥ*] came forward and stood before the LORD, saying, "I will entice him." And the LORD said to him, "By what means?" And he said, "I will go out, and will be a lying spirit [*rûaḥ*] in the mouth of all his prophets." And he said, "You are to entice him, and you shall succeed; go out and do so." Now therefore behold, the LORD has put a lying spirit [*rûaḥ*] in the mouth of all these your prophets; the LORD has declared disaster for you. (1 Kgs 22:19–23; compare 2 Chr 18:18–22)

---

2. This point is not contradicted by passages that refer to angels as men and that have them performing physical acts (e.g., Gen 6:1–4; 18:1–8, 16, 22; 19:1, 10–11, 16; 32:24 [compare Hos 12:4]). When angels interact with human beings, appearance in human form or actual embodiment is normative in Scripture. Without taking some form that could be detected and parsed by the human senses, angelic presence and interaction would be incomprehensible. The words of Jesus in Matt 22:23–33 do not forbid the inclusion of Gen 6:1–4 on this point. Jesus was speaking about angels *in heaven* (v. 30)—the spiritual world—not on earth among humans. Jesus could just as well have said angels do not eat or breathe in heaven, since there is no need for a stomach, lungs, and heart in the spiritual world. On understanding Gen 6:1–4 as part of the supernatural worldview of the biblical writers, see Michael S. Heiser, *The Unseen Realm: Recovering the Supernatural Worldview of the Bible* (Bellingham, WA: Lexham Press, 2015), chapters 12–13, 23. For a discussion of Gen 6:1–4 against the backdrop of its ancient Mesopotamian context, see Michael S. Heiser, *Reversing Hermon: Enoch, the Watchers, & the Forgotten Mission of Jesus Christ* (Crane, MO: Defender Publishing, 2017), 37–54.

There are two important observations to make in this passage. First, the members of the host of heaven are identified as spirit beings in this passage (v. 21). Second, this spirit being is sent by God to "be a lying spirit" in the mouth of Ahab's prophets (vv. 22–23). We are therefore *not* supposed to read this passage as though its point was that God gave Ahab's prophets some sort of internal emotional anxiety or psychological confusion—as though God was troubling *their* individual spirits, their minds and thoughts. While *rûaḥ* can certainly be used to describe a person's intellect and emotional state (e.g., Mal 2:16; Ps 32:2; Prov 15:13),[3] 1 Kings 22:19–23 clearly identifies the lying spirit as a member of "all the host of heaven," who await instruction from their King. This spirit either took control of the minds of Ahab's prophets or influenced them to speak unanimous deception to the wicked king.[4]

The divine throne room scene in 1 Kings 22:19–23 is therefore useful for considering other instances where *rûaḥ* may point to an unembodied entity but where ambiguity exists. In this regard, the following passages are relevant:

Abimelech ruled over Israel three years. And God sent an evil spirit [*rûaḥ*] between Abimelech and the leaders of Shechem, and the leaders of Shechem dealt treacherously with Abimelech. (Judg 9:22–23)

Now the Spirit of the LORD departed from Saul, and a harmful spirit [*rûaḥ*] from the LORD tormented him. And Saul's servants said to him, "Behold now, a harmful spirit [*rûaḥ*] from God is tormenting you. Let our lord now command your servants who are before you to seek out a man who is skillful in playing the lyre, and when the harmful spirit [*rûaḥ*] from God is upon you, he will play it, and you will be well." (1 Sam 16:14–16)

The next day a harmful spirit [*rûaḥ*] from God rushed upon Saul, and he raved within his house while David was playing the lyre, as he did

---

3. *HALOT*, 1199–1200.

4. Some readers may have difficulty with God's use of deception to judge evildoers, but it is plainly taught in Scripture. At times the deception is in the context of warfare (Josh 8:1–9). In other instances, God uses deception to set the stage for his judgment (1 Sam 16:1–5). It is up to the righteous Judge to determine how evil is punished. By definition, his punishment of evil is just and not unjust. See Walter C. Kaiser, Jr., *Toward Old Testament Ethics* (Grand Rapids: Zondervan, 1983): 225–27; Geoffrey David Miller, "The Wiles of the Lord: Divine Deception, Subtlety, and Mercy in I Reg 22," *ZAW* 126.1 (2014): 45–58; Robert B. Chisholm, Jr., "Does God Deceive?" *BSac* 155.617 (1998): 11–28.

day by day. Saul had his spear in his hand. And Saul hurled the spear, for he thought, "I will pin David to the wall." But David evaded him twice. (1 Sam 18:10–11)

The princes of Zoan have become fools,
    and the princes of Memphis are deluded;
those who are the cornerstones of her tribes
    have made Egypt stagger.
The Lord has mingled within her a spirit [*rûaḥ*] of confusion,
    and they will make Egypt stagger in all its deeds,
    as a drunken man staggers in his vomit. (Isa 19:13–14)

When the servants of King Hezekiah came to Isaiah, Isaiah said to them, "Say to your master, 'Thus says the Lord: Do not be afraid because of the words that you have heard, with which the young men of the king of Assyria have reviled me. Behold, I will put a spirit [*rûaḥ*] in him, so that he shall hear a rumor and return to his own land, and I will make him fall by the sword in his own land.'" (Isa 37:5–7)

In each of these passages, a "spirit" (*rûaḥ*) is sent from God and that spirit affects an individual or group in an adverse way. Are these descriptions best understood as God in some way affecting the internal state of mind of the individuals in view or dispatching an unembodied entity to affect behavior?

One could easily conclude, based on the usage of *rûaḥ* to describe a person's thoughts, feelings, and decisions, that the latter perspective makes sense. However, in light of 1 Kings 22:19–23, which uses quite similar language to that found in these passages, it is at least possible that unembodied divine spirits in the service of Yahweh are in view.[5]

---

5. For our purposes, there is no need to launch into a detailed exegetical defense of a divine entity interpretation and rebuttal of the alternative. Rather, these and other passages are clear enough to establish the fact that the Old Testament presents the members of the heavenly host as spirits in the same way the New Testament will. In Rev 1:4, for example, the seven angels of the churches addressed in Rev 1–3 are referred to as spirits. As Aune notes, "A second important view, in my opinion certainly the correct one, understands the seven spirits as the seven principal angels of God. In early Jewish literature the term 'spirits' was used only rarely as a synonym for 'angels' (*Jub.* 1:25; 2:2; 15:31–32; *1 Enoch* 61:12, 'spirit of light'), or of various types of heavenly beings (*1 Enoch* 75:5, 'the spirit of the dew'; see *2 Enoch* 12:2 [J], 'flying spirits'; 16:7, 'the heavenly winds, and spirits and elements and flying angels'). ... The seven ἄγγελοι, literally 'angels,' are those to whom the seven proclamations in Rev 2–3 are addressed" (David E. Aune, *Revelation 1–5* [WBC 52A; Dallas: Word, Inc., 1997], 34, 108).

A potential ambiguity of another sort is produced by the fact that the Hebrew word *rûaḥ* can also mean "wind."[6] This semantic possibility produces uncertainty in regard to interpreting Psalm 104:4.

Bless the LORD, O my soul!
O LORD my God, you are very great!
You are clothed with splendor and majesty,
covering yourself with light as with a garment,
stretching out the heavens like a tent.
He lays the beams of his chambers on the waters;
he makes the clouds his chariot;
he rides on the wings of the wind [*rûaḥ*];
he makes his messengers [*mal'akim*] winds [*rûḥôṯ*],
his ministers a flaming fire. (Ps 104:1–4)

The term *mal'akim* is the plural of the Hebrew word translated "angels" throughout the Hebrew Bible (*mal'ak*). In the ESV translation, that plural is rendered "messengers." These messengers are referred to as "winds" in the ESV, but the Hebrew (*rûḥôṯ*) could just as easily be translated "spirits."

It isn't uncommon for commentators to understand Psalm 104:4 as referring only to winds—elements of nature or the weather—and not divine beings. The ESV reflects this perspective, as its translation effectively has God poetically making the winds his messengers. Goldingay's comments are representative of this approach: "Other aspects of creation then form the means whereby God affects other aspects of this management. The clouds are Yhwh's limousine, the winds its means of propulsion, both the winds and the lightning Yhwh's aides and officers (Ps 104:3–4)."[7] This perspective is what leads scholars like Aune to conclude, "The plural term רוחות, *rûḥôt* 'spirits,' is never used of *angels* in the OT."[8]

---

6. *HALOT*, 1198–99. Job 4:15 is another instance where *rûaḥ* may refer to either a spirit or a wind. Alden notes: "It is not certain whether the 'spirit' should be understood as a divine spirit or whether we should read 'breeze/wind'" (Robert L. Alden, *Job* NAC 11; [Nashville: Broadman & Holman, 1993], 87).

7. John Goldingay, *Old Testament Theology, Volume One: Israel's Gospel* (Downers Grove, IL: InterVarsity Press, 2003), 84–85. Another scholar notes: "These prophets knew that many forces exist in nature which can affect humans. But they believed that these were under God's control. Wind (Exodus 10:13; Psalm 104:3–4; Isaiah 59:19) and water (Genesis 6:17; Psalm 29:3; Isaiah 40:12), fire (Exodus 13:21–22; 1 Kings 18:24; Jeremiah 21:14) and frost (Psalm 78:47; Zechariah 14:5–6)" (David Francis Hinson, *Theology of the Old Testament* [London: SPCK, 2001], 59).

8. Aune, *Revelation 1–5*, 33.

This interpretation of Psalm 104:4 is unconvincing. The preceding psalm and comparative ancient Near Eastern descriptions of angels compel the conclusion that Psalm 104:4 is describing angels as spirits. Psalm 103:20–22 reads:

> Bless the LORD, O you his angels [*mal'akim*],
> > you mighty ones who do his word,
> > obeying the voice of his word!
> Bless the LORD, all his hosts,
> > his ministers, who do his will!
> Bless the LORD, all his works,
> > in all places of his dominion.
> Bless the LORD, O my soul!

The observation to make here is that the angels are referred to as "ministers" (v. 21). The Hebrew word thus translated is identical to that which occurs in Psalm 104 ("his ministers a flaming fire," v. 4). Why translate *mal'akim* as "angels" in Psalm 103:20 but "messengers" in Psalm 104:4? The angels in Psalm 103:20 are also called "mighty ones" who obey the command of God, obeying his voice. "Mighty ones" (*gibborim*) is a term used of human warriors throughout the Hebrew Bible. It is nowhere else abstracted to speak of the forces of nature. It does not seem reasonable to make Psalm 104:4 an exception, especially since, as we'll discuss below, angels are described as men and as a warrior host in the Old Testament.[9]

Further, other scholars have pointed out that another descriptor in Psalm 104:4, that God has made his ministers "a flaming fire" (*'eš lahaṭ*), is vocabulary used to describe divine servants in ancient Near Eastern texts. For instance, two messengers of Yamm sent to a meeting of Canaanite El, the high god of Ugarit, are called "two flames." Miller writes:

> The messengers of Yamm appear as warriors, flaming and with swords. There is no reason in this instance to assume that the figures represent lightning, but they indicate that both sides in the Baal—Yamm conflict were disposed to use fire of some sort. There can be

---

9. This is hardly an idiosyncratic perspective. For example, Kraus writes: "In Ps. 103:20 and 148:2 the מלאכים ('angels') belong to the circle of heavenly powers around Yahweh who praise and honor him. But God also sends out 'messengers' and 'servants' (Ps. 104:4). He charges his angels to protect his servants in all their ways (Ps. 91:11)" (Hans-Joachim Kraus, *Theology of the Psalms* [Minneapolis: Fortress Press, 1992], 49).

no question that these messengers are warriors. ... This suggestion was made ... by Father D. Shenkel, who also relates the messengers of Yamm to the messengers of Yahweh called *'ēš (wā) lahaṭ* in Ps 104:4.[10]

## 2. "Heavenly Ones" (*šamayim*)

The Hebrew word *šamayim* occurs over four hundred times in the Hebrew Bible. In nearly all cases, the referent is either the visible sky, the space above the earth (Gen 1:8; Deut 4:32; 33:26) or the spiritual realm beyond or above the visible sky in which God dwells (Ps 115:3; Isa 66:1). The Hebrew word is found always in plural form.[11] In a handful of passages, *šamayim* describes the members of God's supernatural host and should be translated (though it often is not) as "heavenly ones" for clarity on that point.[12] This usage should be no surprise, since it makes perfect sense that members of the heavenly host should be called "heavenly ones." Psalm 89:5–7 (vv. 6–8 in Hebrew) is a case in point:

> Let the heavens [*šamayim*] praise your wonders, O LORD,
>     your faithfulness in the assembly of the holy ones!
> For who in the skies can be compared to the LORD?
>     Who among the heavenly beings is like the LORD,
> a God greatly to be feared in the council of the holy ones,
>     and awesome above all who are around him?

As we will discuss momentarily, this passage clearly speaks of the heavenly host as a council or assembly in the service of Yahweh, the God of Israel. This divine council has many "holy ones" as its constituent members. In verse 5, these holy ones are set in parallel structure to *šamayim*. The holy ones are "heavenly ones."[13] Goldingay comments on the meaning of *šamayim* in this context:

> Alongside the parallelism of "wonders" and "truthfulness" is that of "the heavens" and "the congregation of the holy," the latter giving

---

10. Patrick D. Miller, *Israelite Religion and Biblical Theology: Collected Essays* (Sheffield: Sheffield Academic Press, 2000), 19.

11. The pointing of the lemma gives it the appearance of a dual form, but as *HALOT* notes, "שָׁמַיִם [is] apparently a dual, but in reality a pl[ural]" (*HALOT*, 1560; see also GKC §88d; *GBH* §91ff).

12. M. Hutter and M. de Jonge, "Heaven," *DDD* 390.

13. The ESV "heavenly beings" in verse 6 is not a translation of *šamayim*, but of *benê 'ēlîm* ("sons of God"). See the ensuing discussion on that term.

precision to the former. It is the body called "the divine assembly," the assembly of the "gods," in 82:1.[14]

Job 15:15 is another example where *šamayim* should be understood as spiritual beings:

Behold, God puts no trust in his holy ones,
 and the heavens [*šamayim*] are not pure in his sight.

While the impurity of "the heavens" could be abstracted to mean that the spiritual world God inhabits has been tarnished in some way by the holy ones, the Hebrew parallelism makes it clear that "the heavenly ones" are not pure in God's sight. The apparent meaning is that the heavenly beings of God's host or council are imperfect, and so God cannot completely trust them. This is reasonable given divine rebellion's presence in the biblical storyline (Gen 3; 6:1–4; Ps 82).

Deuteronomy 32:43 is well known to scholars as an instance of *šamayim* used to describe divine beings. Here is the passage in that translation:

Rejoice with him, O heavens [*šamayim*];
 bow down to him, all gods [*'elōhîm*],
for he avenges the blood of his children
 and takes vengeance on his adversaries.
He repays those who hate him
 and cleanses his people's land.

The ESV follows the reading of the Dead Sea Scrolls in this verse. The evidence from the Dead Sea Scrolls here and for Deuteronomy 32:8 shows that "gods" is demonstrably the correct reading.[15] The stanza in Moses' poetic song very clearly aligns *šamayim* with *'elōhîm*, and so a translation of "heavenly ones" is appropriate.

## 3. "Stars" (*kōkebîm*)

Since the members of God's heavenly host are referred to as "heavenly ones," it should come as no surprise that they are also called "stars"

---

14. John Goldingay, *Psalms, Volume 2: Psalms 42–89*, BCOT (Grand Rapids: Baker Academic, 2006), 670.

15. See Michael S. Heiser, "Monotheism, Polytheism, Monolatry, or Henotheism? Toward an Assessment of Divine Plurality in the Hebrew Bible," *BBR* 18.1 (2008): 1–30 (9–10); idem, "Deuteronomy 32:8 and the Sons of God," *BSac* 158 (2001): 52–74.

(*kōkeḇîm*). Indeed, the very designation "host" draws on descriptions of celestial bodies in the Old Testament (e.g., Gen 2:1; Jer 8:2):

> The identification of personified stars with angels of the heavenly hosts is well accepted within a totally monotheistic religious system: the stars stand in God's presence, to the right and the left of His throne (1 Kgs 22:19; 2 Chr 18:18); they serve Him (Ps 103:21; Neh 9:6). ... At the head of the heavenly hosts stands a "Prince of the army" (Josh 5:14–15; Dan 8:11), probably the highest star and the farthest from the earth, even if the actual leader is God, to whom the starry army belongs. From this conception derives the syntagm "Lord/God of hosts" (*Yhwh 'ĕlōhê ṣĕḇā'ôt*) occurring in numerous biblical passages.[16]

Perhaps the most familiar passage in this regard is Job 38:5–7, where God asks Job:

> Who determined [the earth's] measurements—surely you know!
>     Or who stretched the line upon it?
> On what were its bases sunk,
>     or who laid its cornerstone,
> when the morning stars sang [*kōkeḇê bōqer*] together
>     and all the sons of God shouted for joy?

As we'll note later in our discussion, "sons of God" is a term for the divine members of God's divine family-entourage. The heavenly sons of God who watched the creation of the earth are described as "morning stars." In Isaiah 14:13, the hubris of the king of Babylon is analogized with that of a rebel who sought to displace the God of heaven: "I will ascend to heaven; above the stars of God [*kōkeḇê 'ēl*] I will set my throne on high." Scholars have long known that these lines in Isaiah 14 draw on a tale of divine rebellion present in Ugaritic texts, where the gods of El's council are referred to as the "assembly of the stars [*kkbm*]."[17]

---

16. F. Lelli, "Stars," *DDD* 813; see also Ida Zatelli, "Astrology and the Worship of the Stars in the Bible," *ZAW* 103.1 (1991): 86–99.

17. Michael S. Heiser, "The Mythological Provenance of Isaiah 14:12–15: A Reconsideration of the Ugaritic Material," *VT* 51.3 (2001): 354–59; Mark S. Smith, "When the Heavens Darkened: Yahweh, El, and the Divine Astral Family in Iron Age II Judah," in *Symbiosis, Symbolism, and the Power of the Past: Canaan, Ancient Israel, and Their Neighbors from the Late Bronze Age Through Roman Palaestina*, eds. William G. Dever and Seymour Gitin (Winona Lake, IN: Eisenbrauns, 2003), 265–77; Ulf Oldenburg, "Above the Stars of El," *ZAW* 82.2 (1970): 187–208.

The point of star language for divine members of the heavenly host should be obvious. The members of Yahweh's host are not of earth. They are celestial, transcendent beings whose home is in the heavenly realm, the abode of God.

### 4. "Holy Ones" (*qedōšîm*)

Two passages we considered above that designate the members of God's heavenly host as "heavenly ones" also describe them as "holy ones" (Ps 89:5-7 [Hebrew: vv. 6-8]; Job 15:15). The term *qedōšîm* may be used to describe people (Ps 16:3; Dan 8:24), but it is more often used of spirit beings in Yahweh's service (Deut 33:2-3; Job 5:1; Zech 14:5; Dan 4:17).[18]

As we shall discuss in the next chapter, the designation "holy ones" does not denote some quality of perfection. God does indeed charge his heavenly host with "error" (Job 4:17-18). They are not infallible. "Holy ones" should therefore be understood in much the same way as earthly "holiness" of people, places, and objects. The nature of holiness has to do with proximity to and association with the presence of God.[19]

### 5. "Gods"/"Divine Beings" (*'elōhîm*)

I've written extensively on divine plurality (the reality of multiple *'elōhîm*) in the biblical text.[20] The biblical writers refer to the members of God's heavenly host as gods, lesser divine beings in his heavenly council or assembly.[21] What follows will briefly summarize that prior research.

We have already noted that Psalm 89:5-7 (vv. 6-8 in Hebrew) describes a council or assembly of "holy ones" and "heavenly ones" under the authority of Yahweh, the God of Israel.[22] This council is explicitly

---

18. The instance in Deut 33:2 is actually a singular form (*qōdeš*) that modifies the plural "myriads," a different Hebrew lemma. The word in Daniel 4:17 is *qaddîšîn*, the Aramaic cognate of *qedōšîm*.

19. See J. A. Naudé, "קָדַשׁ (*qādaš*)," *NIDOTTE* 3:877-87.

20. For example: Heiser, *The Unseen Realm*, 21-27; idem, "Monotheism, Polytheism, Monolatry, or Henotheism, 1-30; idem, "Should *elohim* with Plural Predication Be Translated 'Gods'?" *Bible Translator* 61.3 (2010): 123-36; idem, "Does Deuteronomy 32:17 Assume or Deny the Reality of Other Gods?" *Bible Translator* 59.3 (2008): 137-45.

21. See Michael S. Heiser, "Divine Council," *DOTWPW* 112-16; idem, "Divine Council," *LBD*.

22. Other sources include: E. Theodore Mullen Jr., *The Divine Council in Canaanite and Early Hebrew Literature* (Chico, CA: Scholars Press, 1980); Lowell K. Handy, *Among the Host of Heaven: The Syro-Palestinian Pantheon as Bureaucracy* (Winona Lake, IN: Eisenbrauns, 1994); H. W. Robinson, "The Council of Yahweh," *JTS* 45 (1944): 151-57; David Marron Fleming, "The Divine Council as Type Scene in the Hebrew Bible" (PhD diss., Southern Baptist Theological Seminary, 1989); Min

placed "in the skies" (v. 6; _baššaḥaq_), eliminating the common interpretation that the sons of God in Yahweh's divine council are human beings, Israelite judges. The unambiguous nature of this passage is echoed in Psalm 82:1, 6:

> God [ _'elōhîm_] has taken his place in the divine council [ _'adat 'ēl_];
> in the midst of the gods [ _'elōhîm_] he holds judgment. ...
> I said, "You are gods [ _'elōhîm_],
> sons of the Most High [_benê ' nê_ '], all of you..."

In Psalm 82:1 the word _'elōhîm_ occurs twice. The form (morphology) of _'elōhîm_ is plural. The meaning (semantics) of the term, however, is most often singular.[23] In the case of Psalm 82:1, both meanings, singular and plural, are present. The first instance of _'elōhîm_ has the singular participle _niṣṣab_ ("stands" or "to take one's place") as its grammatical partner. That the second _'elōhîm_ must be understood as plural in meaning is indicated by the preposition ("in the midst of"; _beqereḇ_) that precedes it. You can't be "in the _midst_ of" a singular entity.

The plurality of the second _'elōhîm_ in Psalm 82:1 is made obvious by Psalm 82:6. God tells the other _'elōhîm_, "you are gods ( _'elōhîm_), all of you." Both pronouns ("you") in the statement are grammatically plural. These _'elōhîm_ are "sons" (plural) of the Most High, who must be the God of the Bible, as there is none higher.

Many scholars use these passages to argue that the biblical writers at one point in Israelite history were polytheists. This thinking is misguided and rooted in a mistaken notion of what the word _'elōhîm_ means. We tend to presume that the biblical writers thought about _'elōhîm_ in the same way we think about capitalized G-o-d. When we see the word "God," we instinctively assign a unique set of attributes (e.g., omnipresence, omnipotence, sovereignty) to the letters G-o-d. But this presumption is incorrect and leads our thinking astray when we encounter instances where _'elōhîm_ is intended to describe a group of beings instead of the lone God of the Bible.

---

Suc Kee, "The Heavenly Council and Its Type-Scene," _JSOT_ 31.3 (2007): 259–73; S. B. Parker, "Sons of (The) God(S)," _DDD_ 798; G. Cooke, "The Sons of (the) God(s)," _ZAW_ 35 (1964): 22–47.

23. As a Hebrew morphological-syntax search with Bible software reveals, the Hebrew noun _'elōhîm_ occurs with a singular verb/predicator for grammatical agreement over two thousand times in the Hebrew Bible.

We know this presumption about *'elōhîm* is mistaken by virtue of how the biblical authors used the word *'elōhîm*. Briefly, one will find *'elōhîm* in the Hebrew Bible employed to describe spiritual beings that are clearly lesser than the God of Israel. While *'elōhîm* is used thousands of times for the singular God of Israel, it is used for spiritual beings judged by the God of the Bible (Ps 82:1, 6), gods and goddesses of surrounding nations (Judg 11:24; 1 Kgs 11:33), territorial spirits (Hebrew: *shedim*, often translated "demons"; Deut 32:17), and the spirits of deceased people (1 Sam 28:13).

No biblical author would think that the deceased dead or territorial spirits shared the same attributes and power as the God of Israel. The term is not intended to speak of a unique set of attributes, as though the God of Israel was just one of many equals. Biblical writers were not expressing polytheism; they used *'elōhîm* in contexts that require a plural meaning for the term:

- "Demons" (Hebrew: *shedim*; Deut 32:17)
- The deceased Samuel (1 Sam 28:13)
- Angels or the Angel of Yahweh (Gen 35:7)[24]

The fact that biblical writers label a range of entities as *'elōhîm* that they elsewhere take pains to distinguish as lesser than Yahweh tells us quite clearly that we ought not understand *'elōhîm* as having to do with a unique set of attributes possessed by only one Being. A biblical writer would use *'elōhîm* to label any entity that is not embodied by nature and is a member of the spiritual realm. This "otherworldliness" is an attribute all residents of the spiritual world possess. Every member of the spiritual world can be thought of as *'elōhîm* since the term tells us where an entity belongs in terms of its nature. The spiritual realm has rank and hierarchy: Yahweh is the Most High. Biblical writers distinguish Yahweh from other *'elōhîm* by means of other descriptors exclusively attributed to him, not by means of the single word *'elōhîm*:

> Biblical writers also assign unique qualities to Yahweh. Yahweh is all-powerful (Jer 32:17, 27; Pss 72:18; 115:3), the sovereign king over the other *'elōhîm* (Psa 95:3; Dan 4:35; 1 Kgs 22:19), the creator of the other members of his host-council (Psa 148:1–5; Neh 9:6; cf. Job 38:7;

---

24. Heiser, *The Unseen Realm*, 29–30.

Deut 4:19–20; 17:3; 29:25–26; 32:17; Jas 1:17) and the lone *'elōhîm* who deserves worship from the other *'elōhîm* (Psa 29:1). In fact, Nehemiah 9:6 explicitly declares that Yahweh is unique—there is only one Yahweh ("You alone are Yahweh").[25]

This perspective is consistent with very conservative Jewish thinking in the Second Temple (intertestamental) period, which followed the Old Testament era. For instance, there are nearly 180 instances in nonbiblical material from Qumran's Dead Sea Scrolls where the terms *'elōhîm* and *'ēlîm* (also "gods") describe members of Yahweh's heavenly host.[26]

To summarize our findings thus far, Old Testament writers describe the nature of the members of Yahweh's heavenly host with terms such as "spirits," "heavenly ones," and "gods, divine beings." We'll first encounter the more familiar "angel" in the next category.

## TERMS THAT DESCRIBE STATUS IN HIERARCHY

Psalms 82 and 89 both refer explicitly to the members of God's heavenly host comprising a council or assembly under God's supreme authority.[27] A range of terms in the Old Testament describe this heavenly bureaucracy:[28]

- "assembly" (lemma: *'ēdāh*; construct form: *'adat*)
- "council" (*sōd*)

---

25. Heiser, *The Unseen Realm*, 32.

26. Michael S. Heiser, "Monotheism and the Language of Divine Plurality in the Hebrew Bible and the Dead Sea Scrolls," *TynBul* 65.1 (2014): 85–100. The approach taken here to *'elōhîm* is also contrary to Mormon doctrine. I have critiqued Mormonism's understanding of Psalm 82 and divine plurality elsewhere (at invitation): Michael S. Heiser, "You've Seen One *Elohim*, You've Seen Them All? A Critique of Mormonism's Use of Psalm 82," *Foundation for Ancient Research and Mormon Studies Review* 19.1 (2007): 221–66.

27. What is being described in the biblical council of Yahweh is not a polytheistic pantheon. See Heiser, "Divine Council," *DOTWPW* 112–16; idem, "Divine Council," *LBD*; idem, *The Unseen Realm*, 21–37; Stephen F. Noll, *Angels of Light, Powers of Darkness* (Downers Grove, IL: InterVarsity Press, 1998), 37–38, 126–27.

28. In addition to these lemmas, all of which occur in the Hebrew Bible in at least one context of a gathering of divine beings such as the throne room of God, mention should be made of *dôr* ("circled camp, generation"). This term is not used in the context of a divine bureaucracy, but its Northwest Semitic cognate, *dr*, certainly is. For examples in Canaanite inscriptions, see *KAI* 26A iii.19: *dr kl bn 'lm* ("whole assembly of the sons of the gods"); *KAI* 27:12: *dr kl qdšn* ("whole assembly of the holy ones"). Ugaritic examples include: *dr 'il*, "assembly (circle) of El" (*KTU*² 1.15.III:19; 1.39:7; 1.162:16; 1.87:18); *dr bn 'il*, "assembly (circle) of the sons of El" (*KTU*² 1.40:25, 33–34); *dt šmm*, "assembly (circle) of those of heaven" (*KTU*² 1.10.I: 3, 5); *dr 'il wphr b'l*, "the assembly (circle) of El and the assembly of Baal" (*KTU*² 1.39:7; 1.62:16; 1.87:18). See *DULAT* 1:279–80; *DNWSI* 1:259.

- "congregation" (*qāhāl*)
- "assembly, assembled meeting" (*mô ʿēd*)
- "court" (Aramaic: *dîn*)

The term *ʿēdāh* appears nearly 150 times in the Hebrew Bible. It refers to a variety of assemblies, throngs, and communities (e.g., Ps 22:17; Num 16:5; Prov 5:14).[29] Its use in Psalm 82:1 is clearly describing a group of divine beings (cf. vv. 6–7), as many scholars have noted exact parallels to the phrase in the texts of Ugarit, whose language bears close relation to that of Biblical Hebrew.[30]

Hebrew *sōḏ* is less common (21 occurrences) than *ʿēdāh*, but biblical writers employed it more often for references to a "council of holy ones" under Yahweh. We have already cited Psalm 89:7 in this regard, but the following references make mention of Yahweh's divine council: Job 15:8; Jeremiah 23:18, 22; and Amos 3:7.[31] Certain specifics of these passages with respect to the function of the council will be considered below.

In addition to *sōḏ*, Psalm 89:5 utilizes the word *qāhāl* ("assembly of the holy ones"). This assembly includes the "sons of God" and meets "in the skies" (Ps 89:6). Hebrew *qāhāl* occurs over 120 times and, like *ʿēdāh*, elsewhere describes a variety of groups: mass groups of people (Num 20:4; Deut 5:22; 1 Kgs 8:14) and military companies (Ezek 17:17; 23:46; 38:15).

The noun *mô ʿēd* refers generally to a meeting place.[32] The notion that the assembly of the gods meets at a "cosmic mountain" is common across ancient Near Eastern literature.[33] At Ugarit the "mount of assembly"

---

29. *HALOT*, 789–90.

30. It is from the texts of Ugarit that scholars have been better able to understand biblical references to El, Baal, and Sheol, for example. At Ugarit the phrase *ʿdt ʾilm* ("assembly of El / the gods") occurs twice (*DULAT* 1:152; see *KTU²* 1.15.II: 7, 11). On the broad subject of the relationship between Ugaritic and the Hebrew Bible, see A. H. W. Curtis and J. F. Healey, *Ugarit and the Bible* (Münster: Ugarit-Verlag, 1994); Peter C. Craigie, "Ugarit and the Bible: Progress and Regress in 50 Years of Literary Study," in *Ugarit in Retrospect: Fifty Years of Ugarit and Ugaritic*, ed. Gordon D. Young (Winona Lake, IN: Eisenbrauns, 1981), 99–111.

31. In regard to Amos 3, see especially: David E. Bokovoy, "שמעו והעידו בבית יעקב: Invoking the Council as Witnesses in Amos 3:13," *JBL* 127.1 (2008): 37–51.

32. *HALOT*, 557.

33. See Richard J. Clifford, *The Cosmic Mountain in Canaan and the Old Testament* (Cambridge, MA: Harvard University Press, 1972); Heiser, *The Unseen Realm*, 44–49; W. A. VanGemeren, "Mountain Imagery," *DOTWPW* 481–83; Edwin Kingsbury, "The Theophany Topos and the Mountain of God," *JBL* 86.2 (1967): 205–10; M. Selman, "הַר, *har*," *NIDOTTE* 1:1051–55; N. Wyatt, *Space and Time in the Religious Life of the Near East* (Sheffield: Sheffield Academic Press, 2001), 148–54.

varies with the deity and his council. In biblical thought (Isa 14:12), the "mount of assembly" (*har mô 'ēd*) is the place where the "stars of God" meet with the Lord in "the far north" (*yarketê ṣāpôn*).[34]

The Aramaic lemma *dîn* occurs five times in Ezra and Daniel. Each occurrence has something to do with justice or rendering judgment. In Daniel 7:9–10, amid the heavenly scene where "a thousand thousands ... and ten thousand times ten thousand stood before [the Lord]," the seated Ancient of Days, "thrones" are put in place and the "court" (*dînā*; council) "sat in judgment."[35]

Many scholars have pointed out that there is a discernible hierarchy within the divine council. All council members, including Yahweh, are heavenly spirit beings (*rûḥôṯ*; *šamayim*; *'elōhîm*).[36] However, a careful comparison of the council terminology sketched here with texts from ancient Canaan, particularly Ugarit, and the terms "sons of God" (*benê [ha] 'elōhîm/ 'ēlîm*) and "angel" (*mal 'āk*), allows one to discern three tiers within the council.

The term "prince" (*sar*) is also relevant for hierarchy. Not all members of the heavenly host bear this title. As I discussed at length in *The Unseen Realm*, the "princes" of the supernatural realm are to be identified with the "sons of God" assigned to the nations of the world in divine judgment by the Most High (Deut 32:8–9 [Qumran, LXX]).[37] These are the "princes" over nations that oppose Yahweh and his people (Dan 10:13, 20).[38] These

---

34. W. G. E. Watson comments: "In particular *hr m 'd*, 'mount of the assembly' and *yrkty ṣpwn*, 'heights of Ṣaphon' (v. 13) which correspond to Ug[aritic] *pḥr m 'd*, 'plenary session' (*KTU* 1.2 i:14) and *mrym ṣpn*, 'heights of Ṣaphon' (*KTU* 1.3 iv:1) respectively" (W. G. E. Watson, "Helel," *DDD* 394).

35. *dînā* is the determined form of the Aramaic lemma *dîn*.

36. The hierarchy referred to here is not to be superimposed on theological terms like Father, Son, and Holy Spirit. Since all members of the Trinity are of the same essence, the godhead forms and occupies the highest tier of the council.

37. Heiser, *The Unseen Realm*, 110–22. The sons of God allotted to the nations, the divine princes of Daniel, are the conceptual point of origin for Paul's terminology of geographical rulership in the New Testament (i.e., terms such as "principalities," "powers," "rulers," "thrones," "dominions," "authorities"). See *The Unseen Realm*, 328–31. For a lengthy overview of Paul's terminology and its relation to the Deuteronomy 32 worldview, see Ronn Johnson, "The Old Testament Background for Paul's Principalities and Powers" (PhD diss., Dallas Theological Seminary, 2004). For brief discussions of the relevant terms, see D. G. Reid, "Principalities and Powers," *DPL* 746–52. In addition, as Aune notes, "The term *archontes* used as a designation for angelic beings first occurs in the LXX Dan 10:13, and seven times in Theod. Dan 10:13, 20–21; 12:1, where the LXX has *stratēgos*, 'commander,' 'magistrate,' all translations of the Aram *śar*, 'prince'" (see D. E. Aune, "Archon," *DDD* 82–85).

38. Textual critics of the Hebrew Bible are unanimous in agreement that the Qumran reading (in brackets) is superior to the Masoretic text in Deut 32:8, which reads *bny yśr 'l* ("sons of Israel"). See for example, P. W. Skehan, "A Fragment of the 'Song of Moses' (Deut 32) from Qumran," *BASOR* 136

sons of the Most High are later judged for corruption and rebellion in Psalm 82, thereby defecting from Yahweh's service.[39] More positively, the princely terminology is used to describe the "commander (*sar*) of the army of the LORD" (Josh 5:14).[40] The term "chief princes" obviously suggests tiered authority. Michael, the "prince" of Israel (Dan 10:21; 12:1) is one of the "chief princes" (Dan 10:13). As Collins notes:

> The origin of this [prince] idea is to be sought in the ancient Near Eastern concept of the Divine Council. The existence of national deities is assumed in the Rabshakeh's taunt: "Who among all the gods of the countries have delivered their countries out of my hand that the LORD should deliver Jerusalem out of my hand?" (2 Kgs 18:35 = Isa 36:20).[41]

Detailed discussions of the evidence for the hierarchal structure within the divine council may be found elsewhere.[42] "Sons of God" is familial language. "Angel" is the English translation of Hebrew *mal'ak* ("messenger"). This language is intentional. Sonship language in the context of royal ideology conveyed the notion of high-ranking administration. The children of the king were not mere messengers; they outranked messengers. The sons of the king were an elite level of authority; they were extensions of kingly authority, granted that status by the king himself. The king's governance would include hundreds, even thousands, of

---

(1954) 12–15; Julie Duncan, "A Critical Edition of Deuteronomy Manuscripts from Qumran, Cave IV. 4QDt^b, 4QDt^e, 4QDt^h, 4QDt^j, 4QDt^b, 4QDt^k, 4QDt^l," (PhD diss., Harvard University, 1989); Jeffrey H. Tigay, *Deuteronomy*, The JPS Torah Commentary (Philadelphia: Jewish Publication Society, 1996), 514–18; Heiser, "Deuteronomy 32:8 and the Sons of God," 52–74; Jan Joosten, "A Note on the Text of Deuteronomy xxxii 8," *VT* 57.4 (2007): 548–55.

39. Divine beings in a hostile, adversarial relationship to Yahweh are by definition no longer in his service. While still being part of the spiritual world, membership in Yahweh's council means obedient service to him. Divine beings such as Satan and the fallen sons of God of Gen 6:1–4 and Deut 32:8 are now under judgment and no longer part of how God administers his sovereign oversight.

40. See chapter 3 for a discussion of the identity of this prince.

41. John J. Collins, "Prince," *DDD* 663.

42. For a detailed discussed of the terminology and motifs that describe a hierarchy within the Israelite divine council and its terminological overlap with the Ugaritic/Canaanite divine council, see Mark S. Smith, *The Origins of Biblical Monotheism: Israel's Polytheistic Background and the Ugaritic Texts* (Oxford: Oxford University Press, 2001), 41–61. See also Mullen, *The Divine Council in Canaanite and Early Hebrew Literature*, 175–208; Handy, *Among the Host of Heaven*, 65–168; Ellen White, *Yahweh's Council: Its Structure and Membership* (Tübingen: Mohr Siebeck, 2014), 105–37. Most scholars see four tiers in the council of Ugarit but note that evidence for a fourth tier in Israel is quite weak. See the next chapter for more discussion of the divine council.

individuals, but authority was tiered. Family members (immediate and extended) had high ranking.

The hierarchy of the divine council is illustrated by the functional terminology for the members of God's heavenly host, to which we now turn.

## TERMS THAT DESCRIBE FUNCTION

There are a number of Hebrew words that denote what the members of the heavenly host do, or which provide a profile of activity. It might help the reader to think of these terms as job descriptions or attributes related to some task.

### 1. "Angel" (*mal'āk*; plural: *mal'ākîm*)

As noted above, the Hebrew word *mal'ak* means "messenger."[43] It is therefore not surprising that the related noun *melākah* refers generally to a "business journey" or "trade mission" in the Hebrew Bible.[44] In terms of the word's form, it is very likely that *mal'ak* derives from the Semitic verb *l'k* ("to send"), though this verb is not attested in the Hebrew Bible. This has led some scholars to suspect *mal'ak* was brought into Biblical Hebrew vocabulary from an external Semitic language.[45]

The meaning of "messenger" for Hebrew *mal'ak* is quite apparent from passages where human messengers are sent to deliver a message (Gen 32:3, 7; Deut 2:26; Neh 6:3; 2 Sam 11:19) or to bring back a message or report (Josh 6:17, 25). Human beings sent from God are also described with *mal'ak* (prophets: Hag 1:13; 2 Chron 36:15; priests: Mal 2:7). These examples (e.g., priests, those initially sent out without a message to deliver) show us that the primary idea behind the term is not a message but being *sent out* to serve God. Supernatural spirit beings sent from God

---

43. *HALOT*, 585.

44. *HALOT*, 585.

45. Meier writes in this regard: "The *mēm-* prefix and a-vowels of Heb *mal'āk* conform generally to what is expected for an instrumental noun (*maqtal*) identifying the vehicle or tool by which the action of the verb is accomplished (in this case, the means by which a message is sent, hence 'messenger'). Because the verb is not attested in Hebrew, some suspect that this noun is a loan word from another language. However, since the root is widely attested in the Semitic languages, and since even the verb is attested in north-west Semitic (Ugaritic), it is best to see the Hebrew noun as a relic of a once more generative root that otherwise disappeared in Hebrew because of a semantic overlap with a preferred and less specific term ŠLḤ 'send.'" See S. A. Meier, "Angel I," *DDD* 45.

are the most frequent referent of the term. The English translation "angel," which is actually drawn from the Greek New Testament (*angelos*) serves to distinguish supernatural messengers from human ones.

It is interesting to note that angelic messengers are at times explicitly described as "men" (*'ănāšîm*) in the Old Testament (e.g., Gen 18:1–8, 16, 22; 19:1–22).[46] Human form can more or less be assumed in other passages, as it would seem necessary for a human being to be able to comprehend that divine beings were present (e.g., Gen 28:12; 32:1).[47] There are exceptions to this template (Gen 21:17; 22:11), and so it cannot be said that human form was necessary for angelic interaction with people. Human form for God himself is also common in the Old Testament.[48]

The term "angel," then, is basically a job description—a spirit being from God's heavenly host sent by God to deliver or receive a message. This is a particular subset task of the broad service the members of the heavenly host render to God. As we shall see later, the term also factors into discussions of hierarchy in the supernatural world of the Old Testament.

## 2. "Minister" (verb: *šrt*, Piel stem: *šērēt*)

We encountered this job description earlier in our survey of terminology. Psalm 103:20 refers specifically to angels, then adds "Bless the LORD, all his hosts, his ministers [*mešortāyw*],[49] who do his will!" (Ps 103:21). Translating *mal'akim* per our earlier discussion, Psalm 104:4 tells us that God "makes his angels [*mal'akim*] winds, his ministers [*mešortāyw*] as flaming fire."[50]

---

46. Note that in Gen 19:1–22 the Hebrew text alternates between describing the angelic messengers as "angels" (*mal'akim*) and as "men" (*'ănāšîm*). Compare vv. 1 and 15 (*mal'akim*) with vv. 10, 12, and 16 (*'ănāšîm*).

47. In biblical material there are no instances where angels are described as women. This likely reflects an Israelite culture that, for the most part, assigned leadership roles to men. Zechariah 5:9 is often offered as an exception to his portrayal, but it is not. See chapter 8 for discussion.

48. Genesis 18–19 is perhaps the most well-known instance where Yahweh comes to people as a man. See the extended discussion involving the Angel of the Lord (Yahweh) in *The Unseen Realm* (chapters 16–18). There are a number of recent studies of this scriptural phenomenon: Benjamin D. Sommer, *The Bodies of God and the World of Ancient Israel* (Cambridge: Cambridge University Press, 2009); Esther J. Hamori, *"When Gods Were Men": The Embodied God in Biblical and Near Eastern Literature* (Berlin: De Gruyter, 2008); Anne K. Knafl, *Forming God: Divine Anthropomorphism in the Pentateuch* (Winona Lake, IN: Eisenbrauns, 2014).

49. The Hebrew *mešortāyw* is a plural participle (Piel) of the verb *šērēt* suffixed by a pronoun.

50. Author's translation.

The Hebrew verb *šrt* has been broadly defined as "attending to the service of God."[51] The two instances in Psalms 103 and 104 are the only occasions where the verb is used to describe angelic service. Daniel 7:10 conveys the same "ministering" idea, though with an Aramaic verb (*šmš*): "a thousand thousands served [*yešammešûn*] him."

The verb is used frequently of priestly service in Israel ("to minister to God"; e.g., Deut 10:8; 21:5; Jer 33:21; Ezek 40:46), and so a more nuanced understanding is possible:

> Given the basic meaning "to attend (a superior)," it is understandable that the most important category for the theological use of *'bd*, "to serve God with one's entire being," does not occur with the verb *šrt* (Piel). Rather, the meaning corresponding to the verb *šrt* (Piel) does not refer to people but to God, the performance of the cult. *šrt* (Piel) is the specific verb for this activity.[52]

The fact that most of the Old Testament usage is linked to priestly service contributed to the development of the notion of an angelic priesthood in Second Temple Judaism.[53] However, the Old Testament concept of angelic mediation (considered below) is also an important element of that concept.

## 3. "Watcher" ( *'îr*; plural: *'îrîn*)

The Aramaic term *'îr* occurs three times in the Old Testament (Dan 4:13, 17, 23 [Aramaic vv. 10, 14, 20]):

> I saw in the visions of my head as I lay in bed, and behold, a watcher [ *'îr*], a holy one,[54] came down from heaven. (v. 13)

> The sentence is by the decree of the watchers [ *'îrîn*], the decision by the word of the holy ones. (v. 17)

---

51. *HALOT*, 1662.

52. *TLOT*, 1406.

53. Carol Newsom, "He Has Established for Himself Priests: Human and Angelic Priesthood in the Qumran Sabbath Shirot," in *Archaeology and History in the Dead Sea Scrolls: The New York University Conference in Memory of Yigael Yadin* (Sheffield: Sheffield Academic Press, 1990), 101–20; Joseph L. Angel, *Otherworldly and Eschatological Priesthood in the Dead Sea Scrolls* (Leiden: Brill, 2010).

54. The ESV correctly renders the Aramaic phrasing *'îr wĕqaddîš* as "a watcher, a holy one" instead of the more common "a watcher and a holy one." The *waw* conjunction between the two nouns should be understood as creating apposition between them. This is certain from the context—only one heavenly being speaks with Daniel in the passage. In addition, the singular participles that follow, which are used for the heavenly figure's proclamation in Dan 4:14, point to one entity.

And because the king saw a watcher [ *'îr*], a holy one, coming down from heaven ... (v. 23)

As we shall see in a subsequent chapter, this Aramaic term is found much more frequently in Second Temple Jewish literature.

Scholarly understanding of the meaning of *'îr* depends on the presumed Semitic root from which one presumes it derived. Dahood proposed that the term came from Ugaritic *ġyr* ("to protect").[55] Murray initially believed that a better option was Akkadian *êru* ("be wakeful"), but changed his mind after Kaufman's important work on Akkadian influences in Aramaic couldn't find primary source data for the connection.[56] As Collins notes, however:

> Some biblical precedents for the notion of angelic beings as "watchful ones", but with different terminology, have been proposed. The most noteworthy is Zech 4:10 which refers to seven "eyes of the LORD which range through the whole earth". The Watchers, however, never have this function in Daniel or the non-canonical literature.[57]

More recent research by Amar Annus leads to the conclusion that the term does indeed have a connection to Akkadian material—specifically, the supernatural *apkallu*, the central figures in the Babylonian story that is the specific backdrop to the infamous episode in Genesis 6:1–4.[58] Annus writes:

> Figurines of *apkallu*s were buried in boxes as foundation deposits in Mesopotamian buildings in order to avert evil from the house. The term *maṣṣarē*, "watchers," is used of these sets of figurines in Akkadian incantations according to ritual texts. This appellation matches the Aramaic term *'yryn*, "the wakeful ones," for both good angels and the Watchers.[59]

---

55. Mitchell Dahood, *Psalms I: 1–50* (AYB 16; New Haven: Yale University Press, 1965), 55.

56. Robert Murray, "The Origin of Aramaic *'îr*, Angel," *Orientalia* 53.2 (1984): 306. See Stephen A. Kaufman, *The Akkadian Influences on Aramaic* (Chicago: University of Chicago Press, 1974).

57. John J. Collins, "Watcher," *DDD* 894.

58. In addition to the work of Annus, see my detailed description of the relationship between Gen 6:1–4 and the Mesopotamian *apkallu* in *Reversing Hermon*, 37–54.

59. Amar Annus, "On the Origin of Watchers: A Comparative Study of the Antediluvian Wisdom in Mesopotamian and Jewish Traditions," *JSP* 19.4 (2010): 277–320.

As the work of Annus and other scholars demonstrates, Second Temple Jewish literature, particularly 1 Enoch and The Book of Giants, draws on Mesopotamian material for its retelling of events associated with the flood.[60] "Watchers" is the overwhelming choice of term for the fallen sons of God in Genesis 6:1–4 in this later literature; the connection to the Akkadian *maṣṣarē* provides a secure basis for understanding the meaning of *ʿîr* to be "vigilant watchfulness." This, of course, is consistent with being wakeful and a guardian role.

## 4. "Host" (*ṣabà*; plural: *ṣebàôt*); "Mighty Ones" (*gibborîm*, *ʾabbîrîm*)

It is best to consider these Hebrew terms as a group, since they ostensibly pertain to the same functional service to Yahweh: that of serving in his heavenly army. The broadest is *ṣabà*, a common noun that generally refers to a multitude of people (Ps 68:12), compulsory labor (Isa 40:2; Job 7:1), conscripted military service (Num 1:3; 31:3), or an army (Num 2:8; 2 Sam 3:23).[61]

"Host" terminology overlaps with several of the Hebrew words we've studied. As we saw in 1 Kings 22:19, God is surrounded by the heavenly host (*ṣabà*) of spirit beings. His ministers in Psalm 103:21 are called "his hosts" (*ṣebàāyw*). The same term is used in parallel to "angels" in Psalm 148:2. Since the spirit beings in God's service are called "stars," it is no surprise to see them collectively referred to as the "host of heaven" (Jer 33:22; Neh 9:6; Dan 4:35).

The most familiar association of "host" terminology with God's loyal heavenly agents is "Lord of hosts." The phrase is highly controversial in Old Testament scholarship, mainly because it is quite unusual in Biblical Hebrew to link the divine name with another noun. Some scholars argue that it is grammatically impossible.[62] Consequently, scholars have

---

60. In addition to Annus, see Loren Stuckenbruck, *The Book of Giants from Qumran: Text, Translation, and Commentary* (Tübingen: Mohr Siebeck, 1997); Ida Fröhlich, "Mesopotamian Elements and the Watchers Traditions," in *The Watchers in Jewish and Christian Traditions*, eds. Angela Kim Harkins, Kelley Coblentz Bautch, and John C. Endres (Minneapolis: Fortress, 2014), 11–24.

61. *HALOT*, 994–95.

62. The more technical (and accurate) way of expressing this issue is that it has long been thought that Hebrew grammar forbids the divine name in a construct phrase. The problem is that in the phrase "Lord of hosts" the divine name is in the Hebrew construct position, something that for many years was considered grammatically impermissible. The opinion of Joüon and Muraoka is

proposed a variety of translations of the combination other than the traditional "Lord of hosts."

As Mettinger points out, opinion on this matter has shifted, mainly because clear instances of the divine name in the Hebrew construct position in phrases have surfaced in extrabiblical texts:

> The traditional understanding, viz. as a construct relation, "Yahweh of ṣĕbāʾôt" seems the most probable solution and is made less problematical by the epigraphic attestation of analogues such as "Yahweh of Teman" and "Yahweh of Samaria" in Kuntillet Ajrud. But, even if this is the case, the construct relation itself allows for various interpretations of the Zebaoth element.[63]

For our purposes, Mettinger's point is well taken. The traditional translation can stand, but its meaning needs a bit more attention. What exactly does Lord "of" hosts mean? Certainly, it speaks of Yahweh as commander in chief. It is not disputed that the hosts are his and he commands them. Perhaps the most fruitful of the alternative translation attempts is to consider the second element of the phrase, which Hebrew grammarians call "an intensive plural abstract."[64] The result would be that the phrase *means* "Yahweh, the Almighty." The phrase therefore conveys "a characteristic designation for the God-King enthroned on the cherub throne" as uncontested lord of all heavenly powers (1 Sam 4:4; 2 Sam 6:2; Pss 80:2; 99:1).[65]

Angels are referred to as *gibborîm* in one passage, Psalm 103:20 ("Bless the LORD, O you his angels, you mighty ones [*gibborîm*] who do his word"). The wider context isn't overtly military. That acknowledgement does not eliminate the possibility that the psalmist was influenced by the divine warrior motif when he chose the term. It is true that *gibborîm* frequently describes warriors (e.g., Isa 21:17; 2 Kgs 24:16; Ps 33:16),[66]

---

representative: "In the divine name צְבָאוֹת יהוה, the first noun, being a proper noun, cannot be constructed on the second" (*GBH* §1310.)

63. T. N. D. Mettinger, "Yahweh Zebaoth," *DDD* 920.

64. *TLOT,* 1045.

65. *TLOT,* 1045.

66. The term *gibbôr* is often over-read as "giants" due to its presence in Gen 6:4 in concert with *nephilîm*. That the lemma does not inherently point to members of the sinister giant clans associated with the *nephilîm* (Deut 2–3; Num 13:32–33) is easily demonstrated. For example, Israelite warriors under Joshua who fought against these feared enemies are described as *gibborîm* (Josh 6:2; 8:3). David is as well (1 Sam 16:18). Even God is called *gibbôr* in Deut 10:17.

but this is not always the case. The term is occasionally employed to describe community leaders or upstanding citizens (Ruth 2:1; Ezra 7:28). Had Psalm 103:20 described the heavenly *gibborîm* as "those who defeat God's enemies," a warfare context would be clearer. But the lack of an explicit context here does not undo a warrior perspective. Readers would have quite naturally read the term as a reference to members of Yahweh's heavenly army.

The description of heavenly beings as *'abbîrîm* in Psalm 78:25 must be approached in a similar fashion. As part of his lengthy recollection of Israel's obstinate behavior in the wilderness the psalmist wrote:

> And he [God] rained down on them manna to eat
> and gave them the grain of heaven.
> Man ate of the bread of the angels (*'abbîrîm*);
> he sent them food in abundance. (Ps 78:24–25)

The immediate context is not militaristic. Yet *'abbîr* (singular) is used of warriors (Jer 46:15; Lam 1:15), but the term broadly refers to virility and strength (Job 24:22; 34:20; Ps 76:5 [Hebrew, v. 6]; Isa 10:13). "Able-bodied" is likely an appropriate understanding of *'abbîr*. This characterization would of course be required of a soldier, so usage of the term for fighting men makes good sense.

This brief survey of usage may create the impression that the ESV translation of *'abbîrîm* as "angels" is idiosyncratic. The choice is not as odd as one might suppose. Manna was called the "bread of heaven" (Exod 16:4; Neh 9:15). The plural *'abbîrîm* can be understood as an instance of metonymy, "a figure of speech consisting of the use of the name of one thing for that of another of which it is an attribute or with which it is associated."[67] Plural "mighty ones" associated with heaven, the dwelling place of God, would make "angels" an option for translators. But as metonymy, this instance of *'abbîrîm* contributes little to the military metaphor.[68]

---

67. *Merriam-Webster's Collegiate Dictionary*, 11th ed., s.v. "metonymy."

68. The lone occurrence of *šin'ān* ("archers") in Ps 68:17 (Heb, v. 18) occurs in a militaristic context but is problematic. The term may be cognate to Ugaritic *ṯnn*, itself related to Akkadian *šanannu* ("archer, chariot archer"). The Hebrew phrase *'alpê šin'ān* would therefore mean "thousands of warriors." This was Albright's position. However, there is another alternative based on arguments of ancient Semitic phonology (a glide marker) that prevents Albright's proposal from being decisive. This alternative would produce a lemma that simply produces a meaning of "incalculable thousands" with no military nuance. LXX reads *euthēnountōn* ("rejoicing ones") which may indicate a Hebrew reading of *š'nn*, a reading found in one Hebrew manuscript (Sang Youl Cho, *Lesser Deities in the*

## 5. "Mediator" (mēlîṣ)

In Job 33, Elihu, one of Job's "miserable comforters" rebukes him as follows:

> Man is also rebuked with pain on his bed
>> and with continual strife in his bones,
> so that his life loathes bread,
>> and his appetite the choicest food.
> His flesh is so wasted away that it cannot be seen,
>> and his bones that were not seen stick out.
> His soul draws near the pit,
>> and his life to those who bring death.
> If there be for him an angel,
>> a mediator, one of the thousand,
>> to declare to man what is right for him,
> and he is merciful to him, and says,
>> "Deliver him from going down into the pit;
>> I have found a ransom …" (Job 33:19–24)

The verse of interest for our study is Job 33:23: "If there be for [a man] an angel, a mediator." The Hebrew term translated "mediator" is mēlîṣ.[69] It occurs in the phrase mal'āk mēlîṣ, a grammatical construction that is *not* a construct phrase that would require a translation like "a messenger/ angel of a mediator."[70] Rather, as Meier notes, "they are either in apposition, function as poetic parallels, or the first noun is modified by the second adjectival participle."[71] The result is that Job 33:23 puts forth the concept of angelic mediation for human beings.

As we will learn in the next chapter, mediation can be understood as "turning" to someone for an explanation of God's activity. This would

---

Ugaritic Texts and the Hebrew Bible: A Comparative Study of their Nature and Roles [Piscataway, NJ: Gorgias Press, 2007], 238). See HALOT, 1596; William Foxwell Albright, "A Catalogue of Early Hebrew Lyric Poems (Psalm LXVIII)," HUCA 23.1 (1950): 1–39 (25, 38).

69. The Septuagint oddly presents the mediator of Job 33:23 as a "death-bearing" angel, likely on the basis of how the śaṭan of Job 1–2 kills Job's children. See John G. Gammie, "The Angelology and Demonology in the Septuagint of the Book of Job," HUCA 56 (1985): 1–19 (5–6).

70. Morphologically tagged databases of the Hebrew Bible vary on their parsing of mēlîṣ, some having it as a noun, others as a Hiphil singular participle functioning as a noun (appositionally) or adjectivally modifying mal'āk.

71. S. A. Meier, "Mediator," DDD 554.

make good sense in Job's case, but the coherence of the idea requires understanding participation within the divine council.

## 6. "cherubim" (*kerubîm*); "seraphim" (*śerāpîm*)

It may seem strange to find these familiar words considered together in the section focused on functional terms. In fact, both Hebrew terms describe the same function: guardianship of the presence of God. Hartenstein notes:

> Seraphim and cherubim both belong to the so-called "Michwesen," *hybrid figures.* This means they are *combining attributes from various animals and from humans.* ... We find such beings in the ancient Near East especially in contexts necessary *to represent power* and *to prevent evil.* ... [In Mesopotamia] the powers of the universe were concentrated in the main city. The inhabitants of that city were (on a mythical level) identical with the cosmic abodes of the gods. This spatial symbolism involves distinctions between the higher and lower regions of the world (*vertical dimension*) and outer areas (*horizontal dimension*). When the ancient mind travels (in reality or imagination) through peripheral regions, the inhabitants of distant lands seem to be strange and dangerous. So the [hybrid figures] often were depicted as non-humans and monsters in opposition to men. ... When tracing the traditional background of the biblical cherubim and seraphim, this symbolism of time and space should be remembered.[72]

Hartenstein's point is that cherubim and seraphim would be viewed as a blessing (protection) by those welcome in the sacred space they guarded, but as a terror to those unwelcome.

These terms could be considered as describing the nature of heavenly beings, since cherubim and seraphim are divine creatures. Both are said to have wings, though the number varies (Exod 25:20; 37:9; Isa 6:2). Cherubim are at times assigned four faces and both human and bovine body parts (Ezek 1; 10). Seraphim is the plural form of *śārāp,* a Hebrew word also translated "snake" (Num 21:6, 8; Isa 14:29). These descriptions

---

72. Friedhelm Hartenstein, "Cherubim and Seraphim in the Bible and in the Light of Ancient Near Eastern Sources," in *Angels: The Concept of Celestial Beings—Origins, Development and Reception,* eds. Friedrich V. Reiterer, Tobias Nicklas, and Karin Schöplin (Berlin: De Gruyter, 2007), 154–88 (157, 158). Italics are Hartenstein's.

are reflected in iconography from the biblical period.[73] Neither is ever qualified with the term *mal'āk*, and so it is incorrect to think of cherubim and seraphim as angels.[74]

In Alice Wood's detailed treatment of the Hebrew term in her major study on cherubim,[75] she notes:

> Shades of meaning that are attributed to the cherubim in the biblical texts can be further accentuated by means of a comparison with the corresponding Semitic data. It is the form *kurību,* derived from the Akkadian *karābu* "to pray", which provides us with the closest lexical parallel to the biblical כְּרוּב. If the two words are etymologically related, then the Akkadian evidence highlights the apotropaic[76] qualities of the cherubim. ... The cherubim are placed at the boundary between the sacred and the profane, to protect the holy from contamination.[77]

Protecting the sanctity of God's presence is obviously a functional role. While this meaning is elicited from comparative Akkadian material, it is Egyptian literature which informs us that seraphim perform the same function.[78]

It is common for interpreters to presume the lemma behind seraphim is the verb *śārap*, which means "to burn."[79] As recent research has shown, this is only part of the picture. As I noted in *The Unseen Realm*, "It is more likely that *seraphim* derives from the Hebrew noun *śārap* ("serpent"), which in turn is drawn from Egyptian throne guardian terminology and conceptions."[80] As recent research demonstrates, the Egyptian

---

73. Othmar Keel and Adolphe Gutbug, *Jahwe-Visionen und Siegelkunst: eine neue Deutung der Majestätsschilderungen in Jes 6, Ez 1 und 10 und Sach 4* (Stuttgart: Verlag Katholisches Bibelwerk, 1977); O. Keel and C. Uehlinger, *Göttinnen, Götter und Gottessymbole. Neue Erkenntnisse zur Religionsgeschichte Kanaans und Israels aufgrund bislang unerschlossener ikonographischen Quellen* (Freiburg: Herder, 1992).

74. In concert with earlier note 45, the conclusion drawn from this textual circumstance is that, contrary to centuries of tradition, angels (*mal'ākîm*) are never described in the Bible as having wings. See Chapter 8 for that topic.

75. Alice Wood, *Of Wings and Wheels: A Synthetic Study of the Biblical Cherubim* (Berlin: De Gruyter, 2008).

76. The term "apotropaic" means "to avert from evil" (which, by extension, refers to the pollution of sanctity).

77. Wood, *Of Wings and Wheels*, 155. See also Hartenstein, "Cherubim and Seraphim," 161–62.

78. See Hartenstein, "Cherubim and Seraphim," 165–66, for examples.

79. *HALOT*, 1358–59.

80. Heiser, *The Unseen Realm*, 297 n. 4.

Uraeus serpent, drawn from two species of Egyptian cobras, fits all the elements of the supernatural seraphim who attend Yahweh's holy presence in Isaiah 6. The relevant cobra species spit "burning" venom, can expand wide flanges of skin on either side of their bodies—considered "wings" in antiquity—when threatened, and are (obviously) serpentine.[81] As Joines notes, the protective nature of the uraeus cobra is evident: "A function of the uraeus is to protect the pharaoh and sacred objects by breathing out fire on his enemies."[82]

## SUMMARY

Our brief overview of Old Testament terms for God's heavenly host and its members ought to make clear that talk of "angels" in the Old Testament is both too simplistic and incomplete. We are of course accustomed to that term, but it fails to do justice to the how an Israelite would have thought about the spiritual world. As we proceed chronologically into the Second Temple and New Testament eras, we'll discover how the variegated vocabulary of the Old Testament outlook was lost, providing some explanation for our own contemporary ignorance of the complexities and nuances of an Old Testament theology of the heavenly host. Our immediate task is far from complete, though. Now that we have a grasp of the Old Testament terminology for God's divine council and its members, we need to get into specifics: what they actually do.

---

81. Philippe Provençal, "Regarding the Noun שׂרף [śārāp] in the Hebrew Bible," *JSOT* 29.3 (2005): 371–79; Karen R. Joines, "Winged Serpents in Isaiah's Inaugural Vision," *JBL* 86.4 (1967): 410–15. Quoting Keel, Provençal writes (376): "According to Keel, the שׂרפים that are mentioned in Isaiah 6 are theriomorphic lower deities. The fact that they are described as having legs and hands/claws does not, for Keel, invalidate this understanding since he is able to show iconographic examples taken from Egyptian archaeology of Uraeus-serpents in cobra form clearly having human-like limbs and head." The Egyptian context for portions of the book of Isaiah is well known to scholars. Several seals bearing the name Hezekiah, for example, use the familiar winged *kheper* beetle as royal iconography. The names of Isaiah 9:6 are often compared to the pharaonic fivefold titular. On Hezekiah's seal, see Meir Lubetski, "King Hezekiah's Seal Revisited," *BAR* 27.4 (2001): 24–36. Lubetski writes (p. 24): "The image is a direct borrowing from Egyptian iconography and can be understood as adaptation by the great Judahite king to advance his own national agenda." On the possible Egyptian contributions to understanding the names in Isaiah 9, see Máire Byrne, "The Influence of Egyptian Throne Names on Isaiah 9: 5: A Reassessment of the Debate in Light of the Divine," in *A Land Like Your Own: Traditions of Israel and Their Reception*, ed. Jason M. Silverman (Eugene, OR: Pickwick Publications, 2010), 87–100; J. J. M. Roberts, "Whose Child Is This? Reflections on the Speaking Voice in Isaiah 9: 5," *HTR* 90.2 (1997): 115–29.

82. Joines, "Winged Serpents," 412.

# CHAPTER 2

# The Heavenly Host in Service to God

As noted in the last chapter, the label "angel" is just a job description—a particular service rendered on God's behalf by certain members of the heavenly host. The same is true of "cherubim" and "seraphim," both of which describe guardianship of the divine presence. But there is more to what angels and other members of the heavenly host do in God's service than these terms convey.

An accurate understanding of how the members of the heavenly host serve God must derive from the biblical text. Our goal is to build upon our earlier survey of relevant terms, beginning with some general observations about the abilities of members of the heavenly host.

## SHARED ABILITIES FOR SERVICE

The biblical vocabulary makes it clear that the members of the heavenly host are by nature unembodied spirit beings. Their normative domain is the spiritual world. They were present with God before the creation of the world and human beings.[1] This "otherness" raises questions for many Bible readers:

- Are the members of the heavenly host eternal?
- Are they impersonal forces or persons (i.e., do they have personality?)

---

1. For additional discussion on angelic abilities, see chapter 8.

- What attributes and limitations do they possess?
- Do they have free will, or are they "spiritual robots"?

The first question is the easiest to answer. In biblical theology, there is only one Spirit Being who is eternal—having no beginning and no end, never described as being created, whose existence preceded creation and is therefore "from everlasting to everlasting" (Ps 90:2).

All other 'elōhîm were created by the lone, uncreated God of the Bible.[2] He is the creator of the other members of his host council (Ps 148:1–5, esp. v. 5). Since the members of the host of heaven are identified with the stars (Job 38:7) or called stars (Isa 14:12), passages that describe the creation of the heavens "with all their host" speak to the belief of the biblical writers that *everything* in the heavens came to be from God alone (Gen 2:1; Neh 9:6; Ps 33:6). Consequently, the members of the heavenly host aren't eternal since they had a beginning.[3]

The members of the heavenly host also aren't everlasting or immortal, at least in terms of their unchangeable, intrinsic attributes. Their immortality is dependent on God's will. Psalm 82:6–7 is explicit proof of this limitation. The 'elōhîm spirit beings in rebellion against Yahweh will have their existence terminated in God's own time and at God's discretion. These beings "are gods ('elōhîm), sons of the Most High, all of you; nevertheless, like men you shall die, and fall like any prince." The theological point is transparent. God is the single being whose existence is entirely under his own control. No other being can take it away. That is not true of other spirit beings.

As created beings, the members of the heavenly host therefore are not exhaustive "attribute replicas" of God. They have inherent limitations in many respects in comparison to God. Like human beings, whatever the

---

2. Yahweh of Israel is singled out as unique among all 'elōhîm in other ways. Yahweh alone is all-powerful (Jer 32:17, 27; Pss 72:18; 115:3), the sovereign king over the all that he has made, including other 'elōhîm (Pss 83:18; 95:3; Dan 4:35; 1 Kgs 22:19; Isa 37:16, 20). Yahweh therefore is the only 'elōhîm who deserves worship from his creations (Pss 29:1–2; 86:10; 148:13; Exod 22:20; Isa 26:13). In fact, Nehemiah 9:6 specifically declares that Yahweh is unique—there is only *one* Yahweh ("You are the LORD [Yahweh], you alone").

3. "Eternal" is not synonymous with "everlasting." The latter speaks of something having no end, not something having no beginning. An eternal being has no beginning and no end. See Alan Cairns, *Dictionary of Theological Terms* (Belfast; Greenville, SC: Ambassador Emerald International, 2002), 157; Millard J. Erickson, *The Concise Dictionary of Christian Theology* (Wheaton, IL: Crossway, 2001), 60.

'elōhîm of the heavenly host are, they are less than God. And what they are (and what we are) is contingent upon God's own decision to create them and share his attributes with them.

This connection to humanity is not a mere convenience. The idea is scriptural, deriving from the plural language in Genesis 1:26 ("And God said, 'Let us create humankind in our image and according to our likeness,'" LEB). In *The Unseen Realm* I devote a good deal of space to discussing the exegetical basis for this passage being an announcement by God to the members of his council and not an oblique reference to the Trinity and for interpreting the image as representation of God, not as a specific attribute given to humans or the members of God's council.[4] The plural language links God both to us and to the members of the council, to whom he is speaking.[5] They, like us, are reflections of their Creator. Humans and intelligent spirit beings are representatives of God in their respective domains.

Other scholars have taken note of this connection and its implications. For example, Patrick D. Miller observes:

> "Let us make humankind in our image, after our likeness" (Gen. 1:26). While other interpretations are possible, the most plausible understanding of these first person plural verbs and suffixes is that God's words are a directive to the divine council. At the point in the text where the narrative speaks of a close relation between the divine world and the human world and suggests that the human partakes of the divine in some fashion, it refers not simply to the deity but to the whole divine world, the divine beings. The human is both a

---

4. Heiser, *The Unseen Realm*, 38–45, 58–60. Not only is there is no exegetical basis to restrict the plural group addressed by God to two other persons, but sound biblical theology requires us to assert that all members of the Trinity are co-equal in all attributes. Consequently, God would have no need to announce or inform the other members of a Trinity that he intended to create humanity—they would already know that, or they would not be equally omniscient. Appeal to Jesus' inability to know certain things (e.g., Matt 24:36) as the Second Person of the Trinity to explain presumed Trinitarian ignorance in Gen 1:26 fails coherence, as this limitation is of necessity linked to incarnation. The incarnation is not in play in Gen 1:26.

5. This connection is also evident when one compares Gen 3:5 ("For God knows that when you eat of it your eyes will be opened, and you will be like God [ 'elōhîm], knowing good and evil") with Gen 3:22 ("Then the LORD God said, 'Behold, the man has become like one of us in knowing good and evil'"). The phrase "like one of us" clearly informs us that we ought to read 'elōhîm in v. 5 as a plural ("you will be like gods"). In both verses the following participle ("knowing") is grammatically plural. As I discuss in *The Unseen Realm* (pp. 62–63), both humans and the members of God's divine host share God's attribute of intelligence and freedom to choose. However, until humanity made a willing, conscious decision to disobey God (i.e., act autonomously), they had no knowledge of rebellion.

consequence of Yahweh's decision in and to the council and a reflection of the divine world as it is embodied in the heavenly assembly. The *ben 'ādām* ["son of man; human one"] is like the *ben 'ĕlîm* ["son of God; divine one"], a notion expressed explicitly also in Psalm 8. … The creation of the human creature is the establishment of a representative from the divine world to rule the created order. The image of the divine ones is placed on earth to embody and represent the divine ones in subduing, ruling, and governing the earth. The creation of male and female provides for the sustaining of that rule in the perpetuation of the creation.[6]

The implication of this connection is that, if we desire to know what the members of the heavenly host are like, we should consider ourselves analogous. Psalm 8:5, the passage cited by Miller, informs us that God has made us "a little lower than the heavenly beings [*'elōhîm*]."[7] Yet God shared his attributes with us as he first did with them. What are members of the heavenly host like? They are like God and like us. Think about these attributes that we share with our Creator: intelligence, creativity, emotions, rationality, and volition. Our fellow imagers, the members of the heavenly host, have them as well, because they are also his imagers.

Our embodiment naturally means we live with significant limitations that unembodied intelligent beings don't. Because of what happened in Eden, our lifespans are severely curtailed. We die after a brief existence in the world God made for us. It is only at that point that we experience the presence of God, presuming we are part of his family through redemptive grace. We are thus far less intelligent, creative, and wise than the members of the spiritual world. We simply do not know what they have

---

6. Miller, *Israelite Religion and Biblical Theology*, 434. The translation of the transliterated Hebrew was supplied by this author. For specific exegetical details for reading Gen 1:26 as an announcement by God to the members of his council, see Patrick D. Miller, *Genesis 1–11: Studies in Structure and Theme* (Sheffield: University of Sheffield, 1978), 9–18. Not only does seeing the Trinity in Gen 1:26 ignore the grammar and syntax of the passage, but it means reading the New Testament back into the Old Testament. The result is an interpretation foreign to the thinking of the original writer and his readers. The "plural of majesty" is also not an option. As Joüon and Muraoka note, "The *we* of majesty does not exist in Hebrew" (see *GBH*, 347 [§114e]). The point here is that the plural of majesty does exist for nouns (see *GBH* §136d). The plurality of Gen 1:26 does not derive from the nouns—the issue is the verbal forms. See also John C. Beckman, "*Pluralis Majestatis*: Biblical Hebrew," *EHLL* 3:145–46.

7. Hebrews 2:7 has "a little lower than angels [*angelous*]." See the discussion of New Testament terminology for why the writer of Hebrews translates *'elōhîm* with *angelous* (Greek masculine accusative plural).

learned through access to God and lifespans of many eons. But what they are and know is part of our own destiny in Christ.[8]

Free will is part of this attribute matrix. The interest in free will as it relates to members of the heavenly host arises from questions about how and when Satan turned against God, or whether angels still can, at some future time, rebel. There is no scriptural indication in either the Old or New Testament that the ability to rebel against God's authority was "turned off" at any time. Consequently, they can still conceivably fall. But one would suspect that, given the fate of divine rebels recounted in Scripture, those who remain faithful would be much less inclined toward rebellion.[9]

This brief foray into the attributes heavenly beings possess by virtue of their status as representatives of their Creator helps us to grasp what they do. Their service to God can be expressed in three broad categories: participation in God's heavenly council, obedience to God's decisions, and praise of the Most High. We will consider each with its respective aspects.

## PARTICIPATION IN GOD'S HEAVENLY COUNCIL

Our discussion of Yahweh's divine council in the previous chapter made brief mention of council roles, mostly in regard to how the role messengers (mal'ākîm; angels) provided evidence for tiered authority in the council.[10] Council members do more than just run the heavenly

---

8. This destiny, to be like the stars as it were, has deep Old Testament roots. The key passage is Gen 15:5, that the offspring of Abraham would be like the stars. Paul quotes this passage in Rom 4:18 as part of his argument, which includes the statement that Abraham and his offspring would inherit the kosmos (Rom 4:13). Most Bible interpreters take the promise of Gen 15:5 as a numerical one. This is certainly the case, but there is a noteworthy stream of Second Temple Jewish interpretation—culminating in the New Testament—that considers the promise qualitative as well. The point is that believers, the children of Abraham through faith in the promised messianic seed, would not only be as numerous as the stars but would be made divine, as stars, the members of the heavenly host, were considered to be. Being made "like the stars" is part of the biblical theology of glorification or theosis. For the relevant primary sources and academic secondary literature, see David A. Burnett, "Abraham's Star-Like Seed: Neglected Functional Elements in the Patriarchal Promise of Genesis 15," MA thesis, Criswell College, 2015.

9. See Heiser, The Unseen Realm, chapters 8–15; Heiser, Reversing Hermon, chapters 1–2 and the discussion of 1 Cor 11:10 in chapter 8.

10. Some recent work on demons by evangelical scholar John Walton requires some comment, as it potentially creates misunderstanding on the nature of the divine council and its tiered structuring. See John Walton, "Demons in Mesopotamia and Israel: Exploring the Category of Non-Divine but Supernatural Entities," in Windows to the Ancient World of the Hebrew Bible: Essays in Honor of Samuel Greengus, ed. Bill T. Arnold, Nancy L. Erickson, and John H. Walton (Winona Lake, IN;

mail room. They engage with God as a functioning bureaucracy, a role nuanced in three ways.

## 1. Contributing to Council Resolutions

We looked briefly at 1 Kings 22:19–23 in the previous chapter. Our goal then was to establish that the members of Yahweh's host were spirit beings. There is more to observe in the passage:

> I saw the LORD sitting on his throne, and all the host of heaven standing beside him on his right hand and on his left; and the LORD said, "Who will entice Ahab, that he may go up and fall at Ramoth-gilead?" And one said one thing, and another said another. Then a spirit came forward and stood before the LORD, saying, "I will entice him." And

Eisenbrauns, 2014), 229–46. Walton's goal in this essay is to articulate a taxonomy of divine beings that allows alignment between the spiritual worldviews of Mesopotamia and Israel. Consequently (and unfortunately), he excludes civilizations like that of Egypt and ancient Canaan (e.g., Ugarit) from focus. Though Walton is clear that he is focusing on Mesopotamia, these exclusions are noteworthy. To make claims about Israel's divine council as Walton does without appeal to Ugaritic material—which all scholars in the field note constitutes the closest parallels to the Israelite divine council—will produce statements that can be misconstrued. For example, Walton's taxonomic hierarchy (based on Mesopotamian analogies) includes several classes, the first two of which are: "gods" (class I), defined as those who receive sacrifices; and "functionaries" (class II), where he assigns *mal'akim* ("angels"), cherubim, and seraphim. Walton believes, "There is no precedent for class II spirits to be equated with the class I members of the divine council, even after they are largely domesticated in later Mesopotamian literature" (see pp. 239–40, footnotes 46 and 49). This statement could be confusing in that its wording suggests that angels (*mal'akim*—a class II term in his scheme) are not part of the divine council. Such a claim would, of course, be disputed by a number of studies on the divine council and the closer parallels to Israelite material from Ugarit. Elsewhere Walton seems to understand the divine council as being comprised only of those entities in the spiritual world that have decision-making rank. This again violates the tight parallels between the terminology of the Hebrew Bible and Ugaritic material. The problem is a semantic one. The divine council need not *necessarily* be conceptually restricted to decision makers. Indeed, the analogy of human government in civilizations that had a conception of a divine council makes the point clear. Not all members of a king's government would be directly involved in decision making. There are layers of advisors who have input. But these governments had service staff or lesser bureaucrats who were nevertheless part of the king's administration. Perhaps a modern analogy of government in the United States will help make the point: We can speak of the federal legislature, by which we mean that branch of government responsible for passing laws. The term "Congress" is a synonym. However, our Congress has two parts: the Senate and the House. Decision-making members of these two bodies, and hence the Congress, are elected. The House and Senate both have service staff (e.g., "guardian officers," like the sergeant at arms). Though they have no decision-making power, they are nevertheless part of Congress in certain contexts where that term is used. For example, saying that "Congress was not in session" does not mean that all service staff were given the day off. "Congress" can therefore refer to only those elected officials who make laws or to the entire bureaucratic apparatus of the federal legislature. As we will see in this discussion, the heavenly bureaucracy (council) is layered and its members serve God in different but related ways. For other potential problems in Walton's discussion and more detail on these immediate items, readers are directed to the tab for chapter 4 at http://www.moreunseenrealm.com.

the Lord said to him, "By what means?" And he said, "I will go out, and will be a lying spirit in the mouth of all his prophets." And he said, "You are to entice him, and you shall succeed; go out and do so." Now therefore behold, the Lord has put a lying spirit in the mouth of all these your prophets; the Lord has declared disaster for you.

This glimpse into a heavenly council meeting is framed by the wickedness of King Ahab of Israel. It is clear from verse 20 that God has decided that it is time for Ahab to die. The members of the host of heaven are described as "standing" (Hebrew, ʿāmad; עָמַד) in attendance to the seated King-Judge. This language is stock vocabulary for attending to a superior. "Standing" in this setting is not a passive act. Rather, the posture speaks of being available, ready, and willing to carry out the superior's commands. Martens summarizes the idea:

> A more technical, somewhat idiomatic use of the vb. עָמַד relates to government, especially royalty, before whom persons "stand" as messengers or ministers, prepared to take directives (Dan 1:4). As for God, King over all, he can deploy prophets, priests, and others who stand before Yahweh as his messengers. True prophets, for example, are privy to the decisions made in the divine council where they stand (עָמַד) (Jer 23:18, 22; cf. 18:20). Elijah introduces himself as the prophet of Yahweh, "before whom I stand" (1 Kgs 17:1; 18:15). God raises up prophets to serve him ("stand before him," Deut 18:5, 7; cf. Jer 15:1). Priests, Levites especially, are acknowledged ministers before the Lord (Deut 10:8; 18:7; Zech 3:1; cf. 2 Chron 29:11) who "perform their service" (עָמַד) (1 Kgs 8:11 NIV; cf. Ps 134:1; 135:2). In the heavenly court, hosts are at God's right and left hand (2 Chron 18:18). To be in God's service is a high honor.[11]

When the council meeting commences, God asks the spirit beings present *how Ahab's death should be accomplished.* God had decreed Ahab was going to die at Ramoth-Gilead, but he allows debate and participation when it comes to the means of Ahab's demise. One of the spirit beings proposes a plan (vv. 21–22): "I will go out, and will be a lying spirit in the mouth of all his prophets." God approves, knowing full well that

---

11. E. Martens, "עָמַד (ʿāmad)," *NIDOTTE* 3:432.

the plan will succeed. Had the omniscient God of Israel known the proposition would fail, he would have heard another one or proceeded on his own account.

The text presents us with a clear instance where God has sovereignly decided to act but allows his lesser, intelligent servants to participate in how his decision is carried out. God wasn't searching for ideas, as though he couldn't conceive of a plan. He allowed those who serve him the latitude to propose options. In other words, *the members of the host were involved in the divine decree.* As Miller has observed:

> The symbol of the divine council is a quite concrete if multi-faceted one. Yahweh is seen as seated upon his throne of kingship in a temple or palace surrounded by a nameless host of divine beings who are sometimes portrayed as present before or beside Yahweh (e.g. 1 Kgs 22:19–21) and elsewhere as coming in to take their position in the presence of Yahweh (Job 1:6; 2:1). The assembly, or members of it, whether the "divine ones" or the "holy ones" or particular groups within the whole, for example, the seraphim, are sometimes depicted as serving or worshiping the Lord, a part of the holy array that gives God glory (Isa. 6:1–3). At other times, they converse among themselves or the Lord converses with them, for example, in the prologue to the book of Job and in the vision of Micaiah in 1 Kgs 22:19–23. … The Lord takes counsel with the council, commissions them with certain tasks. They sit as a court or governmental body in which the Lord judges a case or utters a decree.[12]

There is no hint that the suggestion of the spirit being to deceive Ahab was preprogrammed. God was also not bound to it. Had a member of the heavenly host proposed an idea God in his omniscience knew would not succeed, he could have vetoed it. The criterion was simple: will it succeed? The omniscient God knew the suggestion would succeed and approved it.

The fact that God was seated in 1 Kings 22:19 is also of interest. While standing is the normative description for attendants, sitting can be presumed as the posture of the one rendering judgment. The Old Testament certainly utilizes this description in the context of rendering judgment

---

12. Miller, *Israelite Religion and Biblical Theology*, 425.

(Judg 4:5; Joel 4:12; Prov 20:8), but there are also interesting exceptions—
in the divine council. Daniel 7:9–10 reads:

As I looked,

thrones were placed,
> and the Ancient of Days took his seat;

his clothing was white as snow,
> and the hair of his head like pure wool;

his throne was fiery flames;
> its wheels were burning fire.

A stream of fire issued
> and came out from before him;

a thousand thousands served him,
> and ten thousand times ten thousand stood before him;

the court sat in judgment,
> and the books were opened.

The seated (v. 9) Ancient of Days is obviously the leader of the council.
But "thrones" are set in place for at least some members of the council
("court"; v. 10).[13] The council members occupying the other thrones are
part of the decision-making process. This is quite evident from Daniel
9:26: "But the court shall sit in judgment, and his dominion shall be
taken away, to be consumed and destroyed to the end." The verdict on
the fourth beast is connected to the *court* sitting in judgment.

The seated council in Daniel 7:9–10 is therefore not just window
dressing. In ancient Israelite thought, the party (or parties) seated in an
assembled meeting had decision-making authority.[14] The seated posture

---

13. Multitudes of the host are also said to be standing (v. 10). The plural thrones are not, as Jewish
tradition wants to argue, for the messianic son of man and the Ancient of Days. While the latter is
seated, at no point does the son of man sit. There is clearly a council in session and multiple thrones,
not merely two and one unoccupied!

14. Some scholars have used Old Testament "standing" vocabulary to Ps 82 to argue that the psalm
is proof of Israelite polytheism. The argument can be summarized as follows: The "God" (*'elōhîm*)
who "stands" (*niṣṣāb*) in the divine council (*'adat 'ēl*) is not the "Most High" (*'ēl-'elyōn*) of verse 6.
Elyon was, so the argument goes, an epithet of El, and so the deity of 82:1 bringing accusation is not
the one who ran the council. The unnamed deity of Ps 82:1 who "stands" is Yahweh. He is bringing
accusation against the "sons of the Most High" who are corrupt (vv. 2–5). The judge of the council is
El-Elyon. Consequently, Yahweh and El-Elyon are not the same, and Israelite religion had a higher
god than Yahweh. The argument is based on several assumptions: (1) That Elyon is seated as judge in
the council and thus the "standing" Yahweh is acting as prosecutor in the divine council; (2) in legal
settings, judges always sit; (3) Yahweh could not be both prosecutor and judge in the divine council.
I have addressed this line of thinking and its presumed evidence in two articles. The data marshaled

of the council expresses a participatory role. But the other details of 1 Kings 22:19–23 and Daniel 7:9–10 are equally significant. The council neither acts alone nor without a Head. The members of the heavenly host partner with God in carrying out his will. They are not autonomous.

## 2. Bearing Witness to God's Decrees

In addition to participating in divine decisions, members of God's heavenly host also bear witness to God's decrees. We have already encountered two such instances. In Job 38:4–7, the morning stars/sons of God bear witness to the majesty of the creation event. In Genesis 1:26 God announced to the assembled council host his decision to create humankind. That the purpose of the declaration "let us create" was to announce intention, not solicit help in creating, is evident in Genesis 1:27, where the verbs of creation are all grammatically singular.[15] The members of the heavenly host perform an endorsement role, not in terms of authorizing God's decision, but rather validating or confirming its goodness, wisdom, and desirability.[16]

Perhaps less well known, but just as transparent in the biblical text, is the idea that the law was delivered by angels (Acts 7:53; Gal 3:19; Heb 2:2).[17] This belief derives from the Septuagint version of Deuteronomy 33:1–4,

---

to create the picture is actually not consistent. God is depicted as standing to judge (Isa 3:13; Amos 7:7–9; 9:1–4). Elsewhere, Yahweh is a seated judge (cf. Pss 7:6; 9:19; 94:2), and so it is possible to see Yahweh as both the standing deity (*'elōhîm*) of 82:1 and the deity asked to rise up (which requires a seated position) in 82:8. The approach advocated here lets the text stand as it is, in the context of the wider Hebrew Bible. The biblical writers explicitly identify Yahweh and El (e.g., 2 Sam 22:31–32; Pss 10:12; 18:2; 31:5; [esp] 50:1; 118:27). Why would someone read Ps 82 in a way that avoids these other passages and this explicit identification? The answer is that the idea of an evolution from polytheism to monotheism is *presumed* and brought to the passage. That is, texts are read through the filter of this assumption, not in the wider canonical context. The evolutionary presumption itself is based on circular reasoning. See Michael S. Heiser, "Does Divine Plurality in the Hebrew Bible Demonstrate an Evolution from Polytheism to Monotheism in Israelite Religion?" *JESOT* 1.1 (2012): 1–24; idem, "Are Yahweh and El Distinct Deities in Deut. 32:8–9 and Psalm 82?" *HIPHIL* 3 (2006), http://see-j.net/index.php/hiphil/article/view/29; posted October 3, 2006.

15. The same observation holds for all other passages that describe the creation of humanity—the act of creating humans, regardless of lemma, is described with grammatically singular verb forms.

16. There is, of course, a discernible ancient Jewish tradition that puts forth the idea that one council member was displeased with humanity's elevated status of imaging (representing) God on the newly created earth. This divine being would rebel against the Most High and cause humanity's fall. For example, see the first-century-AD Jewish pseudepigraphical text the Life of Adam and Eve 12–14.

17. In *The Unseen Realm* (166–67) I propose that the "intermediary" mentioned along with angels in Gal 3:19 is the angel of the Lord. For a survey of ancient Jewish texts connecting the law and angels, see Terrance Callan, "Pauline Midrash: The Exegetical Background of Gal. 3:19b," *JBL* 99.4 (1980): 549–67.

which has a multitude of divine beings at Sinai (v. 2), whereas the Hebrew Masoretic text does not.[18] The Septuagint version of Deuteronomy 33 has angels (its translation of qedōshîm, "holy ones," in v. 2) accompanying God when he gave the Law to Israel. The Masoretic text instead suggests that the "holy ones" are the Israelites receiving the law.[19]

The biblical text makes it clear that the giving of the law was a covenantal act between Yahweh and Israel (Exod 19:5–6; 24:1–8). Members of Yahweh's assembly are present to bear witness to the covenant enactment.[20] Miller again summarizes the implication well: "The rule of the cosmos is in the hands of Yahweh, but the context in which that rule takes place is the activity of the council where Yahweh's decrees directing the human community and the divine world are set forth and through whom they are communicated or enacted."[21] The ultimate expression of this idea was the Sinai covenant between Yahweh and his own people.

Council participation as witnesses to covenant stipulations is quite consistent with ancient Near Eastern covenant structures:

These treaties also typically listed those "third parties" who would witness the enactment of the treaty. It is of especial interest that the witnesses were exclusively deities or deified elements of the natural world. The list of deities was frequently so lengthy as to justify the conclusion that it was intended to be exhaustive: all gods relevant to *both* parties were called upon as witnesses, so that there was no god left that the vassal could appeal to for protection if he wanted to violate his solemn oath. ... The witnesses were those entities that were called upon to observe the behavior of the party under oath and

---

18. The Septuagint is the ancient Greek translation of the Hebrew Bible. However, differences such as this one in Deut 33 are not always mere translation idiosyncrasies. The Septuagint translators used a Hebrew text that diverges from the Masoretic Hebrew text. Other scholars concur that Deut 33:1–2 is behind the New Testament statements about angels being present at the giving of the law: "With God were the members of his divine council, *holy ones* and *warriors of God* (cf. 32:8). In the NT interpretation of the law of Moses, it is probably this verse (v. 2; cf. LXX) that stands behind the view that the law of Moses was mediated through angels (see Acts 7:53; Gal. 3:19; Heb. 2:2)" (Peter C. Craigie, *The Book of Deuteronomy*, NICOT [Grand Rapids: Eerdmans, 1976], 393).

19. The two texts in translation are compared side by side in Heiser, *The Unseen Realm*, 165–66.

20. P. R. Williamson, "Covenant," *DOTP* 149–51.

21. Miller, *Israelite Religion and Biblical Theology*, 426. Other scholars debate whether Ps 89:35–37 involves a member of the divine council as covenant witness. See E. Theodore Mullen, Jr., "The Divine Witness and the Davidic Royal Grant: Ps 89: 37–38," *JBL* 102.2 (1983): 207–18; Paul G. Mosca, "Once Again the Heavenly Witness of Ps 89: 38," *JBL* 105.1 (1986): 27–37; Timo Veijola, "The Witness in the Clouds: Ps 89: 38," *JBL* 107.3 (1988): 413–17.

to carry out the appropriate rewards and punishments (the blessings and curses) connected with the treaty (see below). The fact that these enforcers are all supernatural beings reflects the underlying idea that in this covenant ideology strenuous (if not pretentious) efforts were made to place the entire covenant complex outside the realm of political and military coercive force, and into the realm of a voluntary acceptance of a commonality of interest between suzerain and vassal. In other words, there is expressed here the hope that the vassal's obedience will be "self-policing," i.e., based upon a conscientious regard for higher principles (the gods) than simply upon the fear of superior military force.[22]

Set against this backdrop, it is not surprising that the members of the heavenly council also serve as witnesses in another biblical-theological context: "lawsuits" taken up by God against his guilty people for covenant violation.[23] The following passages are illustrative:

"Hear, O my people, and I will speak;
  O Israel, I will testify against you.
  I am God, your God.
Not for your sacrifices do I rebuke you;
  your burnt offerings are continually before me." ...
But to the wicked God says:
  "What right have you to recite my statutes
  or take my covenant on your lips?
For you hate discipline,
  and you cast my words behind you." (Ps 50:7–8, 16–17)

And this second thing you do. You cover the Lord's altar with tears, with weeping and groaning because he no longer regards the offering or accepts it with favor from your hand. But you say, "Why does he not?" Because the Lord was witness between you and the wife

---

22. George E. Mendenhall and Gary A. Herion, "Covenant," *ABD* 1:1181.

23. The particulars of the covenant lawsuit genre are disputed among scholars. Few would deny the genre altogether given the clear vocabulary used in legal dispute contexts. See Kirsten Nielsen, *Yahweh as Prosecutor and Judge: An Investigation of the Prophetic Lawsuit (Rîb-Pattern)* (Sheffield: University of Sheffield, 1978); Marjorie O'Rourke Boyle, "The Covenant Lawsuit of the Prophet Amos: III 1–IV 13," *VT* 21 (1971): 338–62; Herbert B. Huffmon, "The Covenant Lawsuit in the Prophets," *JBL* 78 (1959): 285–95; Richard M. Davidson, "The Divine Covenant Lawsuit Motif in Canonical Perspective," *Journal of the Adventist Theological Society* 21/1–2 (2010): 45–84.

of your youth, to whom you have been faithless, though she is your companion and your wife by covenant. (Mal 2:13–14)

Occasionally as part of God serving as a witness in his own legal dispute against his people, an unidentified group is also called on to bear witness to God's accusations and the validity of the pronounced verdict. The plurality (i.e., a group) is evidenced in the Hebrew text by the use of *plural* imperatives (underlined):

Proclaim [*hišmî'û*] to the strongholds in Ashdod
    and to the strongholds in the land of Egypt,
and say ['*imrû*], "Assemble yourselves on the mountains of Samaria,
    and see the great tumults within her,
    and the oppressed in her midst."
"They do not know how to do right," declares the LORD,
    "those who store up violence and robbery in their
        strongholds." ...
"Hear [*šim'û*], and testify [*hā'îdû*] against the house of Jacob,"
    declares the Lord GOD, the God of hosts,
"that on the day I punish Israel for his transgressions,
    I will punish the altars of Bethel,
and the horns of the altar shall be cut off
    and fall to the ground. (Amos 3:9–10, 13–14)

In a recent study of Amos 3, David Bokovoy explains the judicial thrust of the passage this way:

This reading of Amos 3:13 as a summoning of God's assembly coheres with the general judicial role fulfilled by the council throughout ancient Near Eastern traditions. Reflecting secular institutions, the heavenly council of the gods in ancient Near Eastern thought formed an important judicial body, governing the affairs of the cosmos. As Richard J. Clifford has explained concerning the Phoenician depiction of the assembly, "as elsewhere in the ancient Near East, the assemblies are pictured as subordinate to individual gods, although the assembly's consent seems necessary for important decisions.[24]

---

24. David E. Bokovoy, "שמעו והעידו בבית יעקב: Invoking the Council as Witnesses in Amos 3:13," *JBL* 127.1 (2008): 37–51 (42–43).

Other passages do that as well, including an interesting nuance. Isaiah 40:1–2 read as follows (the plural imperatives once again underlined):

Comfort [naḥamû], comfort [naḥamû] my people, says your God.
Speak [dibberû] tenderly to Jerusalem,
    and cry [qir'û] to her
that her warfare is ended,
    that her iniquity is pardoned,
    that she has received from the LORD's hand
    double for all her sins.

In this set of plural imperatives, Yahweh is calling for someone in an unnamed group to comfort his people, whose exile is portrayed as ending.[25] As the chapter continues, a voice from among the addressed group cries out (v. 6a: "A voice says, 'Cry!'"), which the prophet answers (v. 6b: "And I said, 'What shall I cry?'"). The prophet thus becomes part of the conversation between God and his heavenly council.

Commentators agree that Isaiah 6 and 40 have a number of connections. In Isaiah 6, only God, Isaiah, and the divine throne guardians (seraphim) are in the room. God addresses the assembled divine host by asking a rhetorical question: "Who will go for us?" (v. 8). God isn't asking Isaiah directly; the prophet is a spectator. A conversation ensues within the council in Isaiah 40:3–6, wherein the prophet becomes a participant (reading "and I said" with the Dead Sea Scrolls text of the passage at v. 6). This is very similar to Isaiah 6, where, after the "Who will go for us?" question, the prophet responds, "Here am I, send me" (v. 8).[26] In that

---

25. On these plural imperatives and the assembled divine council in Isa 40, see Frank Moore Cross, "The Council of Yahweh in Second Isaiah," *JNES* 12 (1953): 274–77; Christopher R. Seitz, "The Divine Council: Temporal Transition and New Prophecy in the Book of Isaiah," *JBL* 109.2 (1990): 229–47. Seitz in particular engages in a detailed exegesis of Isa 40:1–11 with the council address as framework. The plural imperatives should not be regarded as God speaking to a group of men. There is no exegetical proof for this, and it mars the close parallels between Isa 40 and Isa 6 (see Seitz in particular). The Septuagint and the Targums arbitrarily supply a human referent—i.e., they insert a group of priests or prophets. The Vulgate is even more problematic, since it has the verses commanding Israel to comfort Israel. In reference to the latter, arguing that the people are the recipient of the command confuses the command's *recipient* with its *object*. The people are the object—the ones God wants comforted. They are not the recipient of the command. That would make them the agent of their own comfort, which makes little sense. Had the writer wanted to convey this idea clearly, he would have used a Hithpael or Niphal imperative.

26. This in turn has implications for vv. 9–11. Many presume the herald in vv. 9–11 is Zion or Jerusalem, an assumption driven by the grammatical gender of *mebaśśeret* (feminine singular participle), since city names are grammatically feminine. However, the noun in question here is of a type where,

passage, one of the seraphim purifies Isaiah's mouth for service as the spokesman for Yahweh (Isa 6:6–7).

The divine council also bears witness to Yahweh's choice of prophets. In biblical theology, prophets are validated by divine encounter, which at times takes place in the divine council. I treat this motif at length in *The Unseen Realm*.[27] Jeremiah 23:16–22 is the classic passage on the pattern:

> Thus says the LORD of hosts: "Do not listen to the words of the prophets who prophesy to you, filling you with vain hopes. They speak visions of their own minds, not from the mouth of the LORD. They say continually to those who despise the word of the LORD, 'It shall be well with you'; and to everyone who stubbornly follows his own heart, they say, 'No disaster shall come upon you.'"
>
> For who among them has stood in the council of the LORD
>> to see and to hear his word,
>> or who has paid attention to his word and listened? …
> I did not send the prophets,
>> yet they ran;
> I did not speak to them,
>> yet they prophesied.
> But if they had stood in my council,
>> then they would have proclaimed my words to my people,
> and they would have turned them from their evil way,
>> and from the evil of their deeds." (Jer 23:16–18, 21–22)[28]

The implications of the passage are that *true* prophets have stood and listened in Yahweh's council, whereas false prophets have not. The divine council bears witness to Yahweh's decision.

## 3. Assisting in God's Governance of the Human World

Unfortunately, church tradition has produced a myopic understanding of the well-known episode in Job 1–2, where a challenge is issued against

---

though *morphologically* feminine, a male individual can be in view. The best example is *qōheleth* ("the preacher," the Hebrew title of Ecclesiastes), who is obviously male (Eccl 1:1), though the form of the noun is grammatically feminine. The best reading for the herald is the prophet—Isaiah becomes the herald to the released people in the vision.

27. Heiser, *The Unseen Realm*, 232–39. See Edwin C. Kingsbury, "The Prophets and the Council of Yahweh," *JBL* 83.3 (1964): 279–86; Fleming, "Divine Council as Type Scene."

28. Heiser, *The Unseen Realm*, 238–39.

God's assessment of the righteous Job by a heavenly adversary (śāṭān) reporting in a divine council meeting.[29] The focus on this figure distracts readers from a larger point of biblical theology—the role of the heavenly host in God's governance of his terrestrial creation.

Job 1–2 describes a gathering of the sons of God in a heavenly council meeting. The śāṭān attends the meeting, describing himself as "going to and fro" (šûṭ) traversing throughout the earth.[30] This activity is not without purpose. As Clines notes:

> The verb שׁוט refers predominantly to going about for a particular purpose (Num 11:8, to search for manna; 2 Sam 24:8, to take a census; Jer 5:1, to see if a righteous man can be found in Jerusalem; Amos 8:12, to seek a word from Yahweh; cf. 2 Chr 16:9; Ezek 27:8, 26; Zech 4:10; only Dan 12:4 and Jer 49:3 appear to be exceptions). … Whether the implication is that the Satan's particular mission has been to assess the piety of humans, as may appear from the next verse, is hard to determine. Most probably the reason for the Satan's movement throughout the earth is simply not specified for dramatic reasons: he has nothing to report, nothing to advise, nothing to initiate; but

---

29. As I discussed in *The Unseen Realm* (p. 57), the śāṭān figure in Job 1–2 (and Zech 3) is not the devil or serpent of Gen 3. This identification, though traditional, violates Hebrew grammar, which (like English) refuses to prefix a definite article (the word "the"; Hebrew *ha-*) to a proper personal name. Every occurrence of śāṭān in Job 1–2 and Zech 3 has the definite article, and so the term is not a proper personal name. Joüon and Muraoka state, "Proper nouns are in themselves determinate since they designate unique beings. Therefore, they do not take any determining element. Thus, they cannot be followed by a determinate (nor indeterminate, §131 n–o) genitive. Likewise, they do not take the article" (*GBH* §137b).

Day comments, "The opening chapter of the book of Job describes a gathering of the 'sons of God', i.e. a meeting of the divine council. Present at this gathering is a being called *haśśāṭān*: this is the common noun śāṭān preceded by the definite article. The definite article makes it virtually certain that śāṭān is not a proper name contra B. Waltke & M. O'Connor, *An Introduction to Biblical Hebrew Syntax* [Winona Lake 1990] 249). … Attributing this force to the definite article of *haśśāṭān* in Job 1:6 would lead us to understand that a certain divine being whose precise identity is unimportant and who has the current and temporary status of accuser is being introduced into the narrative. The advantage of this interpretation is that it is consistent with known Israelite (and Mesopotamian) legal practice in that 'accuser' was a legal status that various people temporarily acquired in the appropriate circumstances, and not a post or office" (P. L. Day, "Satan שׂטן," *DDD* 727–28).

A related noun also offers support for an adversarial role: "The noun śiṭnâ (Ezra 4:6), usually translated 'indictment,' probably means a 'hostile objection' (*TLOT*, 1268). See also Peggy Day, *An Adversary in Heaven: śāṭān in the Hebrew Bible* (Atlanta: Scholars Press, 1988); John H. Walton, "Satan," *DOTWPW* 714–17.

30. The description that the śāṭān "came among them" in Job 1:6; 2:1 is ambiguous in that it does not allow us to say that this figure is also one of the sons of God. Being "among" (*betôk*) a group may or may not evince membership (e.g., Josh 8:22—the residents of Ai were "among" [*betôk*] the Israelites but obviously not Israelites).

he has nevertheless been abroad on earth with his eyes wide open, amassing the reserve of observations which his sovereign can use as he wills.[31]

Why does the *śāṭān* report in the council? The answer is found in the conception that the divine council is God's task force for governing the world. In Zechariah 1:10 we learn that God sends angels "to patrol the earth." Those angels report to the angel of the LORD, "We have patrolled the earth, and behold, all the earth remains at rest" (Zech 1:11).[32] In Psalm 82 the council *'elōhîm* under God's indictment are being judged because of their failure to administrate the nations according to the principles of Yahweh's justice (Ps 82:2–4). The result is chaos on earth ("all the foundations of the earth are shaken"; Ps 82:5). Miller elaborates:

> The maintenance of justice and righteousness is the foundation of the universe, the responsibility of the divine council, and the issue upon which hang both the stability of the universe and the stability and effective reality of the divine world. ... It is against this background that one must look at one of the texts in which the council of Yahweh is most explicitly present, Psalm 82. It takes place entirely in the world of the gods, although what is clear from the story is that that world is totally ruled and controlled by the Lord. The psalm depicts a meeting of the "divine council" (v. 1) in which God rises and pronounces judgment on the gods. The reason for the verdict against them is spelled out in detail and unambiguous. The divine ones, the gods who are supposed to provide for order/righteousness among the peoples of the earth, have utterly failed to do so. They have shown partiality to the wicked and failed to maintain the right of the poor and the weak. The consequence of this is stated to be a shaking of the foundations of the world. ... The text assumes that justice as the center of world order is a responsibility of the divine world as a whole. Failure to bring that about calls into question the divine world. Indeed its consequence is a decree against the divine world that relativizes it and renders the divine ones mortal. The gods are condemned to death.

---

31. David J. A. Clines, *Job 1–20*, WBC 17 (Dallas: Word, 1989), 23.

32. It is interesting that the report is given to this particular angel when one would expect it to be given to God, who sent them (Zech 1:10). See chapter 3 for the identity of the angel of the LORD.

The fate of the divine world, of gods as well as of human beings, is determined in the divine council.[33]

The most dramatic instance of council members participating in God's governance of the world is associated with judgment. According to Deuteronomy 32:8–9, members of the heavenly host were assigned as administrators of the nations:

> When the Most High gave to the nations their inheritance,
>> when he divided mankind,
> he fixed the borders of the peoples
>> according to the number of the sons of God.[34]
> But the LORD's portion is his people,
>> Jacob his allotted heritage.

We learn from Genesis 11:1–9 that humanity was divided up into the nations at the Tower of Babel event. Yahweh's division of humanity into the nations listed in Genesis 10, which descended from Noah's sons after the flood, was a punitive act. God had decided to put his relationship with humanity as a whole on hiatus. After the nations were divided and allotted to lesser divine beings ("sons of God"), God called Abraham to form a new people—his "inheritance" as described in Deuteronomy 32:9.[35] Through this new people, God planned to bless the nations in the future (Gen 12:3; cf. Acts 17:26).[36]

Deuteronomy 32:8–9 is foundational for understanding the remainder of the Old Testament. As Miller notes of the passage, "The order of

---

33. Miller, *Israelite Religion and Biblical Theology,* 427–28, 437–38.

34. As I wrote in *The Unseen Realm* (p. 113): "Most English Bibles do not read 'according to the number of the sons of God' in Deuteronomy 32:8. Rather, they read 'according to the number of the sons of Israel.' The difference derives from disagreements between manuscripts of the Old Testament. 'Sons of God' is the correct reading, as is now known from the Dead Sea Scrolls. Frankly, you don't need to know all the technical reasons for why the 'sons of God' reading in Deuteronomy 32:8–9 is what the verse originally said. You just need to think a bit about the *wrong* reading, the 'sons of Israel.' Deuteronomy 32:8–9 harks back to events at the Tower of Babel, an event that occurred *before* the call of Abraham, the father of the nation of Israel. This means that the nations of the earth were divided at Babel *before Israel even existed as a people.* It would make no sense for God to divide up the nations of the earth 'according to the number of the sons of Israel' if there was no Israel. This point is also brought home in another way, namely by the fact that Israel is not listed in the Table of Nations." On the text-critical data for "sons of God" and against "sons of Israel," see Heiser, "Deuteronomy 32:8 and the Sons of God," 52–74.

35. For the allotment language associated with this episode, see Deut 4:19–20; 29:25–26.

36. See the extended discussion of this passage and the biblical theology (Old and New Testament) that extends from it in Heiser, *The Unseen Realm,* 113–23, 296–306, 326–30.

nations is rooted in the order of heaven."[37] Though readers are given no timeline, eventually the sons of God charged with this task turn adversarial, seducing the Israelites into idolatry (Deut 32:17) and abusing their populations (Ps 82:1–5). God's response is to pronounce their eschatological deaths at the day of the Lord (Ps 82:6–8; Isa 24:21; 34:1–4).[38]

These areas of participation allow us to draw the conclusion that the members of the heavenly host exercise the attributes shared with them by their Creator, among them freedom and intelligence. Again, our own condition and status is analogous. They, like us, do not act autonomously, but God does indeed expect us (and them) to serve as his representatives, utilizing the abilities he has bestowed.

## RESPONSIVE OBEDIENCE TO DIVINE DECISIONS

Decisions made by God and his council required action. Scripture describes members of the heavenly host responding accordingly in a variety of ways.

### 1. Delivering Divine Decrees

In the previous chapter we briefly discussed the term *mal'āk* ("messenger"),[39] often translated "angel" in English Bibles, though that rendering is a transliteration of the New Testament Greek *angelos*. Messengers (*mal'ākîm*) may be human or divine.[40] The task of delivering messages from God is not always evident in passages where a divine *mal'āk* is mentioned (e.g., Gen 32:1; Pss 91:11; 148:2). Certain contexts are overtly military (Exod 23:20, 23; 32:34; 33:2).

Nevertheless, God does send divine *mal'ākîm* to deliver messages (Zech 1:9, 19; 2:3). One particular divine emissary, the *mal'āk yhwh* ("angel of Yahweh/the LORD"), is prominent in this regard.[41] As we will see below,

---

37. Miller, *Israelite Religion and Biblical Theology*, 436.

38. On the relationship of these and other passages to Ps 82 and Deut 32:8–9, see Joel A. Reemstma, "Punishment of the Powers: Deuteronomy 32 and Psalm 82 as the Backdrop to Isaiah 34" (paper presented at the Annual Meeting of the Evangelical Theological Society, San Diego, CA, 2014).

39. *HALOT*, 585.

40. Human examples include Gen 32:3, 6; Num 21:21; Josh 6:17, 25; 7:2.

41. On this figure, see chapter 3. Of the 110 occurrences (per ESV) of *mal'āk* being used of divine messengers, 75 are the *mal'āk yhwh* or the *mal'āk 'elōhîm* ("angel of God"), a synonym for *mal'āk yhwh* (see Judg 6:20–21; 13:3–9). The discussion in the following chapter will include passages that point to this figure without using the phrase *mal'āk yhwh* (e.g., Josh 5:13–15; Dan 3:28; 6:22).

such instances can include vocabulary other than *mal'āk*. The point for consideration extends beyond the lemmas that are utilized by the writer. Members of the heavenly host deliver information from and about God that derive from council decisions or direct decrees from the Most High.

For our purposes, the point is well illustrated in Daniel 4. The chapter records the dream of Nebuchadnezzar in which he saw a stupendously tall tree that reached into the heavens. Part of the dream included a visitation from "a watcher, a holy one" (Dan 4:13, 17, 23). The watcher informed the Babylonian despot that the tree of his dream would be chopped down, leaving only its stump. The divine messenger explained that the tree and its stump were symbolized Nebuchadnezzar and his future fate. The tall tree was emblematic of the king's greatness, while the stump pictured his destiny. God was judging Nebuchadnezzar for his arrogance; he would suffer temporary insanity and become like an animal (Dan 4:13–16). The wordings of Daniel 4:17, 24 in this regard are of special interest.

> The sentence is by the decree of the watchers, and the decision by the word of the holy ones, to the end that the living may know that the Most High rules the kingdom of men and gives it to whom he will and sets over it the lowliest of men. (Dan 4:17)

> This is the interpretation, O king: It is a decree of the Most High, which has come upon my lord the king. (Dan 4:24)

Not only does the watcher deliver the decree of the Most High, but we learn that members of the heavenly host (here called watchers) participated in issuing the sentence upon Nebuchadnezzar.

The passage is clear, however, that input from the members of the heavenly host did not impinge on the sovereignty of God:

> You [Nebuchadnezzar] shall be driven from among men, and your dwelling shall be with the beasts of the field. You shall be made to eat grass like an ox, and you shall be wet with the dew of heaven, and seven periods of time shall pass over you, till you know that the Most High rules the kingdom of men and gives it to whom he will. And as it was commanded to leave the stump of the roots of the tree, your kingdom shall be confirmed for you from the time that you know that Heaven rules. (Dan 4:25–26)

Despite the participation of the holy ones in Daniel 4:17, the text affirms that the Most High is sovereign.[42] The council does not act independently of its Head. Decisions are made and delivered to those affected when that is in concert with God's will. Their duties as emissaries bring us to the next role of members of the heavenly host.

## 2. Explaining Divine Activity

In chapter 1 we learned that angels are referred to as "mediators" (*mēlîṣ*; Job 33:23) and suggested the idea conveyed by the Hebrew term was "turning" to one of the holy ones for an explanation of God's activity. Since members of God's council participate in the issuing of God's decrees (1 Kgs 22:19–23; Dan 7:9) and deliver messages to human affected by those decrees (Gen 19:1–22; Dan 4:13, 17, 24), the concept of explanatory mediation would make sense. It also has implications for grasping the free decision-making ability of the holy ones.

Recall that Job 15:15 taught us that God "puts no trust in his holy ones." Job 4:17–18 and 5:1 are also instructive in the regard:

> Can mortal man be in the right before God?
>> Can a man be pure before his Maker?
> Even in his servants he puts no trust,
>> and his angels he charges with error. (Job 4:17–18)[43]

A few verses later in his dialogue (Job 5:1), Eliphaz demands of Job, "Call now; is there anyone who will answer you? To which of the holy ones will you turn?"

Further, Job 4:17–18 and 15:15 have Eliphaz ridiculing Job. His unrelenting taunts can be paraphrased as: "Who are you to think you're righteous? Are you better than the angels? Will any of them intercede for you? Go ahead; make an appeal to one of the holy ones." The answer to the rhetorical barb is that Job should expect no heavenly advocacy on his behalf.

---

42. As I wrote in *The Unseen Realm* (p. 54): "[The wording of v. 25] is clearly singular. The phrase [in v. 26] 'heaven is sovereign' is interesting because the Aramaic word translated heaven (*shemayin*) is plural and is accompanied by a plural verb. The plurality of *shemayin* can point to either the members of the council or the council as a collective. In any event, the wording is suggestive of the interchange between council and Most High earlier in Daniel 4."

43. This passage speaks to an Old Testament intercessory ministry of angels that we'll consider subsequently.

The notion that heavenly beings were presumed to function as mediators between the leadership of the divine council and mortal humans, in effect functioning as witnesses for humans to plead their case in the context of unjust suffering, is a very ancient one, perhaps going back to divine assemblies at Sumer.[44] As Clines notes:

> We have heard of such beings previously at 5:1, where Eliphaz warned Job that there was no point in calling out to such a heavenly being for deliverance from the web of sin and punishment in which he was now caught. There too the angel was envisaged as a mediator between humans and God who would seek mercy from God for the suffering human. The angel is an "interpreter" or "mediator" (מליץ), apparently meaning that its function is to ... explain God's purpose in the infliction of suffering.[45]

The point of the comments about the holy ones in Job 4:17–18; 15:15 is not indictment for rebellion. Rather, the context of these passages is establishing the perfect wisdom and righteousness of God compared to his other intelligent creatures (Job 15:7–16). Though fallible, the angels are still explicitly called God's servants. That the holy ones are capable of making less than correct (or even optimal) decisions in mediating God's will cannot mean that those fallible decisions were God's decisions, as though the decisions of the holy ones had merely been programmed into them by God. Rather, angels can fail because God allows them to make decisions and they are lesser beings than the perfect God. We saw this in 1 Kings 22:19–23, where God allowed debate within his council. By definition not all the spirit beings came to the same conclusion, which means that some thought errantly or, at the very least, less optimally than others. They weren't preprogrammed spirit robots whose errant thoughts were implanted in their minds by God. That proposition is not only absurd, it tarnishes God's character.

Angels also explain what God is doing or will do in the future, a phenomenon referred to as the "interpreting angel motif" by scholars.[46]

---

44. It is quite clear that the divine council of Sumer considered cases involving both men and gods. See Thorkild Jacobsen, "Primitive Democracy in Ancient Mesopotamia," *JNES* 2 (1943): 159–72; Samuel Noah Kramer, "Sumerian Theology and Ethics," *HTR* 49 (1956): 45–62 (59).

45. David J. A. Clines, *Job 21–37*, WBC 18A (Nashville: Thomas Nelson, 2006), 735.

46. See David P. Melvin, "In Heaven as It Is on Earth: The Development of the Interpreting Angel Motif in Biblical Literature of the Neo-Babylonian, Persian, and Early Hellenistic Periods," PhD diss.,

Daniel's encounters with Gabriel and another unidentified heavenly figure (Dan 8–10) are clear examples.

> When I, Daniel, had seen the vision, I sought to understand it. And behold, there stood before me one having the appearance of a man. And I heard a man's voice between the banks of the Ulai, and it called, "Gabriel, make this man understand the vision." So he came near where I stood. And when he came, I was frightened and fell on my face. But he said to me, "Understand, O son of man, that the vision is for the time of the end." (Dan 8:15–17)

> While I was speaking and praying, confessing my sin and the sin of my people Israel, and presenting my plea before the LORD my God for the holy hill of my God, while I was speaking in prayer, the man Gabriel, whom I had seen in the vision at the first, came to me in swift flight at the time of the evening sacrifice. He made me understand, speaking with me and saying, "O Daniel, I have now come out to give you insight and understanding." (Dan 9:20–22)

> In those days I, Daniel, was mourning for three weeks. I ate no delicacies, no meat or wine entered my mouth, nor did I anoint myself at all, for the full three weeks. On the twenty-fourth day of the first month, as I was standing on the bank of the great river (that is, the Tigris) I lifted up my eyes and looked, and behold, a man clothed in linen, with a belt of fine gold from Uphaz around his waist. His body was like beryl, his face like the appearance of lightning, his eyes like flaming torches, his arms and legs like the gleam of burnished bronze, and the sound of his words like the sound of a multitude. ... Then I heard the sound of his words, and as I heard the sound of his words, I fell on my face in deep sleep with my face to the ground. And behold, a hand touched me and set me trembling on my hands and knees. And he said to me, "O Daniel, man greatly loved, understand the words that I speak to you, and stand upright, for now I have been sent to you." And when he had spoken this word to me, I stood up

---

Baylor University, 2012. Melvin writes (p. 3): "The interpreting angel appears in only a handful of biblical texts, all of them exilic or post-exilic (Ezek 40–48; Zech 1–6; Dan 7–8). In these passages, a human prophet sees a vision which is highly symbolic and complex and which, in many cases, draws on elaborate mythological imagery. The nature of the vision is such that the prophet is incapable of understanding its meaning apart from its interpretation by a heavenly being."

trembling. Then he said to me, "Fear not, Daniel, for from the first day that you set your heart to understand and humbled yourself before your God, your words have been heard, and I have come because of your words. The prince of the kingdom of Persia withstood me twenty-one days, but Michael, one of the chief princes, came to help me, for I was left there with the kings of Persia, and came to make you understand what is to happen to your people in the latter days. For the vision is for days yet to come." (Dan 10:2–6, 9–14)[47]

The book of Zechariah has a number of similar scenes, where angels converse with prophets to explain what the future holds according to God's plan (Zech 1:9–21; 4–5). According to one scholar whose focus is this material:

> The angel who is talking to Zechariah is an intermediary figure. He belongs to the divine sphere. Therefore, he is representing YHWH as an interpreter of the vision. ... Obviously, Zechariah perceives that God is saying something, but he cannot understand the words. Therefore, the angel tells him God's words (Zech 1:14a) and quotes them (Zech 1:14b–15). ... The strange things Zechariah sees in this sequence of visions turn out to be highly metaphorical illustrations that need explanation. The interpreting angel functioning as God's representative provides the visionary with these explanations. This is his primary function.[48]

Lastly, there is some indication that angelic mediation also involved record keeping. I refer here to the notion that either God or his heavenly agents keeps a record of human behavior (Isa 65:6–7; Dan 7:10; 10:21) or suffering (Ps 56:8), or of those who belong to God or not (Exod 32:32; Isa 69:28–29; Jer 17:13; Ps 87:5–7; Dan 12:1; Mal 3:16).[49] While several of these

---

47. The figure in Dan 10 is neither Gabriel nor Michael. The description is noticeably similar to the vision of the God of Israel in Ezek 1:26–28 (cf. Ezek 10:18–20). See the discussion in chapter 3.

48. Karin Schöpflin, "God's Interpreter: The Interpreting Angel in Post-Exilic Prophetic Visions of the Old Testament," in Angels: The Concept of Celestial Beings—Origins, Development and Reception, eds. Friedrich V. Reiterer, Tobias Nicklas, and Karin Schöpflin (Berlin: De Gruyter, 2007), 189–203 (191, 193, 195). As we'll discuss in a subsequent chapter, this role is even more common in the New Testament (e.g., Rev 10:9–11; 17:7–18).

49. Regarding Jer 17:13, note that the word translated "earth" in the phrase "written in the earth" is 'erets, which may also refer to Sheol, the realm of the dead (e.g., Ezek 31:14, 16, 18; Jonah 2:6). See HALOT, 91.

passages have God keeping track of such things, the wider ancient Near Eastern context has such divine record keeping as a duty of the divine council.[50] The metaphor conveys a simple but profound thought: God and his agents will not overlook evil, injustice, and faithfulness.

### 3. Executing Divine Judgment

The now-familiar scene in 1 Kings 22:19–23 is a convenient place to begin our sketch of this next role for the heavenly host. After God asks how Ahab should be seduced into the battle that would result in his death, a spirit being among the host offers, "I will go out, and will be a lying spirit in the mouth of all his prophets" (v. 22). God approves, and the plan to effect God's verdict ultimately came to pass.

1 Kings 22:19–23 is an illustration, via one council member, of a much wider theme in a biblical theology of the heavenly host: the role of the host as warrior agents in service of Yahweh against the wicked whom Yahweh has targeted for judgment. As one scholar notes, "According to some of the religious beliefs of Israelites, Yahweh was not the sole transcendent warrior. Like earthly rulers who have their officers and soldiers, Yahweh had many heavenly subordinates at his disposal."[51] In an essay entitled, "The Divine Council and the Prophetic Call to War," Patrick Miller adds:

> In a few places in the prophets ... there are indications that the divine council participates as a cosmic or heavenly army in the eschatological wars of Yahweh, those military activities associated with the Day of Yahweh, and that these conflicts (or this conflict?) involved a joint participation of human or earthly forces and divine or heavenly armies. ... For from earliest times on Israel viewed its battles as under the aegis of Yahweh and with the participation of the various cosmic forces which he commanded as the divine warrior, general of the heavenly armies.[52]

---

50. See Shalom Paul, "Heavenly Tablets and the Book of Life," in *Columbia University Ancient Near Eastern Studies* (New York: Columbia University, 1973), n.p.; Andrew R. George, "Sennacherib and the Tablet of Destinies," *Iraq* 48 (1986): 133–46.

51. Aleksander R. Michalak, *Angels as Warriors in Late Second Temple Jewish Literature* (Tübingen: Mohr Siebeck, 2012), 2–3.

52. Miller, *Israelite Religion and Biblical Theology*, 397–400.

In succinct terms, the heavenly host is God's army, and he calls that army into service against his enemies, the wicked, who oppress his people and who abhor him and worship other gods. Isaiah 13 is one example:

> The sound of a tumult is on the mountains
>> as of a great multitude!
> The sound of an uproar of kingdoms,
>> of nations gathering together!
> The LORD of hosts is mustering
>> a host for battle.
> They come from a distant land,
>> from the end of the heavens,
> the LORD and the weapons of his indignation,
>> to destroy the whole land.
> Wail, for the day of the LORD is near;
>> as destruction from the Almighty it will come! ...
> For the stars of the heavens and their constellations
>> will not give their light;
> the sun will be dark at its rising,
>> and the moon will not shed its light.
> I will punish the world for its evil,
>> and the wicked for their iniquity;
> I will put an end to the pomp of the arrogant,
>> and lay low the pompous pride of the ruthless.
> I will make people more rare than fine gold,
>> and mankind than the gold of Ophir.
> Therefore I will make the heavens tremble,
>> and the earth will be shaken out of its place,
> at the wrath of the LORD of hosts
>> in the day of his fierce anger. (Isa 13:4–6, 10–13)

Commenting on Isaiah 13, Miller observes:

Using the ancient designation "Yahweh of hosts," the prophet announces that Yahweh has mustered a great army to wipe out the whole earth. The heavenly army is summoned "from the ends of the heavens." If indeed *kol-ha'āreṣ* ["the whole land"] is to be interpreted as the whole earth, as seems to be the case, the picture is one of the final destruction in the Day of Yahweh—a destruction wrought by Yahweh and his heavenly army (v. 5a).[53]

Other passages illustrate the theme well. In Joel 3:11, the prophet insists, "Bring down your warriors (lemma: *gibbôrîm*), O LORD." In Isaiah 40:26 and 45:12, Yahweh musters his heavenly host, calling out their names, commanding the host as an army. Muilenburg states about these verses:

> God, the captain of the host, calls out his myriads upon myriads of stars, and each star takes its appointed place as its name is called. There they stand in their great battalions in response to the call of the captain. Not one is missing; each responds to the call of its own name.[54]

The celestial language of Isaiah 13:10–11 calls to memory Judges 5:20, where "from heaven the stars fought, from their courses they fought against Sisera." In 2 Kings 6:8–19, a servant of the king of Syria sees the heavenly army of Yahweh, a multitude of horses and chariots of fire, surrounding the prophet Elisha. Zechariah's vision of the day of the Lord includes the heavenly host army: "The LORD my God will come, and all the holy ones with him" (Zech 14:5). Isaiah 24:21–23 makes the connection between Yahweh's day of judgment and the divine council explicit:

> On that day the LORD will punish
>> the host of heaven, in heaven,
>> and the kings of the earth, on the earth.
> They will be gathered together
>> as prisoners in a pit;
> they will be shut up in a prison,
>> and after many days they will be punished.
> Then the moon will be confounded
>> and the sun ashamed,
> for the LORD of hosts reigns
>> on Mount Zion and in Jerusalem,
> and his glory will be before his elders.

---

53. Miller, *Israelite Religion and Biblical Theology*, 399–400.
54. James Muilenburg, "The Book of Isaiah, Chapters 40–66: Introduction and Exegesis," *Interpreter's Bible* (Nashville: Abingdon Press, 1956), 5:442.

Yahweh's victory will result in his glorification "before his elders." Who are God's "elders"? They are "senior officials of the divine court."[55] When Yahweh decrees judgment on his enemies, the members of the heavenly host report for duty.

## PRAISING THE MOST HIGH GOD

The final role in this survey of how the loyal members of God's heavenly host serve him is usually where popular treatments of angelology focus: the praise of the Most High God. As we've seen, there's a lot more to the service of God by his divine agents than praise, yet the praise they render is significant.

Psalm 29:1 opens with a series of plural imperatives (underlined), again indicating a command directed at a group:

Ascribe to the Lord, O heavenly beings [benê 'ēlîm],
ascribe to the Lord glory and strength.
Ascribe to the Lord the glory due his name;
worship the Lord in the splendor of holiness.

The recipients of these commands are the supernatural sons of God (benê 'ēlîm) of his divine council (Ps 89:5–7). They are exalted beings, but not deserving of the praise due to their creator and Lord, the Most High God.

---

55. Timothy M. Willis, "Yahweh's Elders (Isa 24,23): Senior Officials of the Divine Court," *ZAW* 103.3 (1991): 375–85 (here, 375).

As I noted in *The Unseen Realm* (p. 356, including note 21): "Scholars who have focused on this unusual language in Isaiah have drawn attention to the divine character of the elders by means of two trajectories: (1) comparative passages about elders in the Old Testament to establish that the term specifically refers to select members of a royal household; and (2) similarities in the descriptions of the elders in Revelation 4–5 and those of divine beings in other heavenly council scenes. [n. 21] … Many scholars seek to identify the elders in this passage with Israel's human elders due to the reference to Zion and Jerusalem, as well as passages like Exod 24:9–11, where Moses, Aaron, Nadab, Abihu, and 70 elders saw the God of Israel. For that reason, some seek to translate 'his elders' as 'its elders' (i.e., the elders of Zion or Jerusalem). If this were the case, one would expect a feminine suffix pronoun to grammatically align with these feminine nouns. The form in Isa 24:23 is the plural noun ('elders') plus third masculine singular suffix. This form occurs in only one other place in the Hebrew Bible, Psa 105:22, where the context is clearly select court officials of the king's (Pharaoh's) household. Additionally, the references to Zion and Jerusalem do not require a literal reading, since those terms are also clearly attested eschatological *concepts* in apocalyptic contexts and, more generally, in New Testament biblical theology" (italics original).

The conclusion of Psalm 103 makes the same demand of the members of the heavenly host. The command "bless" is again grammatically plural.

Bless the LORD, O you his angels,
    you mighty ones who do his word,
    obeying the voice of his word!
Bless the LORD, all his hosts,
    his ministers, who do his will!
Bless the LORD, all his works,
    in all places of his dominion.
Bless the LORD, O my soul! (Ps 103:20–22)

It is interesting to note that the psalmist focuses on those members of the host who do Yahweh's will (v. 21). Divine beings in rebellion are no longer part of God's task force.

Our last example of serving God through praise is Psalm 148:1–5:

Praise the LORD!
Praise the LORD from the heavens;
    praise him in the heights!
Praise him, all his angels;
    praise him, all his hosts!
Praise him, sun and moon,
    praise him, all you shining stars!
Praise him, you highest heavens,
    and you waters above the heavens!
Let them praise the name of the LORD!
    For he commanded and they were created.

The psalm appropriately articulates the lesser, created status of angelic host (v. 5). As Miller aptly observes, "Psalm 148 begins … with a call to 'all his angels … all his hosts' (v. 2).… If all reality finds its ultimate purpose in the praise of God, the divine assembly leads the choir."[56]

Much more could be said about each aspect of this overview. The heavenly host serve their God in both participatory and subordinate ways. The analogy struck earlier between us—as children and imagers of God—and his heavenly host applies here as well. God graciously allows us to participate with him in fulfilling his kingdom plan on earth, yet he is sovereign. In the end, only he will deserve praise.

---

56. Miller, *Israelite Religion and Biblical Theology*, 440–41.

# CHAPTER 3

# Important Angels

THE EMPHASIS OF WHAT THE BIBLE SAYS ABOUT THE INTERSECTION OF heaven and earth is, understandably, God himself. Angels are rarely named or brought to the forefront of divine activity. Though an integral part of how Scripture shows God's will being carried out on earth, the heavenly host's service operates like a computer program running in the background. As we'll see in this chapter, there are exceptions, and they are significant.

## THE ANGEL OF YAHWEH

Perhaps the most well-known angel in the Old Testament is the one described specifically as the *mal'āk YHWH*, the "angel of the LORD."[1] This figure is actually Yahweh himself in the visible form of a man.[2] Consequently, the angel of Yahweh is central to the concept of a Godhead (God being more than one person, each person being the same and not *ontologically* greater or lesser).[3] This concept is at the heart of the ancient Jewish teaching that the Hebrew Bible bore witness to two Yahweh figures—"two powers" in heaven, one invisible and the other visible.

---

1. The most common translation in English translations of the Bible for the divine name (YHWH; Yahweh) is "Lord." The translation, and hence the presence of the divine name, is stylistically telegraphed with small capital letters: LORD.

2. For more on this claim, see Heiser, *The Unseen Realm*, 127–47.

3. "Ontology" refers to the study of being, or what a thing *intrinsically is*.

My position on this is neither idiosyncratic nor novel.[4] As Jewish biblical scholar Benjamin Sommer stated in his study of divine embodiment and multiple persons of Israel's God:

> The God of the Hebrew Bible has a body. This must be stated at the outset, because so many people, including many scholars, assume otherwise. The evidence for this is simply overwhelming. ... We can term this conception *material anthropomorphism*, or the belief that God's body, at least at times, has the same shape and the same sort of substance as a human body. ... What I mean by "a body" in this book [is] *something located in a particular place at a particular time, whatever its shape or substance.*[5]

To understand that the angel of Yahweh is Yahweh himself in human form, we must look at what Old Testament scholars call "Name theology" and how these two Yahweh figures are interchanged in the Old Testament.[6] Exodus 23:20–22 is a fundamental passage in understanding the identity of the angel of Yahweh:

---

4. As I wrote in *The Unseen* Realm (pp. 134–35, n. 1): "The Jewish community that inherited the Old Testament was well aware of this. For centuries Judaism felt no discomfort with the notion of two Yahweh figures. The idea was referred to as the 'two powers in heaven' and was endorsed within Judaism until the second century AD. It is important to note that the two powers were both holy. This is not dualism, where two equal deities exist, one good, the other evil." The major work on Judaism's two-powers teaching was rabbinic studies scholar Alan Segal's *Two Powers in Heaven: Early Rabbinic Reports about Christianity and Gnosticism* (1977; reprint, Waco, TX: Baylor University Press, 2012). My dissertation focused on the roots of two-powers doctrine in the Old Testament as part of the divine council: Michael S. Heiser, "The Divine Council in Late Canonical and Non-Canonical Second Temple Jewish Literature" (PhD diss., University of Wisconsin–Madison, 2004). Besides the work of Sommer, see Hamori, *When Gods Were Men.*

5. Sommer, *The Bodies of God*, 1–2. Italics are Sommer's. Sommer goes on to develop what he calls a "fluidity model" when it comes to the divine body: God's "bodies" can be in more than one place at a time simultaneously—and so God can be more than one personage at the same time. Sommer demonstrates how this concept is present in the wider ancient Near Eastern world and that Christianity's notion of Trinitarianism is compatible with the Hebrew Bible. Summing up his study, Sommer writes: "No Jew sensitive to Judaism's own classical sources, however, can fault the theological model Christianity employs when it avows belief in a God who has an earthly body as well as a Holy Spirit manifestation, for that model, we have seen, is a perfectly Jewish one" (Sommer, *The Bodies of God*, 135).

6. I am aware of various criticisms of Name theology. These criticisms have been rebutted by a number of scholars. A summary of that rebuttal is presented in Michael S. Heiser, "Co-Regency in Ancient Israel's Divine Council as the Conceptual Backdrop to Ancient Jewish Binitarian Monotheism," *BBR* 26.2 (2015): 195–225 (210–17). The work of Hundley is especially telling in terms of the weakness of the arguments for denying Name theology: Michael Hundley, "To Be or Not to Be: A Reexamination of Name Language in Deuteronomy and the Deuteronomistic History," *VT* 59 (2009): 533–55.

Behold, I send an angel before you to guard you on the way and to bring you to the place that I have prepared. Pay careful attention to him and obey his voice; do not rebel against him, for he will not pardon your transgression, for my name is in him. But if you carefully obey his voice and do all that I say, then I will be an enemy to your enemies and an adversary to your adversaries.

On its surface, the description of this particular angel draws interest because this angel seemingly has the authority to withhold forgiveness for the sin of disobedience. The wording is reminiscent of the scene in the Gospels where Jesus claimed that authority. The Pharisees objected: "Who can forgive sins but God alone?" (Mark 2:7; cf. Matt 9:1–8). Their consternation reflected good theology—they were right. As Jesus proceeded to do miraculous acts, he showed that he had such authority, because he was God. The same thought process is applicable to the angel of Yahweh.

A close reading of scriptural references to God's name shows that "the name" (Hebrew, *ha-shem*) is another way of referring to God himself. For example, Isaiah 30:27–28 uses "the Name" as a substitute for "Yahweh" and personifies "the Name":

Behold, the Name [*ha-shem*] of the Lord [*Yahweh*] comes from afar,
    burning with his anger, and in thick rising smoke;
his lips are full of fury,
    and his tongue is like a devouring fire;
his breath is like an overflowing stream
    that reaches up to the neck;
to sift the nations with the sieve of destruction,
    and to place on the jaws of the peoples a bridle that leads astray.

The interchangeability of "Yahweh" and *ha-shem* is quite evident in Psalm 20:1: "May the Lord [*Yahweh*] answer you in the day of trouble! May the name [*ha-shem*] of the God of Jacob protect you!" Isaiah 60:9 makes the correlation equally clear:

For the coastlands shall hope for me,
    the ships of Tarshish first,
to bring your children from afar,
    their silver and gold with them,

for the name of the LORD your God,
  and for the Holy One of Israel,
  because he has made you beautiful.

The prophet states, "*He* has made you beautiful." The preceding lines identifies to whom the prophet refers: "the Holy One of Israel," "the name of the LORD your God."

The book of Deuteronomy is central to Old Testament Name theology, as it repeatedly associates sacred space with the Name. Deuteronomy 12 is representative of this theology (my emphasis in italics):

> You shall surely destroy all the places where the nations whom you shall dispossess served their gods, on the high mountains and on the hills and under every green tree. ... You shall not worship the LORD your God in that way. But you shall seek the place that the LORD your God will choose out of all your tribes *to put his name* and make his habitation there. There you shall go. ... Then to the place that the LORD your God will choose, *to make his name dwell there*, there you shall bring all that I command you. (Deut 12:2, 4–5, 11)

This command points to the future temple that would be built once Canaan was occupied. When God instructed worship to take place in the place where "his name" would dwell, he meant the space his own presence would occupy and sanctify. "His name" was another way of referring to himself.[7]

The importance of this language for Exodus 23:20–22 should be clear. When God describes for Moses the angel he is sending before the people

---

7. Heiser, *The Unseen Realm*, 145. Second Samuel 6:1–2 is also quite interesting in regard to Name theology. In that passage (cf. 1 Sam 4:4; Jer 7:12), we read: "David again gathered all the chosen men of Israel, thirty thousand. And David arose and went with all the people who were with him from Baale-judah to bring up from there the ark of God, which is called by the name of the LORD of hosts [*ʾăšer-niqrāʾ šēm šēm yĕhwâ ṣĕbāʾôt*] who sits enthroned on the cherubim." *The Unseen Realm* (p. 222, note 4) notes: "The word *shem* (שׁם) appears twice in this verse—the ark is called the name, the name of Yahweh of hosts. The point is that the ark is identified with the Name, who is Yahweh, since Yahweh is the one seated on the cherubim. Many English translations obscure the Hebrew text here, rendering something like 'which is called by the name of the LORD of hosts,' which omits one of the occurrences of *shem*. The reason is that many scholars consider the dual occurrence of *shem* to be an accidental repetition by a scribe, what textual critics call dittography. ... While this is possible, there is no inherent interpretive problem with the Masoretic Text as it stands. ... That the ark would be called the name is understandable, since the ark was a placeholder for the very presence of Yahweh, who is the name. The same association (note the anthropomorphic language) is conveyed in 2 Sam 7:2, where the *ark* is said to *dwell* in a tent."

to guide them to the promised land as having his name in him, he is telling Moses that his very presence is within this angel. The angel is the visible form of Yahweh himself. In Judges 2:1 the angel of Yahweh reports that he accomplished the mission: "Now the angel of the LORD went up from Gilgal to Bochim. And he said, 'I brought you up from Egypt and brought you into the land that I swore to give to your fathers.'" The first-person language—the angel of Yahweh says it was he who swore to the earlier patriarchs that they would have the land—identifies him with Yahweh.

Various Old Testament passages validate this proposition. Look at who delivered Israel from Egypt and brought the nation to the land of promise: God (Yahweh) is credited with that accomplishment (Exod 13:5, 11; Lev 25:38 [cf. Gen 15:7]; Deut 6:10–11; 7:1; 9:4; 11:23; Ezek 20:28) by means of his very presence (Deut 4:37–38). Israel was not brought to the land by different deliverers, nor is the angel claiming some separate deliverance of the people in Judges 2:1–3. All of the deliverers are the same deity spoken of in different ways.

Some scholars argue that the angel of Yahweh is interchanged with Yahweh himself because protocol in ancient Near Eastern culture called for the messengers of a king or deity to be treated as that king or deity. While this cultural feature is no doubt in play, biblical language goes beyond this mental substitution. Genesis 28:10–22, the "Jacob's Ladder" story,[8] describes Jacob's first encounter with Yahweh. Jacob sees Yahweh standing, one of the more common anthropomorphisms in the Old Testament for the visible Yahweh (28:13).[9] Jacob named the location of the encounter Bethel ("house of God") and erected a stone pillar to commemorate the event (vv. 18–19). The episode is referenced in Genesis 31:

Then the angel of God said to me in the dream, "Jacob," and I said, "Here I am." And he said, "Lift up your eyes and see—all the goats

---

8. Scholars are in general agreement that the "ladder" (*sullām*) was actually a stairway that was part of a ziggurat tower. *The Unseen Realm* (p. 137, n. 3) notes: "The term is difficult since it is a *hapax legomenon* in the Hebrew Bible (a word that occurs only once). Cognate material has yielded suggestive, but not certain, options for assistance in discerning its meaning. Aside from a ziggurat, another interpretive option is a 'standing stone' (Hebrew: *maṣṣebah*). Both options are consistent with a conceptual or theological connection between God and human mortals." See Alan R. Millard, "The Celestial Ladder and the Gate of Heaven (Gen 28:12, 17)," *Expository Times* 78 (1966/1967): 86–87; C. Houtman, "What Did Jacob See in His Dream at Bethel? Some Remarks on Gen 28:10–22," *VT* 27 (1977): 337–51.

9. Gen 28:13 has Yahweh standing *'ālāyw*, which can be translated "beside him" (i.e., standing next to Jacob) or "above it" (i.e., the stairway).

that mate with the flock are striped, spotted, and mottled, for I have seen all that Laban is doing to you. I am the God of Bethel, where you anointed a pillar and made a vow to me. Now arise, go out from this land and return to the land of your kindred." (Gen 31:11–13)

The angel of God explicitly tells Jacob in verse 13 that he was the God of Bethel. There is no need to posit that the angel isn't Yahweh in visible form because the earlier account in Genesis 28 described Yahweh in human form without the angel of the Lord ever being in the scene. How does it make sense to have the angel in Genesis 31 essentially saying, "I'm the messenger of Yahweh, but consider me Yahweh for the sake of protocol" when no such protocol mediation was necessary in the earlier event *referenced* by the angel? It makes far more sense to take the angel at his word: "I am the God of Bethel—you've seen me before."

In Genesis 32, Jacob encounters a "divine man" once again and a physical struggle ensues. The divine nature of the "man" is assured in vv. 28–30:

> Then he said, "Your name shall no longer be called Jacob, but Israel, for you have striven with God and with men, and have prevailed." Then Jacob asked him, "Please tell me your name." But he said, "Why is it that you ask my name?" And there he blessed him. So Jacob called the name of the place Peniel, saying, "For I have seen God [*elōhîm*] face to face, and yet my life has been delivered."

Hosea 12:3–4 confirms this interpretation but takes the identity further, theologically:

> In the womb he [Jacob] took his brother by the heel,
>     and in his manhood **he strove** *with God* [*elōhîm*].
> **He strove** *with the angel* [*mal'āk*] and prevailed;
>     he wept and sought his favor.
> He met God at Bethel,
>     and there God spoke with us.

This passage links the "man" with whom Jacob wrestled and the encounter at Bethel. Therefore, Genesis 32 is a physical encounter with the visible, embodied Yahweh, who in Genesis 31 is the angel of the Lord. There is little merit in proposing that we should read these passages and pretend that Jacob wrestled with an entity who was a stand-in for Yahweh. The text does not veil or obscure that this figure is Yahweh in human form.

Perhaps the most striking example of how Old Testament writers conflated "the name" (*ha-shem*) with God himself is Genesis 48:14–16 (LEB), part of Israel's (i.e., Jacob's) blessing of Joseph's sons:

> And Israel stretched out his right hand and put it on the head of Ephraim (now he was the younger), and his left hand on the head of Manasseh, crossing his hands, for Manasseh was the firstborn. And he blessed Joseph and said,

> "The God [*ha-'elōhîm*] before whom my fathers, Abraham and Isaac, walked,
> The God [*ha-'elōhîm*] who shepherded me all my life unto this day,
> The angel [*ha-mal'āk*] who redeemed me from all evil,
> may he bless (*yebārēk*) the boys."

The key observation here is the verb ("may he bless"). The form in Hebrew (*yebārēk*) is grammatically *singular*. This means that a translation of "may *they* bless" would violate the grammar. God and the angel are the singular grammatical subject of the request to bless the boys. They are co-identified in the Hebrew text. Had the writer wanted to avoid having his readers think it was theologically permissible to conflate God and his angel, he would have chosen a plural verb form to keep them distinct. This is not what we find in the text.[10]

---

10. New Testament writers at times connect Jesus to the Old Testament's Name theology and the angel of Yahweh. Jesus bears the name of Yahweh and reveals Yahweh's name (John 17:5–12, 24–26; Rev 19:12, 16) and is described as the one who delivered Israel from Egypt (Jude 5). See Heiser, *Unseen Realm*, 268–89, 373. For further study in regard to Jesus as the name and as the angel, see Carl Judson Davis, *The Name and Way of the Lord: Old Testament Themes, New Testament Christology* (Sheffield: Sheffield Academic Press, 1996); Jarl E. Fossum, *The Name of God and the Angel of the Lord: Samaritan and Jewish Concepts of Intermediation and the Origin of Gnosticism* (Tübingen: Mohr Siebeck, 1985); idem., "Kyrios Jesus as the Angel of the Lord in Jude 5–7," *New Testament Studies* 33:2 (1987): 226–43. Arguing that the angel of Yahweh in the Old Testament is Yahweh in human form naturally raises the question about how such a notion relates to Jesus in the context of the doctrine of the deity of Christ (i.e., that Jesus was God). New Testament writers repurpose "two Yahwehs" language in their descriptions of Jesus in an effort to identify him as Yahweh. While the angel of Yahweh is Yahweh in human form, that angel was not Yahweh *incarnate*, a term that speaks of *becoming a human being*. This is an appropriate description of Jesus because he was born of the virgin Mary. Nevertheless, the two ideas are related, and Jesus can legitimately be related to the angel of Yahweh. I would suggest that the way to both align Jesus and the angel of Yahweh and yet honor the uniqueness

## THE COMMANDER OF YAHWEH'S ARMY

Another significant member of the heavenly host is the unnamed commander (*sar*; "prince") of Yahweh's heavenly host-army who appeared to Joshua on the cusp of the conquest:

> When Joshua was by Jericho, he lifted up his eyes and looked, and behold, a man was standing before him with his drawn sword in his hand. And Joshua went to him and said to him, "Are you for us, or for our adversaries?" And he said, "No; but I am the commander of the army of the Lord. Now I have come." And Joshua fell on his face to the earth and worshiped and said to him, "What does my lord say to his servant?" And the commander of the Lord's army said to Joshua, "Take off your sandals from your feet, for the place where you are standing is holy." And Joshua did so. (Josh 5:13–15)

Most readers will recognize the important connection between this passage and the burning bush incident in Exodus 3. The command to Joshua to "take off your sandals from your feet, for the place where you are standing is holy" also is found in Exodus 3:5. In this regard it is important to note that the angel of Yahweh was in the burning bush passage (Exod 3:2). The angel was apparently visible; if he had not been visible, it would make little sense for the writer to note his presence and then have the voice of God coming forth from the bush (as opposed to the voice of the angel; Exod 3:4; cf. Exod 3:14). This reading is confirmed by Acts 7:30–31, where Stephen notes that an angel "appeared" to Moses

---

of the incarnation is to say that the angel of Yahweh was not Jesus of Nazareth but was indeed the Second Person of the Godhead, come to people as a man (i.e., in human form). Jesus of Nazareth was the human being born of Mary, who was also the same Second Person of the Godhead—this time incarnated as a man (see Heiser, *Unseen Realm*, 268–73; cf. 252–53; 294–95). The phrase "angel of the Lord" occurs eleven times in the New Testament. Only once does it occur with the definite article suggesting a translation "the angel of the Lord" (Matt 1:24). It is "the angel of the Lord" (*ho angelos kyriou*) who tells Joseph to marry his betrothed, Mary, because her pregnancy (with Jesus) is from the Holy Spirit. There is no conflict between this occurrence and the idea that Jesus and the angel are the same Second Person of the Trinity. The definite article in Matt 1:24 is used to refer back to the angel who appeared to Joseph in a dream four verses earlier (Matt 1:20), where the phrase lacks the article. The article preceding *angelos* is, in grammatical parlance, *anaphoric*—that is, it "denotes previous reference ... reminding the reader of who or what was mentioned previously ... [which] is the most common use of the article and the easiest usage to identify" (Daniel B. Wallace, *Greek Grammar Beyond the Basics: Exegetical Syntax of the New Testament* [Grand Rapids: Zondervan, 1996], 218). The presence of the article in Matt 1:24 is therefore not to be taken as imitative language of the Old Testament wording.

in the bush and the voice of the Lord emerged from it. The language both tightly identifies the angel of Yahweh and Yahweh (they both occupy the same sacred space) and yet distinguishes them (one is visible, the other is not).

In Joshua 5:13–15, a "man" appears to Joshua, and his words echo those spoken by Yahweh out of the bush in Exodus 3. This signals that Joshua is speaking to the embodied Yahweh, the angel of Yahweh. This suggestion is confirmed by a close examination of how the commander of Yahweh's host is described (v. 13): "a man was standing before him with his drawn sword in his hand." The phrase "his drawn sword in his hand" (ḥarbô shelûphâ beyādô) occurs only two other times in the Hebrew Bible:

> And [Balaam's] donkey saw the angel of the LORD standing in the road, with a drawn sword in his hand [ḥarbô shelûphâ beyādô]. (Num 22:23)

> David lifted his eyes and saw the angel of the LORD standing between earth and heaven, and in his hand a drawn sword [ḥarbô shelûphâ beyādô] stretched out over Jerusalem. (1 Chr 21:16)

In both passages the figure with the "drawn sword in his hand" is the angel of Yahweh. Given how the writer of Joshua 5:13 pointed his readers to the burning bush incident in Exodus 3, it is evident that the commander of the commander of Yahweh's army is the angel of Yahweh.

## THE DESTROYING ANGEL OF PASSOVER

The characterization of the angel of Yahweh as a destroyer in 1 Chronicles 21:16 has ramifications for identifying another mysterious angel in the Old Testament. Let's include verse 15 in the description of the angel, noting the italicized words:

> And God sent the angel to Jerusalem to destroy [shāḥat] it, but as he was about to destroy [shāḥat] it, the LORD saw, and he relented from the calamity. And he said to the angel who was working destruction [mashḥît], "It is enough; now stay your hand." And the angel of the LORD was standing by the threshing floor of Ornan the Jebusite. And David lifted his eyes and saw the angel of the LORD standing

between earth and heaven, and in his hand a drawn sword stretched out over Jerusalem.

All the italicized words share the same root, *shāḥat*. Two are verbs (infinitives); one is a participle. They occur in the same Hebrew verb stem, the hiphil. Not surprisingly, the parallel passage in 2 Samuel uses the same terminology and forms:

> When the angel stretched out his hand toward Jerusalem *to destroy* [*shāḥat*] it, the LORD relented from the calamity and said to the angel who was working *destruction* [*mashḥît*] among the people, "It is enough; now stay your hand." And the angel of the Lord was by the threshing floor of Araunah the Jebusite. Then David spoke to the Lord when he saw the angel who was striking the people. (2 Sam 24:16–17a)

It is clear from both passages that the angel of Yahweh is in view and that he brings "destruction" (*mashḥît*). Interestingly, this is the identical term used to describe the angel of death in the account of the death of the firstborn on the eve of the first Passover:

> The blood shall be a sign for you, on the houses where you are. And when I see the blood, I will pass over you, and no plague will befall you *to destroy* [*mashḥît*] you, when I strike the land of Egypt. ... Then Moses called all the elders of Israel and said to them, "Go and select lambs for yourselves according to your clans, and kill the Passover lamb. ... For the LORD will pass through to strike the Egyptians, and when he sees the blood on the lintel and on the two doorposts, the LORD will pass over the door and will not allow *the destroyer* [*mashḥît*] to enter your houses to strike you. (Exod 12:13, 21, 23)

The *mashḥît* who was the angel of Yahweh in 1 Chronicles 21 and 2 Samuel 24 is here distinguished from Yahweh by the line, "the LORD will pass over the door and will not allow *the destroyer* [*mashḥît*] to enter your houses to strike you." Yet we read elsewhere that it was *Yahweh* who destroyed the firstborn:

> He sent Moses, his servant,
>     and Aaron, whom he had chosen. ...
> He struck down all the firstborn in their land,
>     the firstfruits of all their strength. (Ps 105:26, 36)

For I know that the LORD is great,
   and that our Lord is above all gods. ...
He it was who struck down the firstborn of Egypt,
   both of man and of beast. (Ps 135:5, 8)

Give thanks to the Lord of lords,
   for his steadfast love endures forever. ...
to him who struck down the firstborn of Egypt,
   for his steadfast love endures forever. (Ps 136:3, 10)

Remember: the destroying angel of Yahweh is actually the visible Yahweh. Given that background, these statements are not incompatible. However, Psalm 78:48–51 seems to complicate matters:

He [Yahweh] gave over their cattle to the hail
   and their flocks to thunderbolts.
He let loose on them his burning anger,
   wrath, indignation, and distress,
   a company of destroying angels [mal'akê rā'îm].
He made a path for his anger;
   he did not spare them from death,
   but gave their lives over to the plague.
He struck down every firstborn in Egypt,
   the firstfruits of their strength in the tents of Ham.

The complication is only surface level. The ESV's translation, "destroying angels," is somewhat misleading with respect to the terminology we are attempting to trace. The Hebrew term translated "destroying" is *not* the word mashḥît associated with the destroyer in the passages we saw earlier. We should also observe that Psalm 78:49 does not say the "destroying angels" killed the firstborn. That act is, once again, attributed to Yahweh (v. 51). Yahweh may have sent angels to enact the other plagues, but the death of the firstborn is attributed to him. These angels do not act in the role of the destroyer.

Given the use of the term mashḥît of that angel in other judgments handed down by Yahweh, a coherent way to reconcile all these passages would be to have Yahweh receiving the credit for the judgment on the firstborn by sending out his destroyer (mashḥît), the angel of Yahweh, who elsewhere is identified as being the visible Yahweh. This would be akin to God himself being present in the burning bush yet also having the angel of Yahweh present. These and other passages are the foundation of the later Jewish theology of two powers (two Yahweh figures).[11]

## GABRIEL, MICHAEL, AND THE PRINCE OF THE HOST

Gabriel and Michael are best discussed together, since their appearances are in the same chapters of the book of Daniel. Along with these two, an unidentified "Prince of the host" also appears. Gabriel and Michael are the lone angels mentioned by name in the Bible.[12] They are well known as archangels, though that term is not used in the Old Testament, and only Michael is called so in the New Testament (Jude 9).[13] In the book of Daniel, Gabriel's appearance precedes that of Michael, and so we begin with Daniel 8.

Daniel 8 opens with the prophet's vision of the ram and the goat (Dan 8:1–14). After conquering the ram, the goat's great horn was broken. Out of that horn sprouted four horns (Dan 8:8). From one of those horns came a little horn that grew, high and exalted, to the heavens, where it cast down some of the heavenly host to the ground (Dan 8:9–10). Then, in verse 11, we read that the little horn "became great, even as great as the Prince [*šar*] of the host." This phrase, "prince of the host" is the same in Hebrew as "commander of the army" in Joshua 5:14.

In Daniel 8:15–26 a "man" comes to assist Daniel in understanding the vision:

> When I, Daniel, had seen the vision, I sought to understand it. And behold, there stood before me one having the appearance of a man. And I heard a man's voice between the banks of the Ulai, and it called, "Gabriel, make this man understand the vision." So he came near where I stood. And when he came, I was frightened and fell on my face. But he said to me, "Understand, O son of man, that the vision is for the time of the end." (Dan 8:15–17)

---

11. See Heiser, *Unseen Realm*, 141–48.

12. This observation is with respect to the Protestant canon. Raphael is mentioned in the book of Tobit (Tob 12:11–15) as one of the seven angels who may be in proximity to the glory of God.

13. As we will see in our discussion of Second Temple Jewish material, the identification of Gabriel and other named archangels comes from Second Temple Jewish texts.

The description of this assistance is our focus here, and its wording will prompt us to return to the phrase "prince of the host." The "man" Daniel sees turns out to be the angel Gabriel (v. 16). But Gabriel is commanded to speak to Daniel by the voice of another "man," emanating from between the banks of the Ulai river, where Daniel had been when overcome by the vision (Dan 8:2). The unseen "man" is superior to Gabriel for he commands him. Gabriel appears again to Daniel to interpret a subsequent vision (Dan 9:20–23).

In Daniel 10 the prophet once again sees a vision involving a glorious "man clothed in linen":

> On the twenty-fourth day of the first month, as I was standing on the bank of the great river (that is, the Tigris) I lifted up my eyes and looked, and behold, a man clothed in linen, with a belt of fine gold from Uphaz around his waist. His body was like beryl, his face like the appearance of lightning, his eyes like flaming torches, his arms and legs like the gleam of burnished bronze, and the sound of his words like the sound of a multitude. ... Then I heard the sound of his words, and as I heard the sound of his words, I fell on my face in deep sleep with my face to the ground.
>
> And behold, a hand touched me and set me trembling on my hands and knees. And he said to me, "O Daniel, man greatly loved, understand the words that I speak to you, and stand upright, for now I have been sent to you." And when he had spoken this word to me, I stood up trembling. Then he said to me, "Fear not, Daniel, for from the first day that you set your heart to understand and humbled yourself before your God, your words have been heard, and I have come because of your words. The prince of the kingdom of Persia withstood me twenty-one days, but Michael, one of the chief princes, came to help me, for I was left there with the kings of Persia, and came to make you understand what is to happen to your people in the latter days. For the vision is for days yet to come."
>
> When he had spoken to me according to these words, I turned my face toward the ground and was mute. And behold, one in the likeness of the children of man touched my lips. Then I opened my mouth and spoke. I said to him who stood before me, "O my lord, by reason of the vision pains have come upon me, and I retain no

strength. How can my lord's servant talk with my lord? For now no strength remains in me, and no breath is left in me."

Again one having the appearance of a man touched me and strengthened me. And he said, "O man greatly loved, fear not, peace be with you; be strong and of good courage." And as he spoke to me, I was strengthened and said, "Let my lord speak, for you have strengthened me." Then he said, "Do you know why I have come to you? But now I will return to fight against the prince of Persia; and when I go out, behold, the prince of Greece will come. But I will tell you what is inscribed in the book of truth: there is none who contends by my side against these except Michael, your prince. (Dan 10:4–6, 9–21)

It is important to note several things about this exchange. First, this "man" is *not* identified as Gabriel. Second, the speaking "man" was opposed by the "prince" of Persia (v. 13) and Greece.[14] Third, the "man" is not only distinct from Gabriel; he is also not Michael, since he refers to Michael in the third person (vv. 13, 20). Michael assisted this unidentified figure in his spiritual warfare against the prince of Persia. Fourth, the unidentified figure later touches Daniel (v. 18) to strengthen him, informing him in the first person, "I will return to fight against the prince of Persia," adding that he expects the "prince of Greece" will also be part of the battle (v. 20).

While the "man" is never identified in Daniel 10, it is clear he is neither Gabriel nor Michael. We meet the "man" again in Daniel 12:

At that time shall arise Michael, the great prince who has charge of your people. And there shall be a time of trouble, such as never has been since there was a nation till that time. But at that time your people shall be delivered, everyone whose name shall be found written in the book. ... Then I, Daniel, looked, and behold, two others stood, one on this bank of the stream and one on that bank of the stream. And someone said to the man clothed in linen, who was above the waters of the stream, "How long shall it be till the end of these wonders?" (Dan 12:1, 5)

"The man clothed in linen" takes us back to the initial appearance of this mysterious figure in Daniel 10:5. Who is this "man"? I would argue

---

14. See the comments on *śar* in the preceding chapters.

that he is to be identified with the "prince of the host" mentioned in Daniel 8:11—the one whom the magnified little horn opposed. In this regard, Bampfylde comments:

> Who then is this man? The author does not identify him with Gabriel, which he could easily have done (cf. 8:16; 9:21). Daniel has already met Gabriel (8:16), and would have recognised him if there were a renewed acquaintanceship. The man whom he sees in ch. 10 is to be identified with the one who had spoken to Gabriel and sent him to Daniel: "And I heard a man's voice between the banks of the Ulai, and it called, 'Gabriel, make this man understand the vision' " (8:16). The man whom Daniel sees in ch.10 "clothed in linen" is described again in 12:6 as "the man clothed in linen, who was above the waters of the stream". He is therefore the man whose voice Daniel heard coming from between the banks of the Ulai when he first saw Gabriel. The man is not Michael. Indeed, he appears to have a higher status than Michael, the patron of Israel according to 10:21, "there is none who contends by my side against these except Michael, your prince". This man seems not to be in charge of any particular nation, but supports those who are on "his side." ... He is therefore to be identified with "the Prince of the host" (8:11). This Prince of the host is not Michael, for although Michael is the patron of Israel and an archangel, he is *not chief* of the archangels in intertestamental literature, e.g. 1 Enoch 9:1–10:16; 20:5; 24:6; 54:6; 60:4–5; 68:2; 71:9. In the Book of Daniel there is no possibility that Michael might be the chief Prince. He is known as "one of the chief princes" (Dan. 10:13), whereas the Prince of the host (8:11) is called "the Prince of princes" (8:25). The man described in 10:5–6 is certainly one of the highest angels,—a "Prince" and a heavenly military commander. Neither is he to be identified with Gabriel, for he addresses Gabriel himself.[15]

These observations are important in light of my earlier contention that the commander ("prince") of Yahweh's host in Joshua 5:14 is the

---

15. Gillian Bampfylde, "The Prince of the Host in the Book of Daniel and the Dead Sea Scrolls," *Journal for the Study of Judaism in the Persian, Hellenistic, and Roman Period* 14 (1983): 129–34 (here, 129–30). Bampfylde also notes (p. 131), "The princes are the patron angels of various countries (cf. Dan. 10:13, 20, 21. In Deut. 32:8 these princes are styled 'sons of God')."

angel of Yahweh, the visible embodiment of Yahweh himself.[16] This commander cannot be Michael, because Michael is one among other "chief princes." The visible Yahweh would have no such company. As we will see when we discuss Second Temple Jewish angelology, certain writers of that period conflate the two on the basis of three passages:

- Joshua 5:14 speaks of the "commander" (*śar*) of Yahweh's army
- Michael is Israel's "prince" (*śar*) in Daniel 10:21
- Michael is "the great prince who has charge of your people" in Daniel 12:1[17]

This thought trajectory is of course marred by the description of Michael in Daniel 10:13 ("one of the chief princes"). If Michael is the commander of Joshua 5:14, then that commander is but one of the commanders of Yahweh's host—any of which could presumably have told Joshua to remove his sandals because he stood on holy ground. This suggests in turn that any number of angels could have occupied space with Yahweh in the burning bush or been identified with Yahweh in Genesis 48:15–16. This simply isn't consistent with the way the angel of Yahweh is portrayed. Further, the claim of Joshua 5:14 is that the commander leads Yahweh's *heavenly* host. The prince is not assigned to the people of Israel as in the Daniel passages.

Michael clearly is not the highest authority in the heavenly sphere. He assists the divine "man" who speaks to Daniel (Dan 10:13, 21). As such, it would be this unidentified figure to whom all members of the heavenly host, including Michael, report. Daniel 8:11 suggests that there is a "prince" over the entire host. In addition, Daniel 8:25 refers to a "prince of princes." Michael is but one of the chief princes, and so he cannot be the prince that is over all the other princes. These descriptions are best understood as describing the commander ("prince") of Yahweh's entire

---

16. It is not possible to link either the figure of Dan 3:24–28 or the angel of Dan 6:22 with this heavenly man or the angel of Yahweh. Not only does the description that the fourth "man" in the fiery furnace come from Nebuchadnezzar—hardly a source of Israelite thought—but the term "son of the gods" aligns quite easily with divine "sons of God" terminology used of members of the heavenly host who are not Yahweh. In Dan 6:22, "his angel" is ambiguous (all angels are under God's authority). Both these figures are best understood as "normal" divine agents in God's service, not the angel of Yahweh.

17. Second Temple period sources have Michael leading the great eschatological war for this reason. However, other Jewish thinkers assigned this role to Melchizedek, effectively conflating Michael and Melchizedek. See chapter 5.

host, who is the angel of Yahweh, the second Yahweh figure encountered by Joshua.[18]

There remains another point of proof for this identification. Daniel 8, the passage where the little horn is magnified "even as great as the Prince of the host" (v. 11) and "rise up against the Prince of princes" (v. 25), has an intriguing parallel elsewhere in Daniel. Since most scholars identify the little horn as Antiochus IV, the little horn is the king described in Daniel 11:36–39, a description that fits Antiochus IV well.[19] Putting the respective descriptions side-by-side is revealing:

| Daniel 8:11, 25 | Daniel 11:36–37 |
| --- | --- |
| "[The little horn] became great, even as great as the Prince of the host."<br><br>"[The king representing the little horn] shall become great. Without warning he shall destroy many. And he shall even rise up against the Prince of princes." | "And the king shall do as he wills. He shall exalt himself and magnify himself above every god, and shall speak astonishing things against the God of gods. ... He shall not pay attention to any other god, for he shall magnify himself above all." |

These parallels lead some scholars to suggest that the titles of 8:11 and 8:25 are epithets that refer to God himself. This makes good sense if the "prince of the host" and the "prince of princes" is the angel of Yahweh, the prince of Yahweh's host in Joshua 5:14. The parallels cannot be adequately explained if the phrases in Daniel 8 point to Michael.[20] Michael cannot simultaneously be one of the chief princes and "the God of gods."

---

18. Rowland compares the description of the "man" in Dan 10 with the son of man and ancient of days in Dan 7, the vision of Jesus in Rev 1, and similar descriptions of heavenly figures in the pseudepigraphical texts Apocalypse of Abraham (AA) and Joseph and Aseneth (JA). He argues that "an identification is to be made between the man-like figure and the Ancient of Days" (p. 106). His explanation of the textual relationships, particularly an important LXX variant follows: "It is suggested that AA, JA and Rev. all reflect an exegetical tradition which (a) knew of the identification of the man-like figure with the Ancient of Days ..., (b) identified the human figure of 7.13 as an angelic being, and (c) as a result linked this verse with the parallel angelophany in Dan. 10.6f" (p. 107). See Christopher Rowland, "A Man Clothed in Linen, Dan 10.6ff. and Jewish Angelology," JSNT 24 (1985): 99–110.

19. See for example, John E. Goldingay, *Daniel*, WBC 30 (Dallas: Word, 1989), 210; Stephen R. Miller, *Daniel*, NAC 18 (Nashville: Broadman & Holman, 1994), 226.

20. See Heiser, "The Divine Council," 164–67 for a discussion of how certain scholars see these parallels and still struggle to produce the Michael identification. The problems are resolved when we embrace the paradigm of two Yahweh figures in the Old Testament, including the commander of Yahweh's host in Josh 5:14.

# CHAPTER 4

# The Language of the Heavenly Host in Second Temple Judaism

THE "SECOND TEMPLE PERIOD" REFERS TO THE ERA IN JEWISH HISTORY that began with the founding of Israel's second temple (c. 516 BC) until the destruction of that temple by the Romans in AD 70.[1] The period is often rounded to 500 BC—AD 100. It is also called the "intertestamental period," since most of the period takes place between the end of the events of the Old Testament and those of the New Testament.

Some authors who wrote during this period, such as Josephus and Philo, are well known today. Other writers are unknown; nevertheless, their work received wide readership during the period and into the initial centuries of Christianity. Examples include books of the Apocrypha (Tobit, Wisdom of Solomon, 1–2 Maccabees) and the Pseudepigrapha (1 Enoch, Jubilees).[2] The documents from Qumran that are not biblical manuscripts are also part of this literary output.[3] These documents range

---

1. The building of the second temple is described in the Old Testament book of Haggai.

2. The term "Apocrypha" is used by Protestants for a group of Old Testament books included in the canon by Roman Catholicism. Consequently, Roman Catholics describe these books as "deuterocanonical." The term "Pseudepigrapha" does *not* mean "false writings" in the sense that their content was considered spurious. The term is a modern category label into which are placed literary works whose authors attributed the content to some noteworthy figure (real or imagined). Some of these books were highly regarded by Jews and Christians in antiquity. They were not systematically maligned.

3. Qumran is the archaeological site near the Dead Sea associated with most of the Dead Sea Scrolls.

from treatises about life in the Qumran community (sectarian texts) to expansions of biblical stories (e.g., the Genesis Apocryphon).

These compositions frequently interact with the content of the Hebrew Bible and its theology. Part of that interaction inevitably concerns portrayals of the heavenly host, providing a window into the thinking of Judaism after the Old Testament period on the spiritual world and its activities.

Second Temple Jewish literature was written in Hebrew, Aramaic, and Greek. However, the Second Temple period literary corpus includes translations—namely, the Septuagint (abbreviated LXX), the Greek translation of the Hebrew Bible. While there are some curiosities, the Old Testament range of terms we surveyed in chapter 1 aligns well with the work of LXX translators.[4] With one exception, the actual data don't support certain academic speculations about Second Temple angelology. As we will see in this chapter, this is significant not only for discussing intertestamental Jewish thinking about the heavenly host but also because New Testament writers utilize the LXX so frequently.[5]

## GENERAL CONGRUENCE

The vocabulary of the heavenly host loyal to the God of Israel in Second Temple Jewish literature is largely consistent with Old Testament vocabulary for God's heavenly agents. The chart below compares Hebrew vocabulary we surveyed in chapter 1 with Hebrew, Aramaic, and Greek vocabulary used of supernatural beings in service to God in Second Temple literature. It is representative, not exhaustive.[6]

---

4. The Septuagint (LXX) is the ancient Greek translation of the Hebrew Bible that was produced prior to the days of Jesus and the apostles. The Septuagint translators used a Hebrew text to produce their translation that differed in a number of places with the traditional Hebrew (Masoretic) text.

5. Studies have determined that New Testament writers quote the Old Testament in places where the Masoretic Text (MT) and the Septuagint (LXX) are in agreement with each other about twenty percent of the time. Of the eighty percent where some disagreement between MT and LXX is evident, the New Testament reading agrees with the MT less than five percent of the time. This demonstrates that the NT writers use the LXX most of the time when they quote the Old Testament. See Karen H. Jobes and Moises Silva, *Invitation to the Septuagint* (Grand Rapids: Baker, 2000), 189–93.

6. The transliterated terms in the chart are lemmas, not inflected forms.

| Hebrew Bible | Second Temple Texts | Septuagint (LXX) |
|---|---|---|
| "spirit" (*rûaḥ*; plural: *rûḥôṯ*)<br><br>1 Kgs 22:19–23; Judg 9:22–23; 1 Sam 16:14–16; 18:10–11; Isa 19:13–14; 37:5–7; Ps 104:4 | "spirits" (*pneuma*)<br><br>1 Enoch 15:7,10; 25:4, 6; 37:2; 38:2; 39:2; 40:2; 41:2; 43:4; 46:3; 48:2; 2 Enoch 16:7<br><br>Josephus, *Against Apion* (Extract of Discourse on Hades, 6); Qumran (*rûḥôṯ*): 1 QS iii.18, 24; iv.23; 1QM xii.9; xiii.2, 4, 10; xiv.10; 4Q400 1.i.5; 4Q403 1.ii.7; 4Q404 5.5; 4Q405 23.i.9; 23.ii.6 | *pneuma*<br><br>1 Kgs 22:19–23; Judg 9:22–23; 1 Sam 16:14–16; Isa 19:13–14; 37:5–7; Ps 104:4[1] |
| "heavenly ones" (*šamayim*)<br><br>Ps 89:5; Job 15:15; Deut 32:43 | "sons/children of heaven"[2] (*ouranos*)<br><br>1 Enoch 6:2; 13:8; 14:3; Qumran (*beney šamayim*): 1QS iv.22; xi.8 | *ouranos*<br><br>plural ("heavenly ones"): Ps 89:5; Deut 32:43 |
| "stars"; "hosts"[3]<br><br>Ps 103:21 | "powers (*dynamis*) of heaven"; "stars" (*kokabîn*)<br><br>1 Enoch 18:14–15; 21:3, 6; 46:7; 86:3; 88:3; 90:21; 2 Enoch 29:3; Life of Adam and Eve 15:3 | *dynamis* or *astron*<br><br>"Lord of hosts" is rendered "Lord of mighty powers" using *dynamis*<br><br>Ps 103:21 (plural); Job 38:7 (plural from *astron*) |
| "holy ones" (*qedōšîm*)<br><br>Ps 89:5–7 [Hebrew: 6–8]<br><br>Job 15:15; Deut 33:2–3; Job 5:1; Zech 14:5; Dan 4:17 | "holy ones" (*hagioi*; *qedîšîn*)[4]<br><br>1 Enoch 1:9; 9:3; 12:2; 14:23, 25; 45:1; 47:2; 61:10; Jubilees 17:11; 31:4; 33:12; Qumran: 1QS xi.8; 1QM x.12; xii.1, 4, 7; xviii.2; 1QHa xix.12; 11QMelch ii.9 | *hagioi*<br><br>Ps 88:6; Job 15:15; Zech 14:5 (plural)<br><br>Deut 33:2; Job 5:1 = *angelos* |
| "minister" (verb: *šrt*, piel stem: *šērēt*) | "servant" (*leitourgos*)<br><br>Testament of Abraham (A) 15:1; Prayer of Joseph (frag A) 8; Qumran ("ministers of the Presence"): 4Q400 1.i.4, 8; 4Q401 15.3; 4Q405 23.i.3 | *leitourgos*<br><br>Pss 102:20; 103:4[5] |
| "watcher" (Aramaich: *ʿîr*; plural: *ʿîrîn*)<br><br>Dan 4:13, 17, 23; [Aramaic text: vv. 10, 14, 20] | "watcher" (*egrēgoroi*); Aramaic: (*ʿîrîn*)<br><br>1 Enoch 1:5; 10:7, 9, 15; 12:2, 3, 4; 14:1, 3; 13:10; 15:9; 16:2; Jubilees 4:15; 7:21; 8:3; 10:5; Testament of Naphtali 3:5; 5:6 | *angelos*<br><br>Dan 4:13, 21, 24 |
| "mighty ones" (*gibborîm*, *ʾabbîrîm*)<br><br>Pss 78:25; 103:20 | Qumran: (*gibborîm*): 1QHa xvi.11; xviii.34–35; 1QM xv.14; 4Q402 1.4; 4Q403 1.i.21 | "angels … strong ones in strength" (*angelos, dynatos*; *ischus*), Ps 103:20; "angels" in Ps 78:25 |

1. 1 Sam 18:10–11 is absent in the LXX.

2. See the discussion of "heavenly ones" in L. Dequeker, "The 'Saints of the Most High' in Qumran and Daniel," *Old Testament Studies* 18 (1973): 108–87 (133–37).

3. Excludes the phrase "Lord of hosts" to be more targeted.

4. See Dequeker, "Saints of the Most High," 137–72, for the Qumran material for "holy ones."

5. LXX numbering differs from the Hebrew text.

| Hebrew Bible | Second Temple Texts | Septuagint (LXX) |
|---|---|---|
| "mediator" (*mēlîṣ*)<br><br>Job 33:23 | | "a thousand angels of death"<br><br>(*angelos*)<br><br>Job 33:23 |
| "cherubim" (*kerubîm*)<br><br>Ezek 10 (throughout)<br>"seraphim" (*śerāpîm*)<br><br>Isa 6:2, 6 | "cherubim" (*cheroubim*)<br><br>1 Enoch 14:11, 18; 20:7; Sibylline Oracles 3:1; Apocalypse of Moses 19, 22, 32, 38; Testament of Abraham (B) 10:8, 11; Qumran (*kerubîm*): 4Q403 1.ii.15; 4Q405 20.ii-21-22.3, 8 | *cheroubim*<br><br>Ezek 10 (throughout)<br><br>*seraphim*<br><br>Isa 6:2, 6 |
| "angel"<br><br>(*mal'āk*; plural: *mal'ākîm*)[6]<br><br>(Gen 19:1, 15; 28:12; 32:1; Job 4:18; Pss 78:49; 91:11; 103:20; 104:4; 148:2) | "angel" (*angelos*)<br><br>1 Enoch 6:2; 10:7; 14:4, 21; 18:14; 20:1–7; 21:5, 9, 10; 22:3, 6; 24:6; 32:6; Josephus, *Jewish Antiquities* 1.196; 1.200; 1.325; Philo, *Allegorical Interpretation* III.177; *On the Sacrifices of Cain and Abel* 5; *On Giants* 6:2; *On Flight and Finding* 212; Qumran (*mal'ākîm*): 1QHa ix.11; xiv.13; xxiv.top.4, 7; 1QM i.15; xii.1, 4, 8; xiii.12 | *angelos*<br><br>Gen 19:1, 15; 28:12; 32:1; Job 4:18; Pss 77:49; 90:11; 102:20; 103:4;[7] 148:2 |

6. Of the 213 occurrences of the lemma *mal'āk*, just over half refer to supernatural beings. Most of those instances refer to the angel of Yahweh. There are 10 instances where the plural speaks of supernatural beings, all of which are listed in the chart.

7. The differences in the verse references for certain psalms are due to the fact that the LXX numbering differs from the traditional Hebrew text.

The chart omits the Hebrew vocabulary of "gods" and "sons of God" since the aforementioned point of scholarly conjecture concerns that terminology. Before we turn our attention to that matter, we need to observe a few things about the vocabulary in the chart.

The significant uniformity of the terminology, even in translation (LXX), shows that a number of Second Temple Jewish writers preserved the nuancing of Old Testament terminology. There are exceptions, though. The LXX translators rendered "holy ones" (*qedōšîm*) in Deuteronomy 33:2 and Job 5:1 with *angeloi* ("angels"). The translation isn't unexpected, since plural "holy ones" in God's presence suggests the heavenly host. Something similar occurs in the book of Daniel, where "watchers" become "angels" in LXX, whereas the Greek text of 1 Enoch is more literal (*egrēgoroi*: "watchers"). The choice is perhaps explained by the fact that the watcher sent from heaven in the beginning of Daniel 4 to explain the dream is also called a "holy one." Again, it is not surprising that a "holy one" sent to deliver information would prompt a translation of "angel," since that was what angels typically did in the Hebrew Bible.

It is difficult to know precisely what the translator of Job 33:23 was thinking in rendering *mēlîṣ* ("mediator") as "a thousand angels of death." In his study of the LXX angelology of Job, Gammie offers a coherent, though not certain, explanation:

> It could be argued that the translator did not any longer conceive angels capable of being מליצים (*meliṣîm*), "spokesmen" in behalf of men, as happens, for example, in the Book of Enoch (1 Enoch 15:2). Such a tack, however, would be in error, in my judgment. The translator may rather be recalling the Prologue where the Adversary, ὁ διάβολος (the Devil) is also a death-bearer in the sense that he bears intermediate responsibility for the death of Job's children. What is said in these verses thus more probably reveals the translator's taking into account the Book as a whole. In the term θανατόφοροι "death-bearing," he may be simply reiterating a role already assigned to one of the angels called "The Adversary" earlier in the book.[7]

Gammie takes note of other oddities in LXX Job: "LXX occasionally renders ἄγγελοι on the basis of an MT [Masoretic Text] that contains no obvious reference to angels."[8] A comparative survey of the "angelic" terminology of the Hebrew Bible and the LXX shows that this phenomenon is wider than the book of Job. Of the 213 occurrences of the lemma *mal'āk* in the Hebrew Bible, just over half refer to supernatural beings ("angels") instead of humans ("messengers").[9] Most of the supernatural instances involve the angel of Yahweh. There are 10 instances where the plural *mal'ākîm* speaks of supernatural beings, all of which are listed in the earlier chart. LXX uses *angelos* 292 times, 160 of which refer to supernatural beings. With respect to our focus here, LXX uses a plural form of *angelos* when referring to supernatural beings 23 times in addition to the 10 references in the chart.[10]

---

7. John G. Gammie, "The Angelology and Demonology in the Septuagint Book of Job," *HUCA* 56 (1985): 5–6.

8. Gammie, "The Angelology and Demonology in the Septuagint Book of Job," 1.

9. The statistics are the result of computer searches in the following resources: *The Lexham Hebrew Bible* (Bellingham, WA: Lexham Press, 2012) and the Septuagint with Logos Morphology (A. Rahlfs, *Septuaginta: With Morphology* [electronic ed.; Stuttgart: Deutsche Bibelgesellschaft, 1979]).

10. Those additional instances are: Gen 6:2; Deut 32:8, 43; 33:2; Pss 8:6; 77:25; 96:7; 137:1; Job 1:6; 2:1; 5:1; 36:14; 38:7; 40:11; 40:19; 41:25; Wisdom 16:20; Tobit 8:15; 11:14; 12:15; Ode 2:8, 43; 10:58.

## REJECTION OF DIVINE PLURALITY?

Statistically, then, LXX refers to angels as a group three times as often as the traditional Hebrew text (33 vs. 10). The higher count is partially due to the inclusion of books in the Septuagint that are not part of the Hebrew canon. But the canonical issue cannot completely account for the greater reference to angels (*angeloi*) in LXX. In several instances, the language of divine plurality in the Hebrew Bible (references to "gods" via plural *'ēlîm* or *'elōhîm* and *benê 'ēlîm/ 'elōhîm*) was rendered with *angeloi*. What are we to make of this?

Many scholars believe this indicates a rejection of divine plurality as part of a theological evolution out of polytheism toward a rigid, intolerant monotheism. The idea is basically assumed by scholars who write about Second Temple Period angelology,[11] but it is based on a misunderstanding of divine plurality and a failure to examine the totality of the data. I have addressed the former at length elsewhere; our focus here is the latter.[12]

In assessing the coherence of whether Jewish writers in the Second Temple period saw a problem with the language of divine plurality in the Hebrew Bible, there are two primary sources: the LXX and the Dead Sea Scrolls.

---

11. For example, Carol Newsom interprets plural *'ēlîm* in the Dead Sea Scrolls as "angelic" (Carol A. Newsom, *Songs of the Sabbath Sacrifice: A Critical Edition* [Atlanta: Scholars Press, 1985], 23–24). John J. Collins does the same when he writes of figures in the heavenly temple of Dead Sea Scroll material, "These holy ones are also called 'gods' ( *'ēlîm*), angels, spirits, and princes" (John J. Collins, "Powers in Heaven: God, Gods, and Angels in the Dead Sea Scrolls," in *Religion in the Dead Sea Scrolls*, eds. John J. Collins and Robert A. Kugler [Grand Rapids: Eerdmans, 2000], 9–20 [esp. 12]). Michael Wise devotes over forty pages of analysis to how certain Qumran scrolls elevate the God of Israel above "angels" even though none of the scrolls he discusses contains the term *mal'ākîm* ("angels"), but rather other terms of divine plurality (Michael O. Wise, "מי כמוני באלים: A Study of 4Q491c, 4Q471b, 4Q427 7, and 1QHa 25:25–26:10," *DSD* 7.2 [2000]: 173–219).

12. See chapter 1 for an overview of why the polytheistic perspective is incoherent. Construing multiple *'elōhîm* as polytheism is to read a modern conception back into ancient thought. Divine plurality is no obstacle to adherence to the uniqueness of Yahweh in the minds of the writers of the Hebrew Bible. Modern scholars mistakenly presume that the multiple *'elōhîm* must have been construed as sharing essentially the same attributes, but this is not the case. See Heiser, "The Divine Council in Late Canonical and Non-Canonical Jewish Literature"; idem, "Monotheism, Polytheism, Monolatry, or Henotheism"; idem, "Does Divine Plurality in the Hebrew Bible Demonstrate an Evolution from Polytheism to Monotheism in Israelite Religion?"

# VOCABULARY OF THE HEAVENLY HOST IN THE SEPTUAGINT (LXX)

As noted above, LXX does indeed render the language of divine plurality with *angeloi*. But there are two facts that must be considered before drawing conclusions: the LXX translators do not do this consistently and in most of the places where they do opt for *angeloi*, other texts of the LXX render the divine plurality literally and do not use *angeloi*. The table below lists all the passages that factor into the discussion, showing which ones LXX translators translated as *angeloi*.

| Hebrew Bible<br><br>"gods"/"divine beings"<br>(ʾelōhîm; ʾēlîm)<br><br>"sons of God"<br>(benê ʾēlîm/ʾelōhîm) | LXX renders<br>the Hebrew terms<br>with plural<br>of angelos ("angel") | LXX preserves divine<br>plurality by using a plural<br>form of theos ("god")[1] |
|---|---|---|
| Torah references to other gods (ʾelōhîm). Examples:<br><br>Exod 18:11 ("greater than all gods"; ʾelōhîm)<br><br>Deut 8:19 ("go after other gods"; ʾelōhîm)<br><br>Deut 10:17 ("God of gods"; ʾelōhîm)<br><br>Deut 17:3 ("served other gods"; ʾelōhîm)<br><br>Deut 29:26 ("served other gods ... gods whom they had not known and whom [God] had not allotted to them"; ʾelōhîm twice)[2] | | Plural of theos is ubiquitous in Torah legal literature (over 60 times, including all the verse references to the left): Exod 18:11; Deut 8:19; 10:17; 17:3; 29:26 |
| Exod 15:11 ("among the gods"; ʾēlîm) | | Exod 15:11 (theois) |
| Ps 82:1 ("in the midst of the gods"; ʾelōhîm) | | Ps 81:1 (theous)[3] |
| Ps 86:8 ("among the gods"; ʾelōhîm) | | Ps 85:8 (theois) |
| Ps 95:3 ("great King above all gods"; ʾelōhîm) | | Ps 94:3 (theous) |
| Ps 96:4 ("feared above all gods"; ʾelōhîm) | | Ps 95:4 (theous) |
| Ps 97:9 ("you are exalted far above all gods"; ʾelōhîm) | | Ps 96:9 (theous) |
| Ps 136:2 ("the God of gods"; ʾelōhîm) | | Ps 135:2 (theōn) |
| 1 Sam 28:13 ("I see a god/gods coming up out of the earth"; ʾelōhîm) | | 1 Sam 28:13 (theous) |

1. Some versification numbers in LXX differ from those in the Hebrew MT.

2. On the allotment language, see the ensuing discussion of Deut 32:8.

3. See R. B. Salters, "Psalm 82:1 and the Septuagint," *ZAW* 103.2 (1991): 225–39.

| Hebrew Bible "gods"/"divine beings" (ʾelōhîm; ʾēlîm) "sons of God" (benê ʾēlîm/ʾelōhîm) | LXX renders the Hebrew terms with plural of angelos ("angel") | LXX preserves divine plurality by using a plural form of theos ("god") |
|---|---|---|
| Gen 6:2 ("sons of God"; benê hā-ʾelōhîm) | | Gen 6:2 ("sons of God"; hoi huioi tou theou) |
| Ps 29:1 ("sons of God"; benê ʾēlîm) | | Ps 28:1 ("sons of God"; huioi theou) |
| Ps 89:7 ("sons of God"; bene ʾēlîm) | | Ps 88:7 ("among the sons of God"; en huioi theou) |
| Ps 8:5 ("you have made him a little lower than God/the gods"; ʾelōhîm) | Ps 8:6 ("less than the angels"; brachy ti par' angelous) | |
| Ps 97:7 ("worship him all you gods"; ʾelōhîm) | Ps 96:7 ("all his angels"; pantes hoi angeloi autou) | |
| Job 1:6; 2:1 ("sons of God"; benê hā-ʾelōhîm) | Job 1:6; 2:1 ("the angels of God"; hoi angeloi tou theou) | |
| Deut 32:8 ("sons of God"; benê hā-ʾelōhîm)[4] | Deut 32:8 ("angels of God"; angelōn theou) | |
| Deut 32:43 ("bow down to him, all gods"; ʾelōhîm)[5] | Deut 32:43 ("angels of God"; angeloi tou theou)[6] | |
| Job 38:7 ("sons of God"; benê hā-ʾelōhîm) | Job 38:7 ("all my angels"; pantes angeloi mou) | |
| Ps 138:1 ("before the gods I sing your [Yahweh's] praise"; ʾelōhîm) | Ps 137:1 ("before the angels"; enantion angelōn) | |

4. The oldest Hebrew text of this verse, found among the Dead Sea Scrolls, reads benê hā-ʾelōhîm. The traditional Masoretic Text reads "sons of Israel." For a lengthy discussion of why the scroll reading is superior, see Heiser, "Deuteronomy 32:8 and the Sons of God," BSac 158 (2001): 52–74.

5. This wording is absent from the MT but present in Dead Sea Scroll material. For a discussion, see Heiser, "Monotheism, Polytheism, Monolatry, or Henotheism?," 9–10; Jeffrey Tigay, Deuteronomy, JPS Torah Commentary (Philadelphia: Jewish Publication Society, 1996), 516–17.

6. The LXX also adds "sons of God" to the first stanza of this verse, a phrase not present in the Hebrew material from Qumran. See the ensuing discussion for the implications and Tigay, Deuteronomy, 516–17, for an explanation.

The chart illustrates that there are eight passages where an LXX translator has taken the language of divine plurality and rendered it as "angels." But the chart indicates there are *more* places where the LXX translator decided otherwise, preferring a more literal equivalent. Some of those instances (Pss 29:1; 82:1 89:7; Exod 15:11) are among the most frequently cited passages by scholars seeking to argue that the Hebrew Bible preserves vestiges of polytheism. If Jews of the Second Temple period were concerned that such language might be taken as polytheism, it would make little sense to leave passages like these intact—undisguised as angels. The unevenness of what we find shows that the LXX cannot be regarded as proof for a campaign to erase polytheistic language and downgrade instance of divine plurality to angels.

The argument that the LXX sought to eliminate "polytheistic" language gets even weaker when one investigates the text-critical data for the eight passages that render plural *'ēlîm* or *'elōhîm* and *benê 'ēlîm/ 'elōhîm* with *angeloi*. Of the eight instances noted above where the translator decided to use *angeloi*, there are variant LXX manuscript readings preserving the more literalistic rendering in half of them.[13] This again indicates the lack of a theological concern with the Hebrew terminology within the literate Jewish community. It may be the case that a few LXX translators preferred "angels" to "gods" or "sons of God," but the data show that many had no such concern.

## VOCABULARY OF THE HEAVENLY HOST IN THE DEAD SEA SCROLLS

The view of many scholars—that Jewish writers, concerned about the language of divine plurality, leveled the vocabulary to angels—is dealt an even more severe blow when we come to the Dead Sea Scrolls. One would never know that upon reading statements such as this one:

There are various OT texts which speak of many gods (אלהים; *'elōhîm*). However, at least by the turn of the era these [*'elōhîm*] were regarded as God's *angelic* host. This can be seen in particular in the DSS where אלהים or אלים [*'ēlîm*] is a common way of referring to angels.[14]

---

13. For "angels of God" in Job 1:6; 2:1, the Greek text of Aquila reads "sons of God" (*hoi huioi theou* and *hoi huioi tou theou*, respectively). Aquila and Theodotion also have "sons of God" in place of "all my angels" in Job 38:7. Lastly, for "before the angels" in LXX Ps 137:1 Aquila and the Heptapla column E' have "before the gods" (*enanti theōn*).

14. Crispin H. T. Fletcher-Louis, *Luke-Acts: Angels, Christology, and Soteriology* (Tübingen: Mohr Siebeck, 1997), 3–4.

This statement is erroneous. The data of the Dead Sea Scrolls (DSS) data in fact point us toward the opposite conclusion. I have refuted this idea at length elsewhere in an article on divine plurality in the Dead Sea Scrolls.[15] In the remaining space in this chapter, I'll summarize that refutation.

The Dead Sea Scrolls contain a number of references to the divine council of the Hebrew Bible. Those references utilize the same terminology for the council we surveyed in chapter 1—a council of *'elōhîm* or *'ēlîm*. There are no instances in the scrolls of council terminology that includes the Hebrew term for angels (*mal'akîm*). This omission is curious to say the least if, as Fletcher-Louis and many others suggest, there was a theological trend in Second Temple Judaism to avoid allegedly polytheistic language and these council members were transformed to angels.[16]

According to Abegg's authoritative database of the Qumran sectarian manuscripts,[17] there are 106 instances of plural *'ēlîm* in the scrolls.[18] The phrase *benê 'ēlîm* occurs five times.[19] Nowhere are these terms negative or polemic, and nowhere are these terms accompanied by *mal'akîm* to make the point that the *'ēlîm* are to be understood as angels.

---

15. See Michael S. Heiser, "Monotheism and the Language of Divine Plurality in the Hebrew Bible and the Dead Sea Scrolls," *TynBul* 65.1 (2014): 85–100. Other scholars have noted the same incongruity between such claims and terminology in the scrolls. Though I disagree with connecting the vocabulary of divine plurality with polytheism, see Peter Hayman, "Monotheism—A Misused Word in Jewish Studies?" *Journal of Jewish Studies* 42.1 (1991): 1–15 (esp. 8–9).

16. For the scrolls data behind this conclusion, see Heiser, "Monotheism and the Language of Divine Plurality," 92–93.

17. Martin G. Abegg, Jr., *Qumran Sectarian Manuscripts* (Bellingham, WA: Logos Bible Software, 2003). The label "sectarian manuscripts" designates nonbiblical texts among the Dead Sea Scrolls that dealt with the rules, practices, and biblical interpretations associated with a Jewish sect from the Second Temple period. The identity of the sect is debated. For additional discussion, see Edward M. Cook, "Dead Sea Scrolls, Nonbiblical," *LBD*.

18. 1QM i.10, 11; xiv.15, 16, 17; xv.14; xvii.7; xviii.4, 6; 1QH[a] iii.bottom.8; xv.28; xviii.8; xxiii.bottom.3, 10; xxiv.top.8; xxvi.top.7; xxvi.bottom.3; 1Q22 1.iv.1; 1Q35 1.2; 4Q166 1.ii.6; 4Q181 1.ii.4; 4Q248 1.3; 4Q286 2.2; 7.i.6; 4Q381 15.6; 4Q400 1.i.4, 20; 4Q400 1.ii.9, 17; 2.1, 7; 4Q401 14.i.5 (2x), 7; 16.1; 30.1; 4Q402 4.8; 6.3; 9.2; 4Q403 1.i.14, 18, 21, 26, 31, 33, 34, 35, 38 (2x); 1.ii.26, 33, 35; 4Q404 2.2; 4.6, 7; 4Q405 4–5.1, 2, 3; 13.2, 5; 14–15.i.3; 19.3; 23.i.8; 4Q418 69.ii.15; 81.4; 4Q423 8.4; 4Q427 7.i.8, 11; 7.ii.9; 4Q428 8.2; 9.3; 15.3; 4Q431 i.4, 7, 8; 4Q471b 1a–d.1, 5, 8; 4Q491 8–10.i.13 (2x), 14; 10.ii.15; 13.1; 15. 8, 11; 24.3, 4; 4Q491c 1.5, 7, 11; 4Q496 i.2.1:2; 4Q503 48–50.8; 65.2; 4Q510 1.2; 4Q511 10.11; 16.4; 5Q13 1.6; 11Q11 ii.10; 11Q13 ii.14; 11Q17 iii.5, 9; iv.3, 10; 11Q17 v.7; vi.4; viii.7.

19. 1QH[a] xxiii.bottom.3, 10; 4Q381 15.6; 4Q491 24.4; 5Q13 1.6.

The word *'elōhîm* occurs over five hundred times in the scrolls, seventy of which are semantically plural.[20] These instances are not references to idols. It's evident that the Qumran authors, in concert with the Hebrew Bible, considered them spirit beings based on phrases like "spirits of the gods" (*rûḥôt 'elōhîm*) and "spirits of the living gods" (*rûḥôt 'elōhîm ḥayyîm*).[21]

As I wrote in my study of the scrolls for the language of divine plurality:

> There are nearly 180 instances of explicit divine plurality in the sectarian Qumran scrolls, a number *far greater than in the Hebrew Bible*. Many of these instances are found in unequivocal divine council contexts of the type associated with the allegedly polytheistic stage of the religion of biblical Israel. These gods are found in the heavenly temple-heights praising God and serving him. Angels (מלאבים; *mal'akîm*) are seldom found in these contexts. When they are, there is no clear instance where אלים (*'ēlîm*) or semantically plural אלוהים (*'elōhîm*) are described as מלאבים (*mal'akîm*). The data therefore portray a theological situation quite contrary to what would be expected if Jewish theological thinking was moving away from polytheistic belief toward an intolerant monotheism.

To summarize our findings, the vocabulary of Second Temple Jewish literature is quite consistent with that of the Hebrew Bible, even in translation. Despite this consistency, Second Temple Jewish angelology moves beyond the Old Testament in imaginative ways.

---

20. 4Q400 1.i.2; 1.ii.7; 2.2, 3, 5; 3.i.3; 4Q401 1–2.5; 14.i.8; 4Q402 3.ii.12; 4.7, 9, 10; 4Q403 1.i.2, 32, 33, 36, 40, 43, 44, 46; 1.ii.5, 6, 8, 9, 12, 16, 20; 4Q404 5.5; 4Q405 4–5.4; 6.5, 7; 14–15.i.5, 6, 8; 18.3; 19.2, 4, 5, 6, 7; 20.ii–22.3, 7, 8, 11, 13; 23.i.4, 5, 6, 13; 4Q511 8.12; 11Q17 2.6; 4.8, 10; 5.3, 4, 6; 6.3, 5, 6, 7, 8, 9; 7.5, 10, 11, 13; 8.4, 6, 8.

21. 4Q405 6 7 and 4Q405 20 II–22:11, respectively.

# CHAPTER 5

# Second Temple Jewish Angelology[1]

In her 1926 thesis, Dorothy Leiffer stated, "One of the outstanding features of the Intertestamental literature is the appearance of a well-developed belief in angels."[2] The statement is accurate, though it reads like a dramatic understatement today, since Leiffer did her research over two decades before the discovery of the Dead Sea Scrolls. That material underscores just how much of an obsession angelology became in the Second Temple period.

Members of God's heavenly host are mentioned repeatedly in Jewish literature of the Second Temple period.[3] The Dead Sea Scrolls contain nearly 170 instances of plural ʾēlîm or ʾelōhîm and the related phrases benê ʾēlîm and ʾelōhîm. While these figures are nowhere described as malākîm, that term does appear in the plural over 100 times in the Qumran scrolls.[4]

---

1. I have opted for "angelology" to encompass the varied terminology for members of the heavenly host surveyed in chapters 1 and 4. Having discussed that terminology, readers should be aware that "angelology" is used for convenience. Our survey to this point will lend coherence to Olyan's assessment: "The use of the common term 'angelology' by scholars is problematic. It implies a single, systematic doctrine of angels, something that may have existed for some specific groups (perhaps the Qumran sectarians), but certainly does not exist in rabbinic texts" (Saul M. Olyan, *A Thousand Thousands Served Him: Exegesis and Naming of Angels in Ancient Judaism* [Tübingen: Mohr Siebeck, 1993], 1).

2. Dorothy Leiffer, "Development of Angelology in the Apocrypha and Pseudepigrapha," Masters Thesis, Northwestern University, 1926, 1.

3. Many studies of Second Temple Jewish angelology have demons or the fallen watchers in view, not our focus of the loyal members of God's heavenly host. Exceptions include: Leiffer, "Development of Angelology"; Harold B. Kuhn, "The Angelology of the Non-Canonical Jewish Apocalypses," *JBL* 67.3 (Sept 1948): 217–32.

4. As with the Qumran material figures in chapter 4, statistical counts are based upon searches in Abegg, *Qumran Sectarian Manuscripts*. If one includes singular forms, the lemma is used closer to

The Greek text of the Pseudepigrapha references *angeloi* ("angels") 196 times.[5] The same Greek corpus includes *egrēgoros* ("watcher") 13 times, all in the plural. The Old Testament Apocrypha includes "angel" (9 times), "angels" (38 times), and "spirits" (5 times).[6] In the writings of Josephus, of the 66 occurrences of *angelos*, 22 of them point to a supernatural being.[7]

This sort of frequency indicates a strong interest in the heavenly host. Second Temple literature portrays the abilities and behavior of angels and their service to the Most High in many of the same ways as the Old Testament does, but there are also differences. Both the comparative and contrastive elements in Second Temple portrayals of angels will be our focus in this chapter.

## NATURE AND ABILITIES

Second Temple Jewish texts frequently refer to angels as "holy ones," no doubt due to their proximity to the presence of God. The description of God's heavenly host as "holy ones" occurs repeatedly in the Dead Sea Scrolls (147 times), as well as in Greek texts of the Pseudepigrapha (98 times).[8] The divinity of angels is also put forth when Second Temple writers utilize *rûḥôt* ("spirits") 175 times to describe members of the heavenly host. According to Jubilees 2:2, the spirit members of the heavenly host were created on the first day of creation.[9] Philo famously referred to them as "disembodied souls" (*On the Confusion of Tongues* 34:174). The Dead Sea Scroll 1QH[a] ix.8–11 declares that God "has formed every spirit"

---

150 times. Qumran angelology has been the subject of several studies, including: S. F. Noll, "Angelology in the Qumran Texts," PhD diss., University of Manchester, 1979; Maxwell Davidson, *Angels at Qumran: A Comparative Study of 1 Enoch 1–36; 72–108 and Sectarian Writings from Qumran* (Sheffield: Sheffield Academic Press, 1992).

5. Greek Pseudepigrapha counts are based on searches in Ken Penner and Michael S. Heiser, *Old Testament Greek Pseudepigrapha with Morphology* (Bellingham, WA: Lexham Press, 2008). The singular *angelos* occurs 177 times in the Greek Pseudepigrapha.

6. These texts are also in Greek. The counts are based on a search of Rahlf's Septuagint, which includes the Apocrypha: *Septuaginta: With Morphology* (electronic ed.; Stuttgart: Deutsche Bibelgesellschaft, 1979).

7. Christopher Begg, "Angels in the Work of Flavius Josephus," in *Angels: The Concept of Celestial Beings: Origins, Development and Reception*, eds. Friedrich V. Reiterer, Tobias Nicklas, and Karin Schöpflin (Berlin: De Gruyter, 2007), 525–36. These twenty-two occurrences are one-third of the total instances of *angelos*. The other two-thirds refer to human messengers.

8. The respective terms are *qedôšîn* and *hagioi*. In Aramaic scrolls the *qedôšîn* ("holy ones") are mentioned 22 times.

9. In contrast, 2 Enoch 29 has them created on the second day.

and created all the hosts of heaven "according to your will." The fact that angels are called (fallen) stars also attests to their divine nature (1 Enoch 18:13–16; 21:6; 41:5; 86:1–3; 88:1; 90:21).[10]

Writers of the period leave no doubt as to the lesser status of the members of the supernatural world (holy or fallen) relative to the God of Israel. Citing the texts devoting the most space to angels—1 Enoch and the Qumran scrolls—Davidson writes:

> There is no trace in the Enochic books of a cosmic dualism in which two equal, or nearly equal, heavenly powers are opposed to each other. … The Enochic authors gave no place to any rival to God. Even though angels are very important … no angel ever challenges God to usurp his authority.[11]

This detail is important in light of lengthy academic discussion on the Qumran community's dualism, an easily misunderstood term. In the early stages of the scholarly investigation of the Qumran material, some researchers incorrectly argued that the Rule of the Community (1QS) revealed a cosmic dualism in which God had an equal, evil rival. The mistaken idea was based on a portion of 1QS now referred to as the Two Spirits Discourse. Davidson's words are again appropriate:

> The *Two Spirits Discourse* in the *Rule of the Community* (1QS 3.13–4.26) has occasioned much discussion on this issue, since it involves mutually opposed angels, the Prince of Lights with whom are associated the sons of light, and the Angel of Darkness with whom are associated the sons of darkness and a contingent of other angels (1QS 3.20–21, 24–25). Given the clear statement that God has made all things and ordained their patterns (1QS 3.15–18), it was argued that the *Two Spirits Discourse* presupposes a cosmic dualism, but not one involving equally or nearly equally matched powers. Nor is the opposition to be described simply in terms of God and an evil angel. … The dualism of the Discourse is indeed a variety of cosmic dualism, but with God clearly unequalled.[12]

---

10. The stars of heaven are also distinguished from angels in many passages of 1 Enoch (e.g., 1 En 8:3; 14:8; 18:4; 33:2; 36:3; 43:1; 60:12).

11. Davidson, *Angels at Qumran*, 304–5.

12. Davidson, *Angels at Qumran*, 306–7. 1QH$^a$ xv.26–33; xviii.1–12 are two scrolls that assert the superiority of God with force and clarity. 1QH$^a$ xv.28 echoes Exod 15:11: "Who among the gods ( *'ēlîm*)

Angels ("watchers" in Enochian terminology) might fall due to a lapse in moral judgment or rebel in concert with their own hubris; 1 Enoch suggests both with respect to forbidden unions with human women before the flood.[13] As such, Second Temple Judaism saw the holy ones as imperfect. That the fallen watchers are punished by God (1 Enoch 10) reveals they were considered subject to divine judgment.[14]

Members of God's host also were not considered omniscient. When asked about certain events in the distant future, an angel answers the scribe: "Concerning the signs about which you ask me, I can tell you in part; but I was not sent to tell you concerning your life, for I do not know."[15]

Second Temple Jewish writers considered angels to be immortal. Indeed, part of the rationale in 1 Enoch for condemning the decision of certain angelic beings to cohabit with human women was that they were immortal beings having no need to perpetuate their kind (1 Enoch 15:6–7). The scroll 1QH$^a$ xix.13 speaks of the "everlasting" host of heaven, suggesting that "angels will live on indefinitely."[16] However, as Kuhn notes, their immortality was contingent on God's favor: "They were considered to be deathless, and yet to be capable of annihilation by an intervention of divine judgment."[17]

Angels were also intimately connected with natural forces. Jubilees 2:1–2a is representative:

> For on the first day he created the heavens, which are above, and the earth, and the waters and all of the spirits which minister before him:
>
> the angels of the presence,
> and the angels of sanctification,
> and the angels of the spirit of fire,
> and the angels of the spirit of the winds,
> and the angels of the spirit of the clouds and darkness and snow
>     and hail and frost,

---

is like you, O Lord?" The question is of course rhetorical.

13. See 1 Enoch 6–16.

14. 1QH$^a$ xviii.34–35 from Qumran refers to judgment of "the host of holy ones." This is likely a reference to the Watchers of Enochian texts. See Davidson, *Angels at Qumran*, 209–10.

15. *OTP*, 1:531.

16. Davidson, *Angels at Qumran*, 200.

17. Kuhn, "Angelology of the Non-Canonical Jewish Apocalypses," 220.

and the angels of resoundings and thunder and lightning,
and the angels of the spirits of cold and heat and winter and
    springtime and harvest and summer,
and all of the spirits of his creatures which are in heaven and
    on earth.[18]

This selection from the book of Jubilees associates angels with the behavior of the skies and weather, a thought echoed by 1 Enoch 60:11–13, 17–19:

Then the other angel who was going with me was showing me the hidden things: what is first and last in heaven, above it, beneath the earth, in the depth, in the extreme ends of heaven, the extent of heaven; the storerooms of the winds, how the winds are divided, how they are weighed, how the winds divide and dissipate, the openings of the winds, each according to the strength of its wind; the power of the light of the moon and how it is the right amount, the divisions of the stars, each according to its nomenclature, and all the subdivisions; the thunders according to the places where they fall, and the subdivisions of the lightnings according to their flashing of light and the velocity of the obedience of the whole array of them. … The frost-wind is its own guardian [literally, "angel"] and the hail-wind is a kind messenger [literally, "angel"]. The snow-wind has evacuated (its reservoir); it does not exist because of its strength; there is in it only a breeze that ascends from (the reservoir) like smoke, and its name is frost. And the wind and the mist do not dwell together with them in their reservoirs. But (the mist) has its own reservoir, for its course is glorious. It has light and darkness both in the rainy season and the dry season; and its reservoir is itself an angel.[19]

This thinking amounts to an extrapolation from the biblical association between angels ("sons of God"), the stars, and the sky, as well as God's sovereign control over season and weather (Job 5:10; Pss 107:25; 147:16; 1 Kgs 17:1, 14). As "sky beings," angels would naturally be God's agents for such things.[20] Kuhn notes:

---

18. *OTP*, 2:55.

19. *OTP*, 1:41. See 1 Enoch 61:10 as well.

20. Though certain Second Temple works deny that the stars were angels, the idea persisted in Judaism into late antiquity. The book of 3 Enoch, written in Hebrew and composed in the fifth or

Concerning the function of angels in the natural world, the doctrine is substantially as follows: as "spirits" of the natural powers they are thought of in terms of the elements over which they exercised super-intendence: the sea, frost, hail, mist, dew, and rain. They attend the sun, direct the lightning, control "seasons and years" and direct the course of the vegetative growth on the earth.[21]

For Second Temple Jewish thinkers, angels were supernatural, celestial beings, yet their descriptions went beyond those offered in many biblical scenes where angels interact with people.

## ANGELS AS MEN

According to 1 Enoch 17:1–2, angels are like "flame of fire," but when they desire to do so, they can "appear like men," a consistent feature of Second Temple angelology. It is especially prevalent (and apparently necessary) with respect to interaction with humans.[22] The book of Tobit, composed in the third century BC, is a prime example. Tobit sends his son Tobias to find a travel companion for a journey to Media to collect a debt. Tobias meets a "man" who turns out to be the angel Raphael (Tobit 5:3–6). Raphael does not reveal his true identity until the end of the book.[23] Curiously, Tobit 6:5 suggests that Raphael shared a meal with

sixth century AD, is a good example. In his contribution to Charlesworth's *Old Testament Pseudepigrapha*, Alexander observes that in 3 Enoch "the stars are clearly regarded as animate beings, like angels, and so can be said to possess 'spirits.' Like angels they have fiery bodies ... [and] are sentient beings. ... But in 14:4 and 17:6 they appear to be regarded as inert masses of matter that are moved by the angels" (*OTP*, 1:299, note b).

21. Kuhn, "Angelology of the Non-Canonical Jewish Apocalypses," 225. On the same page Kuhn adds: "The author of Jubilees similarly speaks of ... the angels of the spirit of fire and the angels of the spirit of the winds and the angels of the spirit of the clouds, and of darkness, and of snow and of hail and of hoar frost, and the angels of the voices and of the thunder and of the lightning, and the angels of the spirits of cold and of heat, and of winter and of spring and of autumn and of summer, and of all the spirits of His creatures."

22. Sullivan's study is devoted entirely to this element of Jewish angelology. See Kevin P. Sullivan, *Wrestling with Angels: A Study of the Relationship between Angels and Humans in Ancient Jewish Literature and the New Testament* (Leiden: Brill, 2004).

23. Scholars have noted that the portrayal of Raphael in Tobit "depicts a stage in the development of angelic mediation that stands apart from angelic deliverers in previous Jewish texts, and can be significantly associated with early Christianity's view of Jesus. ... [as] a heavenly being who appears as a nondescript Israelite and brings news of hope, healing and demonic liberation to suffering Israelites" (Philip Muñoa, "Raphael, Azariah, and Jesus of Nazareth: Tobit's Significance for Early Christology," *JSP* 22.1 [2012]: 3).

his human companion, but Raphael attributes the scene to a mere vision in Tobit 12:19.[24]

The first century AD work Joseph and Aseneth features a "heavenly man" who is human in form, save that "his face was like lightning, and his eyes like sunshine, and the hairs of his head like a flame of fire of a burning torch, and hands and feet like iron shining forth from a fire, and sparks shot forth from his hands and feet" (Joseph and Aseneth 14:9).[25] The luminescent angel accepts the hospitality of Aseneth but specifically requests a honeycomb as food, which Aseneth does not have (Joseph and Aseneth 15:14–16:2). The angel instructs Aseneth where to find one, but the honeycomb was one made by "the bees of paradise" from "the dew of the roses of life that are in the paradise of God" (Joseph and Aseneth 16:8–9).[26]

The late first-century Apocalypse of Abraham describes the angel Iaoel (Yahoel) as coming to the patriarch "in the likeness of a man" (Apocalypse of Abraham 10:3).[27] Iaoel appears physically, as he takes Abraham by the hand (Apocalypse of Abraham 11:1), despite the fact that the patriarch sees a body of spectacular radiance when looking upon the angel (Apocalypse of Abraham 11:1–3).

The belief that angels assumed human form, even flesh, was no doubt based on certain Old Testament incidents involving angels where fleshly embodiment is presumed (e.g., Gen 6:1–4; 18–19).[28] First Enoch 6–16 is

---

24. On the ancient Jewish debate over whether angels eat, see D. Goodman, "Do Angels Eat?" *Journal of Jewish Studies* 37.2 (1986): 160–75.

25. *OTP*, 2:225. Sullivan notes, "Most interpreters understand this being as an angel, even though the text does not contain the term [*angelos*]. There are good reasons for this interpretation. The being comes originally as a 'star' (14:1). Within the passage he is called 'a man from heaven' (v. 4), who identifies himself as the 'commander of the whole host of heaven' (v. 7). This title was seen in Josh 5:13–15 and later attributed to primary angels such as Michael. The imagery of his brilliant face and fiery hands and feet (v. 9) is common to angelophanies. Moreover, Aseneth responds by falling to the ground. This is undoubtedly a case where an angel is referred to as a man" (Sullivan, *Wrestling with Angels*, 78).

26. There are other instances of angels accepting meals of hospitality. In the Testament of Abraham, Michael appears to Abraham, Sarah, and Isaac on more than one occasion. In places, the story is reminiscent of the incident in Gen 18, save for creating the impression that Michael does not actually eat the meal offered to him. Instead, God sends "an all devouring spirit" to consume the food to feign Michael's own consumption. See Sullivan, *Wrestling with Angels*, 189–90. Such stories undoubtedly have some relationship to Heb 13:2 ("Do not neglect to show hospitality to strangers, for thereby some have entertained angels unawares"), though the primary referent is almost certainly Gen 18.

27. The name of this angel is sometimes written Yahoel. According to Rubinkiewicz, "Here *yhwh'l* is indicated" (*OTP*, 1:681).

28. See Sullivan, *Wrestling with Angels*, 197–226.

an expanded retelling of the incident of Genesis 6:1–4, where the heavenly sons of God produce offspring (Nephilim) with human women.[29] The same physicality is assumed in the Genesis Apocryphon (col. II.1–26) from the Dead Sea Scrolls.[30] Focusing on Josephus, Begg writes in this regard:

> Josephus' initial mention of angels comes in *Ant* 1.173 where, in line with a LXX reading in Gen 6:2, he alludes to "angels of God" who generate hybrid beings ("giants," 6:4) with human women. … In this instance, Josephus envisages angels as engaging in a very human and physical activity, copulation."[31]

Elsewhere Josephus has angels performing other acts of embodiment, such as fighting (*Ant.* 1.332–33) and wielding a sword (*Ant.* 7.327a), while remaining capable of ascending unaided to heaven (*Ant.* 5.284; 7.327b).

This is similar to what we see in the Old Testament, yet Second Temple descriptions of angels, even when described as "men," are more elaborate. In the Old Testament it is rare for angels to be visibly distinct from humans. Often people who encounter such figures have no idea that they are anything but men (cf. Gen 19; 32:22–32; Judg 6) until some sort of self-revelation. Second Temple texts take more liberty in portraying angels as men with features not common to humans.

---

29. For lengthy treatments of this episode in 1 Enoch, see Annette Yoshiko Reed, *Fallen Angels and the History of Judaism and Christianity: The Reception of Enochic Literature* (Cambridge: Cambridge University Press, 2005); Archie T. Wright, *The Origin of Evil Spirits: The Reception of Genesis 6:1–4 in Early Jewish Literature* (Tübingen: Mohr Siebeck, 2013). See also Heiser, *The Unseen Realm*, 92–109.

30. It is for this reason that demons are referred to as "bastard spirits" in the Qumran literature (4Q510 [= 4QShir$^a$] 1:5; 4Q511 [= 4QShir$^b$] 35:7; 4Q204 [= 4QEnoch$^c$ ar] v.2–3; 11QapocPsa[= 11Q11] ii.3; v.6). In Second Temple Jewish texts, demons are the offspring of the watchers (fallen sons of God) released from the bodies of the giants when slain. See Loren T. Stuckenbruck, "The 'Angels' and 'Giants' of Genesis 6:1–4 in Second and Third Century BCE Jewish Interpretation: Reflections on the Posture of Early Apocalyptic Traditions," *DSD* 7.3 (2000): 354–77; Ida Fröhlich, "Theology and Demonology in Qumran Texts," *Henoch* 32.1 (2010): 101–28; Hermann Lichtenberger, "Spirits and Demons in the Dead Sea Scrolls," in *The Holy Spirit and Christian Origins: Essays in Honor of James D. G. Dunn*, eds. James D. G. Dunn, Graham Stanton, Bruce W. Longenecker, and Stephen C. Barton (Grand Rapids: Eerdmans, 2004), 22–40.

31. Begg, "Angels in the Work of Flavius Josephus," 529. Begg goes on to note with curiosity Josephus' reticence to have angels eating (cf. Gen 18:8). Josephus has the three "men" (in the biblical account, Yahweh and two angels) only seeming to eat. Begg also cites Josephus' use of the term "phantom" when describing angels at certain points. This terminology cannot be taken as a denial of angelic physicality in Josephus for, as Begg's work shows, Josephus interchanges this terminology with "angel" in his affirmation of Old Testament passages that require physicality (Begg, "Angels in the Work of Flavius Josephus," 530).

# NAMING THE ANGELS

One of the more noteworthy innovations in Second Temple Jewish angelology is the naming of angels. In the Bible, Michael and Gabriel are the only holy, celestial servants of Yahweh that bear personal names.[32] This number swells in the Second Temple period. The innovation also operates more widely, as groups of angels also receive names. Olyan's observations capture the development:

> The emergence of angelic names and the designations for angelic divisions ... poses a problem for historians attempting to understand developing belief, and has been widely noted as a salient characteristic of ancient and medieval Judaism in contrast to Israelite religion. Where pre-exilic and exilic biblical texts suggest a divine realm populated by thousands of unnamed angels praising God and serving him in war and in judgment, the materials of ancient and medieval Judaism present a very different picture: The angelic host is beyond counting, named and articulated in detail. ... The developments include the emergence of named angels, classes of heavenly beings, angelic hierarchy, archangels, a complex of heavenly temples and cults, conflict between good and bad angels, expanding roles of angels in the human sphere, and characterization of angels.[33]

In terms of specific names, Barton lists nearly thirty "good angels" given names in "the apocryphal literature."[34] Begg uncovers five additional names in his brief discussion of angelology in Pseudo-Philo.[35] As

---

32. Other divine beings are known via transliterating Hebrew words and recognizing their existence in ancient Near Eastern texts outside the Bible (e.g., *śāṭān*, Rahab, Leviathan) or by virtue of their being foreign deities (e.g., Marduk, Asherah, Baal). These figures are not holy members of Yahweh's heavenly host—they are hostile chaos agents or rival deities. As many Old Testament scholars have noted, the term *śāṭān*, translated in English Bibles as "Satan," is not a proper personal name by rule of Hebrew grammar. See Heiser, *The Unseen Realm*, 56–57; Day, *Adversary in Heaven*; Walton, "Satan," *DOTWPW* 714–17.

33. Olyan, *A Thousand Thousands Served Him*, 2–3.

34. George A. Barton, "The Origin of the Names of Angels and Demons in the Extra-Canonical Apocalyptic Literature to 100 A.D.," *JBL* 31.4 (1912): 156–67. In Barton's essay, "apocryphal literature" is not a technical term, as it includes books from the Pseudepigrapha.

35. Christopher Begg, "Angels in Pseudo-Philo," in *Angels: The Concept of Celestial Beings: Origins, Development and Reception*, eds. Friedrich V. Reiterer, Tobias Nicklas, and Karin Schöpflin (Berlin: De Gruyter, 2007), 537–54.

Olyan's work demonstrates, there are more, and the number increases after the Second Temple era.[36]

The discussion of named angels typically revolves around those heavenly beings identified as archangels, also called "watchers" (*'îrîn*) in 1 Enoch 20:1.[37] Second Temple Jewish literature is not consistent with respect to their number. Primary sources might enumerate four, six, or seven archangels. Commenting in 1 Enoch 9–10, Nickelsburg writes:

> A complement of four, and later seven, named archangels (here "holy ones") appears first in 1 Enoch 9–10 and then becomes something of a staple in Jewish and Christian literature. Their existence and the number four were doubtless inferred from the four living creatures (חיות) in the throne vision of Ezekiel 1–2. The later literature makes an association with Ezekiel 1–2 explicit. In the action of 1 Enoch 9–10, however, the four are not placed at the throne. They go forth from heaven, view the world, approach the divine throne with their petition in behalf of humanity, and are then dispatched to the world to act in God's behalf. … In 1 Enoch 20–36 + 81 the number four is expanded to seven (adding Uriel, Reuel, and Remiel to Michael, Sariel, Raphael, and Gabriel) in order to provide a complement of angels who are associated with the places of Enoch's cosmic tour, rather than God's throne."[38]

Why the upsurge in naming angels in this era? What drive the impulse among Second Temple Jewish writers? Several theories have been put

---

36. In addition, some angel names have more than one form (e.g., Raphael/Rafael vs. Rufael/Rofael). As Barton ("Origin of the Names," 158) notes, "Rufael (i.e. Rôfael) is the Hebrew form; Rafael, the Aramaic."

37. This designation is found in the Ethiopic text: "And these are names of the holy angels who watch" (*OTP*, 1:23). The term "watcher" is usually reserved in Second Temple literature for the divine beings who sinned before the flood, though, as in Dan 4, it is not exclusive to fallen divine beings. In academic literature, some scholars prefer "principal angels" over "archangels."

38. George W. E. Nickelsburg, *1 Enoch 1: A Commentary on the Book of 1 Enoch, Chapters 1–36; 81–108*, Hermeneia (Minneapolis: Fortress, 2001), 207. The difference in listing is related to the textual situation of 1 Enoch. Aside from a few Aramaic fragments of the book found at Qumran, the book is preserved substantially in Greek but only in its entirety in Ethiopic. Michalak (*Angels as Warriors*, 66–67) notes in this regard: "The traditions concerning the numbers of the principal angels differ one from another. The conception of four probably preceded the notion of seven archangels which is testified to, e.g., in *1 En* 20 [which] witnesses a tradition which lists the seven angels of power (Ἄγγελοι τῶν δυνάμεων) whereas in the Ethiopic text [of 1 Enoch] we find only six. The Greek text has Uriel, Raphale, Raguel, Michael, Saraqa'el, Gabriel, and Remiel. Therefore, the expansion includes Raguel, Remiel and Saraqa'el. Remiel does not appear in the Ethiopic mss."

forth. In his extended study of the names of angels and angelic "brigades," Olyan outlines and critiques the approaches thus:[39]

1. Foreign Influence: Religious ideas outside Judaism provided the catalyst for "personalizing" angels and making them more prominent.

2. Magical Practices: Religious rituals aimed at combating demons or practicing divination were thought to be more potent if named angels were invoked.

3. Transcendence of God: The term "transcendence" refers to the idea that Jews thought God less accessible, and so angels took on more of a mediating role. Angels in turn became more personalized.

4. "Gnostic" Trajectories: In terms of specific sects and formulations, the Second Temple era is too early to speak of Gnosticism. However, various elements of gnostic thought were drawn from Jewish mysticism. One such thread was the proliferation of named entities (e.g., aeons).

5. Internal Jewish Development: By this, scholars point to an apparent evasion of anthropomorphic language for God. One example would be how the book of Jubilees inserts an angel in the story of the binding (and near sacrifice) of Isaac in the place of God in the biblical account (Jubilees 17:15–18:19). Other Second Temple texts similarly relieve God of his role in Old Testament stories. This approach is related to the third option noted above. The approach argues that personal angels replaced God in stories as God is perceived as being more remote.

Olyan—and I—find these suggestions unconvincing, though several of them have some worthwhile insights.[40] Olyan views the internal

---

39. Olyan, *A Thousand Thousands Served Him*, 3–9.

40. Briefly, Olyan (pp. 4–5, n. 9, 10) cites H. Ringgren and G. von Rad approvingly when they argue it cannot explain postexilic developments. These scholars prefer to look to Israelite religion's divine council as a better source for the variegated role of angels (H. Ringgren, *Israelite Religion* [Augsburg Fortress, 1966], 310–12; G. von Rad, "B. מַלְאָךְ in the OT," in *TDNT* 1:79). Given the biblical emphasis on the divine council in the Hebrew Bible as agents of God implementing his will on earth it is difficult to see the coherence in the notion put forth by many scholars that angelic activity in the Second Temple period indicates God's withdrawal from human affairs. Olyan notes that Second Temple Jewish works such as the Testament of Solomon, known for demonic exorcism ritual magic, "[is] useful for elucidating many of the more obscure angelic names occurring in Hekalot texts and Jewish theurgical materials from first millennium CE" (pp. 5 [n. 11], 8), but again concludes there are significant aspects of angel names not explained at all by magical practices. With respect to an inaccessible ("transcendent") God, Olyan rightly ponders: how many angels are needed to be conduits

development thesis most favorably, but by this he does not mean misgivings about an anthropomorphic Deity. Rather, he discerns an exegetical development—specifically, that angel names were the product of creative Jewish exegesis of the biblical text. He writes:

> Many names of individual angels as well as angelic divisions were the result of biblical exegesis, particularly of theophanic and angelophanic texts and descriptions of the divine council. ... Exegesis is at least a major aspect, if not the most significant component, of the elusive framework sought by scholars in order to better understand the development of ideas about angels in late biblical and post-biblical texts. ... Many epithets or adjectives describing angels in theophanic/angelophanic settings in the Hebrew Bible became the designations of angelic brigades in some of the more elaborate descriptions of angels."[41]

To briefly explain, Olyan discovered that common words associated with scenes in God's throne room—or rare words, in the same scenes, made confusing by errors in manuscript transmission—were used by Jewish writers to create the names of angelic contingents.[42]

Olyan discovered that Second Temple writers used the same techniques to manufacture the names of specific angels. After surveying ten angel names, he observes:

> Patterns of exegesis emerge from this survey of ten angelic personal names. All appear to be of biblical derivation. ... A number of the

---

to God? Second Temple texts reveal there are few angels who perform such a role, most of whom are "second power in heaven" figures ("hypostases"). The large number of named angels would therefore be superfluous, and so inaccessibility is not a useful explanation. Olyan notes that this view had, by the time of his writing, been "widely discredited, both for the anti-Jewish bias underlying the classic formulations and for a lack of supporting evidence" (p. 8). In like manner, Olyan notes of the gnostic option that it "may explain some features of angelic beliefs, though this remains unproven" (pp. 8–9).

41. Olyan, *A Thousand Thousands Served Him*, 11. The terms "theophanic" and "angelophanic" refer, respectively, to the *appearance* of God or an angel.

42. Olyan provides specific examples: "Parts of the throne complex, often rare or unusual words, and sometimes opaque in meaning, gave rise to angelic orders ('*ôpan* > '*ôpannîm* ['wheels']; *galgal* > *galgallîm* ['wheel']; *ḥašmal* > *ḥašmallîm* ['electrum']; *taršîš* > *taršîšîm* ['chrysolite']). So did words that are otherwise common, but are here associated intimately with the throne of God (*ma'aśêhem* > *ma'aśîm* ['constructions']). ... Corrupt words which are cruces in theophanic. Angelophanic contexts produced angelic brigades through the process of exegesis ('*alpê šin'an* > *šin'ānîm* ['archers']; '*er'ellām* > '*er'ellîm* ['heroes']). ... *Hapax legomena*, textual corruptions, and obscure and perplexing theophanic/angelophanic narrative gave rise to angelic divisions" (Olyan, *A Thousand Thousands Served Him*, 68). *Hapax legomena* are words that occur only once in the biblical text.

names discussed in this chapter appear to have been derived from textual cruces in the [Hebrew Bible], some from *hapax legomena* in particular (e.g., *sidrî'ēl, yepêpiyyâ, dōqî'ēl, keballa'*). Most of these cruces or hapax legomena occur in theophanic/angelophanic or related settings. ... tied closely to God's activity.[43]

## THE HEAVENLY HOST: Soldiers of the Most High

Olyan's choice of a term like "brigades" of angels may strike some readers as odd. Second Temple vocabulary validates such a perspective. The names of angelic groups are often militaristic. A variety of combat terms are attributed to angels, clearly casting them as celestial warriors. For example, texts from Qumran refer to angels as "troops" (*gedûdîm*), "warriors" (*gibborîm*), and "companies, brigades" (*degalîm*).[44]

Other scholars who focus on the angelology of the period have noted that angels are frequently cast in a militaristic role and that such portrayals are frequently part of apocalyptic literature. In his important study on angels as warriors in Second Temple Jewish literature, Michalak notes:

In the apocalyptic works of this time the development of elaborated angelology/ies took place. One of the marks of the identification of apocalyptic literature is the idea that a seer is able to see the heavenly world together with its angelic inhabitants. Therefore it is hardly surprising that in this literature a trend appears which makes a distinction between the various categories of angels and establishes their hierarchy.[45]

This feature of Second Temple angelology is consistent with, and in fact derives from, the portrayal of God's holy ones as a *host* (*ṣebàôt*) led

43. Olyan, *A Thousand Thousands Served Him*, 87.

44. On *gedûdîm* see 4Q529. Davidson (*Angels at Qumran*, 88) also notes the use of the term for fallen angels in the War Scroll (1QM). See the other terms, see Davidson, *Angels at Qumran*, 89–94. Among the scroll references for *gedûdîm* and *gibborîm* are: 1QM xii.7–8; xv.14; 1QH^a xvi.11; xviii.24, 34–35; xix.35–36. The singular of *degalîm* is *degel*, often translated "banner." As G. B. Gray has shown, this meaning cannot be correct in context. Gray opts for "company" as the most coherent option (see G. B. Gray, "The Meaning of the Hebrew Word דגל," *Jewish Quarterly Review* 11 [1899]: 92–101). Michalak notes (p. 91) that LXX renders it mostly with *tagma* ("brigade"). Roland de Vaux also argued that the term described a division of armed forces (Roland de Vaux, *Ancient Israel, Its Life and Institutions* [Grand Rapids: Eerdmans, 1997], 226). Scroll usages of *degalîm* include 1QM 3.6; 4.10; 4Q503 (frags 8–9, 1–5); 4Q405 20 ii–21–22 14.

45. Michalak, *Angels as Warriors*, 57.

by a supernatural commander (*sar;* "prince").[46] Several passages in the Old Testament describe an end-times conflict involving the army of the holy ones unleashing the wrath of God on both his earthly and heavenly enemies (Isa 24:21–24; 34:1–4; Zech 14:1–5). It is quite understandable, then, that Second Temple angelology includes this element of the heavenly host in service to God.

The most obvious instance of supernatural armies in Second Temple literature comes from Qumran's War Scroll (1QM), a lengthy text envisioning human forces fighting side-by-side with angels against wicked men and supernatural powers of darkness. Michalak summarizes its contents:

> The major theme of the work is the eschatological war waged by the sons of light against the sons of darkness under the command of Belial. The main work consists of nineteen columns from Qumran Cave 1. In Cave 4, six manuscript fragments have been found, all of which correspond to 1QM. ... The *War Scroll* improves our knowledge of Jewish angelology. The already mentioned notion of human communion with angels is particularly noticeable in this work. Angels are brothers in arms of the sons of light in the holy war against the "army of Belial".[47]

Davidson, author of another major study of Qumran angelology, adds:

> God's army consists of "a multitude of holy ones" and "hosts of angels" in heaven, and "the elect ones of the holy nation" on earth (1QM 12:1). Both groups are to be mustered for the battle (1QM 12:4–5). ... The writer not only asserts that angels will be with them, but he also believes that God himself, the Mighty One of War, will be too. The thought is similar to that in 1QM 15:13–14, where God raises his hand to act against the wicked spirits, and the angels gird themselves for battle.[48]

---

46. As noted in our earlier discussion (chapter 2), this Hebrew term is commonly used to describe human armies in the Hebrew Bible (*HALOT*, 302; cf. Gen 21:22; Num 1:3; 31:34; 2 Sam 3:23). Davidson adds, "The participation of the angelic armies in this eschatological battle belongs to the traditions of the holy war as it was conceived in Israel" (Davidson, *Angels at Qumran*, 230).

47. Michalak, *Angels as Warriors*, 151–52. Michalak lists the terms used to denote the angelic participants, including: "angels" (*malākîm*), "holy angels" (*malākîm qôdeš*), "gods" (*'ēlîm*), "mighty ones" (*gibbôrîm*), "holy ones" (*qedôšîm*), "armies, hosts" (*ṣebāôt*). See Michalak, *Angels as Warriors* for scroll references, as well as Davidson, *Angels at Qumran*, 334–37.

48. Davidson, *Angels at Qumran*, 230.

Angel armies are also found in the Pseudepigrapha. The watcher-archangels are cast as guardians and "special forces" charged by God with rounding up the fallen, rebellious watchers and destroying their progeny, the giants (1 Enoch 9–10). In the scene where God shows Enoch how he created "all the forces of heaven and earth" (2 Enoch 28:1) God says, "I created the ranks of the bodiless armies—ten myriad angels—and their weapons are fiery and their clothes are burning flames. And I gave orders that each should stand in his own rank."[49]

In a passage that echoes the eschatological judgment of the princes of the nations and their inhabitants (Isa 34:1–4; cf. Ps 82:6–8; Ezek 38–39), 1 Enoch 56–57 describes an angelic assault on the enemy nations:

> In those days, the angels will assemble and thrust themselves to the east at the Parthians and Medes. They will shake up the kings (so that) a spirit of unrest shall come upon them, and stir them up from their thrones. ... In those days, Sheol shall open her mouth, and they shall be swallowed up into it and perish. (Thus) Sheol shall swallow up the sinners in the presence of the elect ones. ... And it happened afterward that I had another vision of a whole array of chariots loaded with people; and they were advancing upon the air from the east and from the west until midday. And the sound of their chariots (was clamorous); and when this commotion took place, the holy ones in heaven took notice of it and the pillars of the earth were shaken from their foundations. (1 Enoch 56:5, 8; 57:1–2a)[50]

Angelic warriors are also prominent in the Testaments of the Twelve Patriarchs, a work, as its title suggests, divisible into twelve separate works, each focused on one of the sons of Jacob.[51] A solitary angel soldier appears on behalf of Judah (Testament of Judah 3:10) and at the request of Levi (Testament of Levi 5:6). Several scholars consider the angel in the latter instance to be Michael. An oblique reference to this same angel occurs in Testament of Dan 6:1, a passage reminiscent of Jude 9. An army of angels is described in Testament of Levi 3:3.

---

49. *OTP*, 1:148.

50. *OTP*, 1:39. Angelic warfare is also portrayed in 1 Enoch 8:1; 69:6; 90:14.

51. The testament genre "concerns works that purport to be the final words ('farewell discourses') of the figure whose name the title bears" (Penner and Heiser, "Introduction to the Testaments of the Twelve Patriarchs," *Old Testament Greek Pseudepigrapha with Morphology*).

Other Second Temple literary works present angels as an attacking force. In 2 Maccabees 3:25–34, we read that God protected the temple treasury from the invading Heliodorus with supernatural warriors (2 Macc 3:24–26 NRSV):

> But when [Heliodorus] arrived at the treasury with his bodyguard, then and there the Sovereign of spirits and of all authority caused so great a manifestation that all who had been so bold as to accompany him were astounded by the power of God, and became faint with terror. For there appeared to them a magnificently caparisoned horse, with a rider of frightening mien; it rushed furiously at Heliodorus and struck at him with its front hoofs. Its rider was seen to have armor and weapons of gold. Two young men also appeared to him, remarkably strong, gloriously beautiful and splendidly dressed, who stood on either side of him and flogged him continuously, inflicting many blows on him.[52]

The incident in 2 Maccabees 3 is not unique. There are similar episodes in 2 Maccabees 4:1–2; 5:2; 10:29–30; 11:6–8; 15:22–23. The third book of Maccabees relates an angelic intervention (along with "the holy face of God") against Ptolemy IV Philopator (3 Macc 6:1–5).[53] Pseudo-Philo describes two named warrior angels who come to the assistance of Kenaz in his struggle against the Amorites (Liber antiquitatum biblicarum [LAB] 27:10). Michalak notes that Kenaz is depicted in a manner similar to the Israelite judges Samson and Gideon.[54] Interestingly, angels appear in Pseudo-Philo's retelling of several of the stories in the Old Testament book of Judges.[55]

---

52. The NRSV includes the Apocrypha.

53. See the discussion in Michalak, *Angels as Warriors*, 196–210. Josephus downplays the activity of angels and so "does not mention any references to angels in his account of the Maccabean revolt" (Michalak, *Angels as Warriors*, 213).

54. Michalak, *Angels as Warriors*, 224.

55. Begg, "Angels in Pseudo-Philo," 541–44. Begg writes (p. 541): "Pseudo-Philo's mention of angel(s) are particularly concentrated (37 out of a total 59 references, i.e., almost 2/3 of these) in the long segment (*LAB* 25–48) that presents his (often dramatically distinctive) version of the personages and events recounted in the Book of Judges."

# THE DIVINE COUNCIL: Scenes of Praise and Judgment

As was the case with the Old Testament theology of the heavenly host, angels in Second Temple literature appear in council with God, both to praise him and discharge his decrees.

In the previous chapter we noted the profound number of instances where the language of divine plurality (multiple *'elōhîm* or *'ēlîm*) is found in the Dead Sea Scrolls, often in scenes of the heavenly throne room, the place of Yahweh's council. Second Temple period literature does not downgrade the biblical idea of a divine council; it embraces it and adds a few innovations.[56]

The language of the divine council is most evident in Second Temple texts from Qumran and certain books of the Pseudepigrapha. For example, the complex angelic liturgies found in the Songs of the Sabbath Sacrifice (4Q400–407; 11Q17; Mas1K) contain important vocabulary of the Hebrew Bible for the meeting place of Israel's divine council.[57] For example, one of the council scenes reads as follows:

> *30* Of the Instructor. Song of the sacrifice of the seventh sabbath on the sixteenth of the month. Praise the God of the heights, you exalted ones among all the

> *31* divinities of knowledge. May the holy ones of God magnify the King of glory, who makes holy with holiness all his holy ones. Chiefs of the praises of

---

56. My dissertation in part dealt with the divine council in the literature of this period: Heiser, "The Divine Council." There has been one similar study: Kathryn Muller Lopez, "The Divine Council Scene in Second Temple Literature," PhD diss., Emory University, 2002. My dissertation cast a wider net than that of Lopez, whose Pseudepigrapha focus was only on 1 Enoch 90.

57. Heiser, "The Divine Council," Section 7.2. The terminology includes: "heights" (*merômîm, mārôm, rāmîm*). There are roughly a dozen references to the council "heights" in the Songs of the Sabbath Sacrifice, none of which uses the term *mal'a'kîm* ("angels"), opting instead for plural *'elōhîm* or *'ēlîm*. The Songs of the Sabbath Sacrifice is "a liturgical document consisting of thirteen distinct compositions, each dated to one of the first thirteen sabbaths of the year. ... Each song begins with a heading and date formula (e.g., 'For the Instructor. Song of the sacrifice of the first sabbath on the fourth of the first month'). Following the heading comes a call to praise, introduced by the imperative 'praise,' followed by a direct object (an epithet for God) and a vocative (an angelic title). The initial call to praise is expanded with one or more parallel calls to praise" (C. A. Newsom, "Songs of the Sabbath Sacrifice [4Q400–407, 11Q17, Mas1K]," *DNTB* 1137).

32 all the gods, praise the God [of] majestic praises, for in the magnif-icence of the praises is the glory of his kingdom. Through it (come) the praises of all

33 gods, together with the splendour of all [his] maje[sty. And] exalt {his} exaltation to the heights, gods of the exalted divinities, and his glorious divinity above

34 all the exalted heights. For h[e is the God of the gods] of all the chiefs of the heights, and king of king[s] of all the eternal councils. {By the will}

35 {of his knowledge} At the words of his mouth a[ll the exalted divin-ities] exist; by what issues from his lips, all the eternal spirits; [by the w]ill of his knowledge, all his creatures

36 in their enterprises. Sing with joy, those of you enjoying [his knowledge, with] rejoicing among the wonderful gods.[58]

The Songs of the Sabbath Sacrifice bear witness to an elaborate angelic hierarchy:

[The Songs are] characterized by repetitious formulas in which the number seven figures prominently, the sixth and eighth songs enu-merate the praises and blessings uttered by the seven chief and deputy princes respectively. The central, seventh song elaborates the initial call to praise into a series of seven increasingly elaborate calls to praise addressed to each of the seven angelic councils. After these calls to praise the song then describes the heavenly temple itself bursting into praise, concluding with a description of the chariot throne of God and the praise uttered by multiple attendant chariot thrones (mer-kābôt), their cherubim and wheels ('ophannîm).[59]

The Pseudepigrapha has similar scenes. The Apocalypse of Zephaniah (Text A) describes Zephaniah's divine council vision in the fifth heaven: "I saw angels who were called lords, and the diadem was set upon them in the Holy Spirit, and the throne of each of them was sevenfold more bril-liant that the light of the sun."[60] Reminiscent of the divine council scene

---

58. The passage is 4Q403 1.i.30–36a. The translation is that of Florentino García Martínez and Eibert J. C. Tigchelaar, *The Dead Sea Scrolls Study Edition* (Leiden: Brill, 1997–1998), 819.

59. Newsom, "Songs of the Sabbath Sacrifice," 1138.

60. *OTP*, 1:508.

in Daniel 7, 1 Enoch 47:3 has Enoch relating, "I saw the Chief of Days when he seated himself upon the throne of his glory, and the books of the living were opened before him; And all his host which is in heaven above and his council stood before him." Second Enoch 20:1 describes a council meeting of "many-eyed thrones" with numerous archangels, dominions, and authorities. Second Enoch has God seated the tenth heaven, so it is clear that these lesser-ranking thrones are for divine council members.

Portrayals of the heavenly host and the divine council in the Pseudepigrapha are no less elaborate than those of Qumran. There are many terms besides the militaristic labeling noted above, and it is difficult to discern what the perceived hierarchical relationships were between the groups.

For example, 1 Enoch 61:10 says, "And he [God] will summon all the forces of the heavens, and all the holy ones above, and the forces of the Lord—the cherubim, seraphim, ophanim, all the angels of governance, the Elect One, and the other forces on earth (and) over the water."[61] Like others we have already considered, this one correlates members of the heavenly host to the throne presence of God and the elements of the natural world. Consequently, we presume that Second Temple Jewish angelology had distinct groups close to God's presence and others in charge of nature. In 2 Enoch 19:1–5, Enoch describes a number of tasks for heavenly beings:

> And those men took me from there, and they carried me up to the 6th heaven, And I saw there 7 groups of angels, brilliant and very glorious, And their faces were more radiant than the radiance of the sun, and there was no difference between their faces or in their dimensions or in the style of their clothing. And these groups carry out and carefully study the movements of the stars, and the revolution of the sun and the phases of the moon, and the well-being of the cosmos. And when they see any evil activity, they put the commandments and instructions in order, and the sweet choral singing and every kind of glorious praise. These are the archangels who are over the angels; and they harmonize all existence, heavenly and earthly; and angels who are over seasons and years, and angels who are over rivers and the ocean, and angels who are over the fruits of the earth and over every

---

61. *OTP*, 1:42.

kind of grass, and who give every kind of food to every kind of living thing; and angels who record all human souls, and all their deeds, and their lives before the face of the LORD.[62]

Here we learn that archangels are over angels, and they seem to be busily in charge of maintaining created order, plotting out times and seasons, and praising the Most High. Other angels record the lives of human beings and, it seems, never depart from God's presence. There is, not surprisingly, much more we could investigate. It is clear that the heavenly bureaucracy of the Second Temple period is complex. Jewish texts from this period refer to "angels of the Presence" (Hellenistic Synagogal Prayers 4:11), "angels of sanctification" (Jubilees 15:27), "archangels" (e.g., 1 Enoch 20–22, 40:8–10); Life of Adam and Eve 25:3–4), "archons" (Testament of Job 49:2; 1 Enoch 6:7–8; 2 Enoch 20:1); "rulers of the stars" (2 Enoch 4:1–2), "satans" (1 Enoch 40:1–8), "powers" (1 Enoch 40:8–10; 65:6–7; 82:8–9), "principalities" (1 Enoch 61:10–11), and "dominions" (1 Enoch 61:10; 2 Enoch 20:1). In 1 Enoch 6:7–8, the labels *archē* and *archōn* are used interchangeably as titles for twenty named watchers.[63]

Speculative as it is, this material still generates logical questions. Are archangels too busy to participate in praising God? Are they so preoccupied with supervising lesser angels and running creation that they don't get much time in God's presence? First Enoch 40:2–4, 9–10 seems to clear up the matter, as the four archangels (Michael, Raphael, Gabriel, and Phanuel) "stand before the glory of the Lord ... blessing the name of the Lord of Spirits ... saying praises before the Lord of Glory" (cf. 1 Enoch 40:9; 54:6; 71:8–9, 13).[64]

Regardless of the lack of hierarchical clarity, Second Temple Jewish angelology is not ambiguous when it comes to the divine council rendering and administering judgment. 1 Enoch 89–90, an allegory referred to as the "Animal Apocalypse" by scholars, contains a provocative divine

---

62. *OTP*, 1:132.

63. Heiser, "The Divine Council," 238.

64. *OTP*, 1:32. Phanuel replaces Sariel/Uriel in 1 Enoch 40:10. The names may have been understood as overlapping. See Geza Vermes, "The Archangel Sariel: A Targumic Parallel to the Dead Sea Scrolls," in *Christianity, Judaism, and Other Greco-Roman Cults: Studies for Morton Smith at Sixty*, ed. Jacob Neusner (Leiden: Brill, 1975), 159–66. Two of the angelic voices in 1 Enoch 40 "intercede and pray" for humans and expel demons, "forbidding them from coming to the Lord of the Spirits in order to accuse those who dwell upon the earth." The ensuing discussion will touch on these duties.

council scene. The Animal Apocalypse is, as its name suggests, a vision of the end of days.[65] Collins describes the content as

> a complex allegory in which people are represented by animals. Adam is a white bull. Cain and Abel are black and red bullocks; Israel are sheep. In the period after the exile, the sheep are given over to seventy shepherds, representing the angelic patrons of the nations.[66]

The seventy shepherds of 1 Enoch 89–90 are the fallen sons of God allotted to the gentile nations at the Tower of Babel event (Deut 32:8).[67] They are given charge over Israel as a punishment. The idea being conveyed in the allegory is that the chief shepherd, the Lord of the sheep of Israel (i.e., Yahweh), handed over the governance of his sheep (Israel) to the seventy angelic under-shepherds put over the nations at the Babel event. Israel is forsaken and would be governed by those lesser agents (i.e., would remain in exile) until the end of days (1 Enoch 89:51–67). The author of 1 Enoch 89–90 seems to be tracking on Jeremiah 25, transforming the human rulers who had conquered and abused Israel into angelic shepherds placed over Israel while in exile.[68] In other words, the Animal Apocalypse frames Israel's apostasy and exile in supernatural terms.

God commands these shepherds to slaughter his sheep (1 Enoch 89:59–60), but they disobediently go beyond the parameters he had set. The severity of Israel's condition until the time of release is therefore the fault of the disobedient patron angels of the nations. This brings us to the divine council scene (1 Enoch 90:20–27).

---

65. The Animal Apocalypse and other Jewish pseudepigraphical works bear an important relationship to Dan 7–9 in that the end time apocalypse is framed as the culmination of human history, divided into discrete periods determined by God (cf. the seventy "weeks" of Dan 9:24–27). See "Excursus: The Chronology of the Vision: Seventy Shepherds Ruling for Seventy Weeks of Years," in Nickelsburg, *1 Enoch 1*, 391–93.

66. John J. Collins, "Enoch, Books of," *DNTB* 315.

67. See the discussion in chapter 1 and Heiser, *The Unseen Realm*, 110–22; Heiser, "Deuteronomy 32:8 and the Sons of God," 52–74.

68. Davidson (*Angels at Qumran*, 108) writes: "This scheme of the seventy angels who rule Israel for seventy periods from the Babylonian conquest till the advent of the eschaton creatively utilizes several OT ideas. Genesis 10 gives the list of seventy nations descended from Noah and Deut 32:8 appears to take this up, stating that an angel was assigned to each ethnic group. Israel, however, was different, Yahweh himself caring for it. Jeremiah 25:17–38 has no doubt also influenced our author, for there the (human) leaders of the nations which have oppressed Israel are referred to as 'shepherds' who will be punished by God (Jer 25:34, 36)."

The Animal Apocalypse combines the judgment of the fallen sons of God (the watchers) of Genesis 6:1–4 and that of the seventy disobedient sons of God who rule as princes over the nations. It is, in effect, the writer's imaginative enactment of the final verdict that the 'elōhîm over the nations are sentenced to "die like men" (Ps 82:6–7). But the human inhabitants of the nations who oppressed Israel are also judged. As in Old Testament theology, the apocalyptic judgment of the day of the Lord is enacted in both the earthly and supernatural realms (Dan 7:1–12; Isa 24:21–24; 34:1–4; Joel 3:11 [Heb 4:11]). Lopez writes:

> As has been previously mentioned, Joel 3 is an earlier example of the connection of divine/human battle with the earthly judgment of all those who oppose Yahweh. Another parallel text is found in Isaiah 24:17–23. ... While the act of judgment is not mentioned directly, as it is in Joel 3, the heavens and the earth are all punished. The implication of these texts, including Daniel 7, is that the judgment of the wicked cannot take place in the heavens. The divine council scene in I Enoch 90 further implies that it is not just the wicked of the earth that cannot enter the heavens; the heavenly beings who have disobeyed God are also forbidden entrance. ... After the books are opened, judgment is carried out against three distinct groups: the fallen stars, the seventy shepherds, and the blind sheep (vv. 24–27). It should be noted that within this one judgment scene separate traditions are maintained. First, there is the judgment of the Watchers, here called the fallen stars. They are mentioned here in the same order as the fall: first the star that is identified with Asael and then the remaining stars who followed. Here the fallen stars are placed alongside the seventy shepherds who did not fall from the heavens (i.e. openly reject God), but rather were appointed by God to rule over Israel. Their reason for punishment is not that they directly rejected God but that they carried out God's punishment more severely than was ordered. The two groups of heavenly beings are judged separately and are sent to "a place of condemnation," and "that abyss of fire." The place of punishment is somewhere at the ends of the earth, and the description of the place of punishment is in keeping with that found throughout I Enoch.[69]

---

69. Lopez, "The Divine Council Scene in Second Temple Literature," 223, 227.

## GUARDING, INTERCEDING, INTERPRETING

In our earlier comments on archangels, we briefly looked at 1 Enoch 20, which described some of the functions of archangels. Two of those duties were "interceding and praying on behalf of those who dwell upon the earth and supplicating in the name of the Lord of the Spirits. … expelling the demons and forbidding them from coming to the Lord of the Spirits in order to accuse those who dwell upon the earth."[70]

The passage brings into focus the angelic ministries of guardianship of God's people and intercession on their behalf.[71] Angelic intercession is described in a range of Second Temple texts. In Tobit 12:12, Raphael reveals that "when you and Sarah prayed, it was I who brought and read the record of your prayer before the glory of the Lord." In the book of 1 Enoch the antediluvian patriarch sees the holy ones who "interceded and petitioned and prayed on behalf of the children of the people" (1 Enoch 39:5) and hears an angel "interceding and praying on behalf of those who dwell upon the earth and supplicating in the name of the Lord of the Spirits" (1 Enoch 40:6).[72] In a scene reminiscent of Revelation 6:9; 8:3–5, where the "prayers of the holy ones" were on a golden altar attended by an angel before the throne of God, under which were "the souls of those who had been slain for the word of God" (Rev 6:9), 1 Enoch 47:1–2 says:

> The prayers of the righteous ascended into heaven, and the blood of the righteous from the earth before the Lord of the Spirits. There shall be days when all the holy ones who dwell in the heavens above shall dwell (together). And with one voice, they shall supplicate and pray—glorifying, praising, and blessing the name of the Lord of the Spirits—on behalf of the blood of the righteous ones which has been shed. Their prayers shall not stop from exhaustion before the Lord of the Spirits—neither will they relax forever—(until) judgment is executed for them.[73]

---

70. *OTP*, 1:32.

71. Angelic intercession before God on behalf of people was thought to involve special angelic language. See chapter 7. For brief surveys of angelic intercession in Jewish literature, see Norman B. Johnson, *Prayer in the Apocrypha and Pseudepigrapha: A Study of the Jewish Concept of God* (Philadelphia: Society of Biblical Literature and Exegesis, 1948), 52–53; Davidson, *Angels at Qumran*, 309–13.

72. *OTP*, 1:31–32.

73. *OTP*, 1:35.

The Testament of Dan 6:1–2 admonishes, "And now fear the Lord, my children, be on guard against Satan and his spirits. Draw near to God and to the angel who intercedes for you, because he is the mediator between God and men for the peace of Israel."[74] Archangels "serve and offer propitiatory sacrifices to the Lord in behalf of all the sins of ignorance of the righteous ones" (Testament of Levi 3:5).[75]

As it relates to individuals, while there are generic references to protection (e.g., in Jubilees 35:17, Rebecca told Jacob he had a "protector" who was mightier than Esau's), the guardianship role of angels in Second Temple Judaism is cast in terms of protective intercession or instruction. With respect to intercession, the role is akin to what we saw earlier in the Old Testament.[76] First Enoch abounds with the motif, as Nickelsburg notes:

> In almost all the strata of 1 Enoch, angels play a crucial role as intercessors for humanity. … The angelic role of intercessor and its context can be traced back into the Hebrew Scriptures, and it continues to be important in early Christian theology. The heavenly intercessor is of some prominence in the Book of Job, where it is envisioned as a legal protagonist in Job's dispute with God. As such the figure is described variously as an "umpire" or arbiter (Job 9:3; cf. 16:21), a "witness" (Job 16:19), a "mediator" (Job 16:20; 33:23), and a "vindicator" or "redeemer" (Job 19:25–27). The concept goes back to the ancient belief that each individual had a personal god who acted in one's behalf in the divine council. … The closest parallel to the Enochic texts occurs in Tob 3:16–17 and 12:12–15. As in Job, at stake is the innocence of the suffering righteous—Tobit and Sarah. Raphael is one of seven holy angels, who present a "reminder" of the prayers of the "holy ones" in the presence of the glory of the Great One and Holy One. As such an intercessor and as the divinely sent healer who will adjudicate the situation, Raphael corresponds to the angelic intercessors and agents of judgment described in 1 Enoch 9–10. … In the story of the sacrifice of Isaac in *Jub.* 17:15–18:16, the biblical account is framed by a Job-like prologue in which the angels of the

---

74. *OTP*, 1:810.
75. *OTP*, 1:789.
76. See chapter 2.

presence praise Abraham's righteousness, while the chief of demons, the prince of Mastemah, accuses him. ... For the author of *3 Baruch*, Michael receives both the prayers of the righteous and their merits (chaps. 11–12). Here, as elsewhere, the mediating of prayer is tied to the upright status of those who pray.[77]

Individuals also receive instruction from angels. Again, there are peripheral instances, such as how angels taught Adam how to work in the garden of Eden (Jubilees 3:15–16). For the most part, however, angelic instruction becomes a developed motif in Second Temple Jewish literature, that of the "interpreting angel." The Old Testament describes a number of occasions when angels deliver messages, but by the time of later books such as Daniel, the messages become more formal, usually revolving around the interpretation of a vision or dream. As Collins notes, this portrayal becomes prominent in the Second Temple period, particularly in apocalyptic literature:

It is possible to trace the evolution of some literary forms from prophecy to apocalypticism. For example, the role of the interpreting angel, the supernatural mediator, appears first in Zechariah, in the late sixth century BC.[78]

Nickelsburg highlights the features noting the Old Testament connections:

The accompanying, interpreting angels in this section of 1 Enoch are an extension and formalization of similar figures in the prophetic books of Ezekiel and Zechariah. In Ezekiel 8–11 an otherworldly figure of brilliant appearance takes the prophet, "in the visions of God" (8:3), from his house in Babylon to Jerusalem, where he escorts him around the temple and comments on the abominations there, before returning him to Babylon. In chaps. 40–48, after Ezekiel is again taken to Jerusalem "in the visions of God" (40:2), the same figure, presumably (40:30), again escorts Ezekiel through the temple

---

77. Nickelsburg, *1 Enoch 1*, 208–9. Corporately, Nickelsburg also comments (p. 209): "In Zech 1:12–17, in the place of a multiplicity of such intercessors, the prophet describes 'the angel of YHWH' as the singular intercessor for the nation of Israel, who raises the question, 'How long?' not to plead the nation's innocence, but to argue the sufficiency of God's punishment." See chapter 3 for how the Old Testament presents this figure as superior to Michael.

78. John J. Collins, "Apocalyptic Literature," *DNTB* 42.

and explains various of its features to him. Noteworthy is the formula, "Brought me ... he said ... this is." In Zechariah 1–6 an angelic interlocutor engages Zechariah in a question-and-answer format relating to the content of the prophet's visions. ... In this section of the Book of the Watchers, the combination of vision, question, and an answer by the interpreting angel is the sole vehicle of revelation, as is already hinted at in the book's superscription ([1 Enoch] 1:2). Moreover, here, as in Ezekiel 40–44, the angel accompanies the seer on his vision journey. The device will continue to structure parts of the Book of Parables ([1 Enoch] 40:8; 52:3; 53:4; 54:4; 56:2; 60:9, 11, 24; 61:2; 64:2). The idea may also be presumed in the Book of Tobit, where Raphael guides Tobias across Mesopotamia and explains the magical properties of the fish's viscera to the inquiring young man ([Tobit] 6:6–8).[79]

The concept of angelic interpretation of course presumes access to divine knowledge about the affairs of humans and human destiny. Some of that knowledge is portrayed as the result of direct access to divine decrees. However, as with the Old Testament, there are allusions in Second Temple literature to divine record keeping. Jubilees 19:9 informs us that Abraham "was found faithful and he was recorded as a friend of the LORD in the heavenly tablets."[80] The same pseudepigraphical book notes that Levi's elevation to priestly duty was "written (on high) as a testimony for him in the heavenly tablets before the God of all" (Jubilees 30:20). Those who break God's covenant are recorded "in the heavenly tablets as enemies ... [and] will be blotted out of the book of life and written in the book of those who will be destroyed and with those who will be rooted out from the land" (Jubilees 30:21–22).[81] First Enoch 47:3 has the Ancient of Days seated on this throne and "the books of the living ones were open before him."[82]

Corporate guardianship is most evident in the way angels are cast as warriors. The contexts of the passages we previously examined typically had something to do with the protection of Israel. In concert with Daniel 10:21; 12:1, Michael is the chief guardian of Israel (Assumption of Moses

---

79. Nickelsburg, *1 Enoch 1*, 294.
80. *OTP*, 2:92. There are references to "heavenly tablets" in Jubilees 3:9–11; 33:10, but these texts seek to cast the Mosaic law as preexisting in heaven.
81. *OTP*, 2:113
82. *OTP*, 1:35.

10:2). In several Greek Pseudepigrapha he is called *archistratēgos* (Testament of Abraham 2:3; 2 Enoch 22:6; 33:10; 71:28; Joseph and Aseneth 14:8 [Grk:7]), a term that denotes military superiority over a *stratēgos*, the normative term for commanding generals in Greek literature. The term *archistratēgos* is how the LXX describes the commander ("prince"; *sar*) of Yahweh's host in Joshua 5:14.[83] At other times an unnamed angel appears who claims to be Israel's guardian (Testament of Levi 5:6).[84] 4Q529, though fragmentary, suggests that angels were assigned by Michael to guard the temple.

Guardianship has a dark side as well. We saw that in the Animal Apocalypse the writer believed that God had turned over his people to judgment at the hands of the patron angels of the nations because of their apostasy. The Syriac Apocalypse of Baruch has Jerusalem being destroyed by four anonymous angels just before the Babylonian attack (2 Baruch 6:4–8:1).[85] In Pseudo-Philo (Liber antiquitatum biblicarum 15:5), Israel's guardian angels are commanded to not intercede for the people but instead afflict them.

## PROMINENT ANGELS AS SECOND YAHWEH FIGURES

In chapter 3 we discussed the identity of the Old Testament's angel of Yahweh as Yahweh himself in human form. This angel, in conjunction with the Old Testament "Name theology," was the foundation behind later Jewish speculation as to the identity of the "second Yahweh" or the second of the "two powers in heaven" motif in Second Temple literature and rabbinic Judaism.[86] The most important study of Second Temple literature with an eye toward this issue is that of Charles Gieschen, whose research reveals that writers of the period cast both exalted (glorified)

---

83. See the discussion of Michael in chapter 3.

84. As Michalak notes, some scholars believe this unidentified angel is Michael because Michael is so often cast in this role. The same rationale leads some scholars to identify Michael as the prince of light in the War Scroll. See Michalak, *Angels as Warriors*, 165–69, 236.

85. See also 4 Baruch 3:2; 4:2.

86. See Heiser, "Co-Regency in Ancient Israel's Divine Council as the Conceptual Backdrop to Ancient Jewish Binitarian Monotheism," *BBR* 26.2 (2015): 210–17. The major work on Judaism's two-powers teaching is Segal, *Two Powers in Heaven*.

humans and angels as the second power in heaven.[87] Criteria for the second power can be summarized as follows:

There are five criteria that scholars agree merit special consideration when seeking to understand exalted vice regency: (1) divine position (Is the figure with or near God and his throne?); (2) divine appearance (Is the figure described in the same ways as God's physical form in the Hebrew Bible?); (3) divine functions (Does the figure perform actions typically ascribed to God?); (4) divine Name (Does the figure bear the name of Yahweh, or is he described as a hypostasis[88] of the Name?); and (5) divine veneration (Is the figure worshipped, or is prayer offered to the figure?). With respect to the last criterion, the exaltation of a figure most often has its roots in Exod 23:20–23; Exod 24:9ff.; Dan 7:9ff.; and Ezekiel 1, 10. It is not a coincidence that these texts are precisely those at the root of the two powers controversy since they evince a second divine personage.[89]

For our purposes, we will focus on angels who fit the criteria most closely.[90]

In Joseph and Aseneth, Aseneth's visitor, the "heavenly man" (Joseph and Aseneth 14:4–17:10) is referred to as a god (*theos*) two times (17:9; 22:3), and yet he is distinguished from God by virtue of his titles: "chief of the house of the Lord and commander of the whole host of the Most High" (Joseph and Aseneth 14:7–8). Many scholars believe the heavenly man is Michael, though the text never says this, nor is Michael ever referred to as *theos* in any Second Temple text.[91]

---

87. Charles Gieschen, *Angelomorphic Christology: Antecedents and Early Evidence* (Leiden: Brill, 1998).

88. It is recognized that "hypostasis nomenclature" has been criticized by scholars in the past. However, the criticisms have been carefully addressed in recent work on Jewish angelology and divine mediation. See Gieschen, *Angelomorphic Christology*, 36–48.

89. Heiser, "The Divine Council," 235. See Gieschen, *Angelomorphic Christology*, 1–46, 51–123; Segal, *Two Powers in Heaven*, 148–49; Christopher Rowland, *The Open Heaven: A Study of Apocalyptic in Judaism and Early Christianity* (Eugene, OR: Wipf & Stock, 1982), 78–112.

90. Metatron deserves special mention, despite exclusion from our discussion. Metatron is arguably the capstone of vice-regent traditions since he bears the name *yhwh hqtn* (the "lesser Yahweh"; 3 Enoch 7; 12:5, 48). Much of the material for Metatron is found in 3 Enoch (written in Hebrew), which scholars date from the second to the fifth centuries AD, outside the normative parameters of the Second Temple period. Third Enoch also has detailed divine council scenes, demonstrating that divine plurality and two-powers theology was alive and well in the rabbinic period.

91. Several manuscripts of this passage show that some scribes were offended by the content. In some manuscripts a scribe added the definite article before *theos*, apparently trying to cast the figure

In making the argument for Michael, scholars take note that the heavenly man is called *archistratēgos* (Joseph and Aseneth 14:8 [Grk: 7]) in this passage, which is the term used in LXX for the commander ("prince"; *sar*) in Joshua 5:14. However, the same title is also used of Raphael (Greek Apocalypse of Ezra 1:4), a slightly later text,[92] and Michael's military functions are not unique to him, being shared by other archangels (1QM 9.15–16; 1 Enoch 20:5; 40; 54; 71: 8–9, 13; 3 Baruch 4:7; Apocalypse of Moses 40; Sibylline Oracles 2:214–37).[93]

A deified figure distinct from Michael does appear in Second Temple literature:

And it came to pass when I heard the voice pronouncing such words to me that I looked this way and that. And behold there was no breath in me, and my spirit was amazed, and my soul fled from me. And I became like a stone, and fell down upon the earth, for there was no longer strength in me to stand up on the earth. And while I was still face down on the ground, I heard the voice of the Holy One speaking, "Go, Ya'el of the same name, through the mediation of my ineffable Name, consecrate this man and strengthen him against his trembling." The angel he sent to me in the likeness of a man came, and he took me by my right hand and stood me on my feet. And he said to me, "Stand up Abraham, friend of God who has loved you, let human trembling not enfold you! For lo! I am sent to you to strengthen you and to bless you in the name of God, creator of heavenly and earthly things, who has loved you. Be bold and hasten to him. I am Ya'el. ... Stand up, Abraham! Go boldly, be very joyful and rejoice. And I (am) with you, for a venerable honor has been prepared for you by the Eternal One. Go, complete the sacrifice of the command. Behold, I am assigned (to be) with you and with the generation which is predestined (to be

---

as God himself and remove the reference to a second deity figure. Other manuscripts read "angel" in place of *theos*. See *OTP*, 2:231, 239.

92. The Greek Apocalypse of Ezra dates from the second to the ninth century AD (*OTP*, 1:562).

93. The closest any Second Temple text comes to deifying Michael is either 1 Enoch 40:1–9 or 69:13–25. The former texts refer to the four "angels of the Presence" (1 Enoch 40:2) and goes on to list Michael as the "first" (1 Enoch 40:9). This descriptive phrase is then taken to Jubilees 1:27–2:2, where an unnamed "angel of the Presence" is clearly identified as "the angel who went before the camp of Israel," (i.e., the Angel of Yahweh). This strategy therefore produces an argument from silence. The second passage (1 Enoch 69:13–25) has Michael being asked to reveal the hidden name of God. The speculation is that Michael must be at the level of Yahweh to know this information.

born) from you, And with me Michael blesses you for ever. Be bold, go!" (Apocalypse of Abraham 10:1–7, 15–17) [94]

The passage is noteworthy since the angel in view bears the name of God, Ya'el ("Yah is El"), he appears as a man, and is explicitly distinguished from Michael (Apocalypse of Abraham 10:17).[95] Not only does this angel bear the divine name, but readers learn later in the same work that Ya'el *is* the God of Israel. In the Apocalypse of Abraham 17:4–13, Abraham is commanded to worship God "on the place of highness" by reciting a song listing God's names (17:4). Abraham obeys with these words:

> Eternal One, Mighty One, Holy El, God autocrat self-originated, incorruptible, immaculate, unbegotten, spotless, immortal, self-perfected, self-devised, without father, without mother, ungenerated, exalted, fiery, just, lover of men, benevolent, compassionate, bountiful, jealous over me, patient one, most merciful. Eli, eternal, mighty one, holy, Sabaoth, most glorious El, El, El, El, Ya'el! (17:8–13)

The point to be made is that the litany of names proclaimed to God includes Ya'el. The co-identification of this angel with God himself is echoed in the Life of Adam and Eve. God is once again addressed as Ya'el:[96]

> When the Lord had said these things, he ordered us cast out of paradise. And your father (Adam) wept before the angels opposite Paradise, and the angels said to him, "What do you want us to do for you, Adam?" Your father answered and said to the angels, "See you are casting me out; I beg you, let me take fragrances from Paradise, so that after I have gone out, I might bring an offering to God so that God will hear me." And they (the angels) came to God and said, "Ya'el, eternal king, command that fragrant incenses from Paradise be given to Adam." And God ordered Adam go come that he might take aromatic fragrances out of Paradise for his sustenance. When the angels allowed him, he gathered four kinds: crocus, nard, reed, cinnamon; and other seeds for his food. And he took these and went

---

94. The Apocalypse of Abraham was composed at the time of the destruction of the second temple or shortly thereafter (*OTP*, 1:683).

95. Or "Yahoel" (*OTP*, 1:692, n. 10b).

96. *OTP*, 2:285.

out of Paradise. And so we came to be on the earth. (Life of Adam and Eve 29:1–6)

It should be apparent that Second Temple angelology bears a strong resemblance to the Old Testament theology of the heavenly host. As we'll see, and as many readers have no doubt discerned, Second Temple thoughts about angels also have clear connections to the New Testament.

# CHAPTER 6

# The Heavenly Host
# in the New Testament

Our examination of vocabulary to this point has revealed a good deal of continuity. Members of the heavenly host are referred to in the Old Testament and Second Temple Jewish literature in much the same way, though some of the vocabulary of the former is not repeated in the latter. There were also innovations in angelology during the Second Temple period along with quite a bit of speculation. The New Testament shows marked differences with respect to both the Old Testament and Second Temple literature. New Testament angelology is rooted in the Old Testament but has much less variety in its vocabulary for the heavenly host. It also shows little interest in innovation and speculation of Second Temple Jewish literature.[1]

## NEW TESTAMENT TERMINOLOGY
## FOR THE HEAVENLY HOST

The vocabulary choices of New Testament authors can be easily misunderstood. For example, the plural of *theos* ("god," "gods") is found in the New Testament only eight times. It would be incoherent to see this as a rejection of Old Testament thinking about the supernatural. Rather, the limited usage is pragmatic. New Testament writers use divine plurality language when needed, such as in citation of an Old Testament passage,

---

1. This is true of "good" members of the heavenly host. When it comes to demonology, which is not the focus of this book, the New Testament follows Second Temple Jewish literature and its development of Old Testament ideas in discernible, important ways.

a reference to pagan (gentile) idols, or some point of gentile religion. It is quite evident that Paul, for instance, considered the gods of the Old Testament to be actual, sinister entities. In 1 Corinthians 8:1–6 Paul tells the Corinthians that there were indeed other gods (*theoi*) and lords (*kurioi*) worshipped by people instead of Yahweh and Jesus, entities that Paul, following the Septuagint of Deuteronomy 32:17, considered demons (1 Cor 10:21–22).[2] Paul feared the Corinthians would be "participants with demons" if they ate the sacrificial meat (1 Cor 10:20).[3]

The same caution about drawing erroneous conclusions in regard to New Testament vocabulary is appropriate given the virtual absence of other terms found in the Old Testament or Second Temple Jewish thought. The New Testament uses "holy ones" only once of celestial, non-human beings (Jude 14), and that instance is drawing on material from a pseudepigraphical book (1 Enoch 1:9). This infrequency of usage would not lead us to the conclusion that New Testament writers didn't think the members of the heavenly host were holy or that God's presence was void of other heavenly beings. New Testament references to "sons of God" or

---

2. When it comes to demonological vocabulary, both the LXX and the New Testament conflate the Old Testament vocabulary for foreign gods and idols to *daimōn/daimonion*. By the Hellenistic era, this term (in Jewish circles) was broadly used for entities hostile to God. English translations regularly obscure Paul's thinking by putting *theoi* in quotation marks, creating the impression that Paul wasn't serious. The same translations regularly take the common Greek lemma (*legō*; "to say, speak") and render it "so-called" to create the same misleading impression. There is nothing cryptic about Paul's statement; 1 Cor 8:5–6 should be straightforwardly translated: "For although there are those called gods and lords in heaven or on earth—as indeed there are many gods and lords—yet for us there is one God, the Father, from whom are all things, and for whom we exist, and one Lord, Jesus Christ." Paul's theology is precisely in line with Old Testament writers who affirm multiple *'elōhîm* but only one Yahweh. That Paul was serious is indicated in his reference to these same gods and lords in 1 Cor 10:21–22, where he calls them demons in quoting the LXX of Deut 32:17, where they are called *'elōhîm* and *šēdîm*. The latter Hebrew term denotes territorial entities to whom Israelites sacrificed in the place of Yahweh. The term makes good sense in the context of the Deut 32:8 worldview of the Old Testament. See Heiser, *The Unseen Realm*, 328–29, 339–40.

3. Paul does not contradict himself here with respect to his conclusion, two chapters earlier, that "we are no worse off if we do not eat, and no better off if we do" (1 Cor 8:8). An idol was indeed nothing (1 Cor 8:4). But the entity who was thought to indwell the idol was a different matter. Paul allowed eating the meat that was sold in the marketplace (1 Cor 10:25), but apparently any connection to the altar (i.e., the sacrificial ritual) meant fellowship with demons (1 Cor 10:18–22). This had to be avoided because it amounted to worship of foreign gods, akin to Israel's failure (1 Cor 10:22; cf. Deut 32:21, which is contextualized by Deut 32:17, where the "demons" (*šēdîm*; LXX: *daimoniois*) are "gods" (*'elōhîm*; LXX: *theoi*). For the logic of idolatry and the difference between the entity and the idol, see Gay Robins, "Cult Statues in Ancient Egypt," in *Cult Image and Divine Representation in the Ancient Near East*, ed. Neal H. Walls (Boston: American Schools of Oriental Research, 2005), 1–2; Michael P. Dick, *Born in Heaven, Made on Earth: The Making of the Cult Image in the Ancient Near East* (Winona Lake, IN: Eisenbrauns, 1999), 33–34.

"children of God" refer to human believers (glorified or not).[4] We would be quite wrong if we concluded that New Testament writers thought that angels were not created by God (as spirit "children") or that they thought there was something theologically amiss about the phrase "sons of God."[5] New Testament writers had their own focus points. There was no need to rehearse Old Testament angelology in their writings.

Ontological language (e.g., "spirits") is frequently employed and qualified with adjectives ("evil spirits") to describe demons, a term that is itself ontological. "Demon" is actually a transliteration of the Greek *daimōn* (or the related *daimonion*), which in classical Greek literature describes any supernatural being without regard to its disposition (good or evil). A *daimōn* can be a god or goddess, a lesser supernatural being, or even the disembodied spirit of a human.[6] Consequently, *daimōn* is semantically akin to Hebrew *'elōhîm*.[7] Gospel writers use *daimōn* in combination with descriptive phrases like "evil/unclean spirits,"[8] and so *daimōn/daimonion* in the New Testament nearly always point to a disembodied entity hostile to God.[9] These supernatural fallen spirits are also cast as fallen or wandering "stars" (Matt 24:29 [cf. Isa 34:4]; Mark 13:25; Jude 13).

---

4. All other references to "sons of God" or "children of God" in the New Testament have believers (glorified or otherwise) in view: John 1:12; 11:52; Rom 8:16, 21; 9:8; Phil 2:15; 1 John 3:1, 10; 5:2.

5. Indeed, as I have explained elsewhere, this language used of believers is intentionally drawn from the Old Testament vocabulary for God's spirit children. See Heiser, *The Unseen Realm*, 23–43, 307–21. For other commentary that contains insights into the divine council/Old Testament background of the "divine sonship" of believers, see Brendan Byrne, *"Sons of God"—"Seed of Abraham": A Study of the Idea of the Sonship of God of All Christians in Paul Against the Jewish Background* (Rome: Pontifical Biblical Institute Press, 1979), 1–69; James Tabor, "Firstborn of Many Brothers: A Pauline Notion of Apotheosis," in *Society of Biblical Literature Seminar Papers 21* (Chico, CA: Scholars Press, 1984), 295–303. Byrne's study subsequently pursues the New Testament sonship language. Other studies have that as their primary focus: James M. Scott, *Adoption as Sons of God: An Exegetical Investigation Into the Background of Yiothesia in the Pauline Corpus* (Tübingen: Mohr Siebeck, 1992); Matthew Vellanichal, *The Divine Sonship of Christians in the Johannine Writings* (Rome: Pontifical Biblical Institute Press, 1977).

6. On the term *daimōn*, see J. E. Rexine, "*Daimōn* in Classical Greek Literature," *Greek Orthodox Theological Review* 30.3 (1985): 335–61.

7. See the discussion in chapter 1.

8. See Luke 8:2, 29; 9:42 (cf. Luke 4:33; Rev 18:2). Demons are also referred to as spirits in Matt 8:16.

9. The one exception is Acts 17:18, where gentiles (Greeks) listening to Paul opine: "He seems to be a preacher of foreign divinities [*daimoniōn*]." The New Testament is silent on the origin of demons. The origin of demons in Jewish texts outside the Bible (such as 1 Enoch) is attributed to the events of Gen 6:1–4. When a Nephilim was killed in these texts, its disembodied spirit was considered a demon. These demons then roamed the earth to harass humans. For the origin of demons, see Wright, *The Origin of Evil Spirits*; Loren T. Stuckenbruck, "Giant Mythology and Demonology: From Ancient Near East to the Dead Sea Scrolls," in *Demons: The Demonology of Israelite-Jewish and Early Christian Literature in Context of Their Environment*, eds. Armin Lange, Hermann Lichtnberger, K.

Outside the Gospels, particularly in the writings of Paul, vocabulary for the powers of darkness is characteristically described with functional or role terminology. Most of Paul's terms for the powers of darkness describe geographical rulership. The word choices make good sense given the content of Deuteronomy 32:8–9 and Psalm 82, which explain the origin (and corruption) of the fallen sons of God assigned to the nations by Yahweh:

> [Paul] understood and presumed the Deuteronomy 32 worldview: "rulers" (*archontōn* or *archōn*); "principalities" (*archē*); "powers"/ "authorities" (*exousia*); "powers" (*dynamis*); "dominions"/"lords" (*kyrios*); "thrones" (*thronos*); "world rulers" (*kosmokratōr*). These lemmas have something in common—they were used both in the New Testament and other Greek literature to denote *geographical domain authority*. At times these terms are used of humans, but several instances demonstrate that Paul had spiritual beings in mind.[10]

With respect to the faithful members of the heavenly host, the vocabulary of the New Testament is more functional than ontological. Ontological vocabulary is occasionally used to describe God's servants. They are occasionally described as "spirits" (Heb 1:14; Rev 1:4; 3:1; 4:5; 5:6),[11] "heavenly ones" (*epouranioi*; 1 Cor 15:48), "glorious ones" (*doksai*; 2 Pet 2:10; Jude 8); "lights" (*phōtōn*; Jas 1:17); "holy ones" (*hagiais*; Jude 14); and (possibly) "stars."[12] New Testament writers seldom qualify the term "angel"

---

F. Diethard Römheld (Tübingen: Mohr Siebeck, 2003), 31–38; idem, "The 'Angels' and 'Giants' of Genesis 6: 1–4 in Second and Third Century BCE Jewish Interpretation: Reflections on the Posture of Early Apocalyptic Traditions," *DSD* 7.3 (2000): 354–77.

10. Heiser, *The Unseen Realm*, 329–30. See Deut 4:19–20; 17:1–3; 29:23–26; 32:17, translating *'elôah* in this last reference correctly, as a plural ("gods"), as in the KJV, NKJV, NLT, NRSV, NET, LEB, NIV [1984]). For Deut 32:8, see our earlier discussion in chapters 1 and 2.

11. The adjective *pneumatikos* is used once in the plural as a general, ontological designation of supernatural beings hostile to God (Eph 6:12; "spiritual forces"). Its remaining plural occurrences the lemma points to or describes spiritual service (1 Pet 2:5), truths (1 Cor 2:13; 9:11), blessings (Rom 15:27), gifts (1 Cor 12:1; 14:1), songs (Eph 5:19; Col 3:16), or human believers themselves (1 Cor 2:13; 3:1; Gal 6:1).

12. On the "star" designation for the angels of the seven churches in Revelation (Rev 1:16, 20; 2:1; 3:1; 12:4), see chapter 7. Not all scholars see the angels associated with the churches as divine beings. Two instances of "spirits" require comment. Hebrews 12:29 (God is the "father of spirits") is either neutral or refers to God as the source of the human spirit/breath. If the former trajectory is followed, the term would credit God with creating all divine beings regardless of their loyal or fallen status. Hebrews 12:23 clearly refers to redeemed (human) souls. James 1:17 refers to God as the "father of lights," a phrase that calls to mind the Old Testament and Second Temple Jewish notion that stars were heavenly beings. See chapters 1 and 4, along with P. W. van der Horst, "Father of

with "holy" (Mark 8:38 [cf. Luke 9:26]; Acts 10:22; Rev 14:10). However, angels are associated with heaven (Matt 22:30; 24:36; Mark 12:25; 13:32; Luke 2:13, 15; Heb 12:22; Rev 10:1; 14:17; 18:1; 20:1).

The functional word "angel" (*angelos*) is by far the principal New Testament moniker for celestial beings in service to God. The label—effectively a job description ("messenger")—communicates assistance from heaven. Only 4 of the 175 occurrences of *angelos* point to fallen divine beings.[13] For New Testament authors, *angelos* is a catchall term for the supernatural agents who faithfully attend God. The varied vocabulary of the Old Testament and Second Jewish literature is therefore largely conflated into *angelos*.

In accord with the Old Testament, the New Testament names only two angels, Michael (Jude 9; Rev 12:7) and Gabriel (Luke 1:19, 26). There is

---

the Lights," *DDD* 328–29. The term *stoicheia* ("elemental principles") is excluded from this list of ontological terms for "good" angels. In the two passages where this term (at least in part) arguably refers to divine beings (Gal 4:3, 9; Col 2:8, 20) instead of (apparently) the material components of the natural world (2 Pet 3:10, 12) or "first principles" of the Mosaic law (Heb 5:12), the referents would be fallen supernatural beings. On this term and these passages, see D. G. Reid, "Elements/Elemental Spirits of the World," *DPL*. As I wrote in *The Unseen Realm* (p. 327, n. 17): "There is no consensus among scholars on Paul's use of the term (Gal 4:3, 9; Col 2:8, 20). The question is whether Paul is using the term of spiritual entities/star deities in Gal 4:3, 9 and Col 2:8, 20. Three of these four instances append the word to 'of the world' (*kosmos*; i.e., '*stoicheia* of the world'), but this doesn't provide much clarity. Paul's discussion in Gal 4 and Col 2 includes spiritual forces (angels, principalities and powers, false gods) in the context, which suggests *stoicheia* may refer to divine beings. He is contrasting *stoicheia* to salvation in Christ in some way. Since Paul is speaking to both Jews and Gentiles, he might also be using the term in different ways with respect to each audience. *Stoicheia* as law would make little sense to Gentiles, though it would strike a chord with Jews. My view is that in Gal 4:3 Paul's use of *stoicheia* likely refers to the law and religious teaching with a Jewish audience in view (cf. Gal 4:1–7). The audience shifts to Gentiles in 4:8–11, and so it seems coherent to see *stoicheia* in Gal 4:9 as referring to divine beings, probably astral deities (the 'Fates'). Galatians 4:8 transitions to pagans since the Jews would have known about the true God. The reference to 'times and seasons and years' (4:10) would therefore point to astrological beliefs, not the Jewish calendar. Paul is therefore denying the idea that the celestial *objects* (sun, moon, stars) are deities. His Gentile readers should not be enslaved by the idea that these objects controlled their destiny."

13. See Matt 25:41; Rev 12:9; 2 Pet 2:4; Jude 6. The reasoning should be clear. If a spirit being isn't serving God, it would be working against God along with other fallen divine beings. The devil, linked in Second Temple literature and the New Testament with the serpent (*nachash*) of Eden, has primary status apparently due to being the original rebel, made ruler of the underworld—the place in ancient cosmology opposite to the abode of God. See Heiser, *The Unseen Realm*, 276–77. A link between the sons of God who fell before the flood (Gen 6:1–4) to the devil becomes prominent in Second Temple Jewish literature. The idea can in fact be tied to the Old Testament if one is aware (as a number of Second Temple Jewish authors were) of the Mesopotamian (Babylonian) background to Gen 6:1–4. See Heiser, *Reversing Hermon*, 1–52. According to *NIDNTTE*, the word *angelos* is "especially frequent in the book of Revelation (67×), the Synoptics (51×), and Acts (21×). It is rarely used of human messengers (Luke 7:24; 9:52; Jas 2:25 [cf. LXX Josh 7:22]; and a quotation from Mal 3:1 in Matt 11:10; Mark 1:2; Luke 7:27)" (*NIDNTTE* 1:122).

therefore far less interest in specific angels than found in Second Temple literature. Unlike the Old Testament's emphasis on the angel of Yahweh, and the space devoted to angelic "second Yahweh" figures (Melchizedek, the Prince of Light, the heavenly man, Yahoel) in Second Temple literature, the New Testament's focus is on Christ.[14] For New Testament writers, the second power became incarnate in Jesus Christ.[15]

The obvious exception to New Testament indifference toward exalted angels is the scant attention paid to archangels. The term *archangelos* is

---

14. The phrase "angel of the Lord" occurs eleven times in the New Testament (Matt 1:20, 24; 2:13, 19; 28:2; Luke 1:11; 2:9; Acts 5:19; 8:26; 12:7, 23). The very similar "angel of God" occurs twice (Acts 10:3; Gal 4:14). In no case can it be exegetically argued that the phrase points to the same figure as the Old Testament angel of the Lord. Part of the problem is the disconnect between the fact that translating the corresponding Hebrew phrase into English requires a definite translation ("*the* angel of Yahweh/the Lord") due to the grammar and syntax of the Hebrew construct relationship with a noun of deity as the *nomen rectum*. That said, there are rare occasions where an English indefinite translation of a Hebrew noun construct phrase referring to a deity could be appropriate. For instance, 1 Sam 16:23; 18:10 have *rûaḥ 'elōhîm*, where the meaning cannot be "*the* Spirit of God" (i.e., the Holy Spirit). Two earlier references (1 Sam 16:15, 16) make the context clear (through modification by an adjective) that *an* "evil spirit" from God is meant. Typically, though, the Hebrew construct relationship involving a specific deity requires definiteness. Greek grammar is more flexible, requiring neither the article for definiteness nor that a phrase involving a deity noun be semantically definite. Greek can omit the article before the noun in syntactical relationship to another genitive case noun, thereby creating the possibility that the first noun is indefinite. The only New Testament instance of the article occurring before *angelos* in the phrase "angel of the Lord" is Matt 1:24. Utilizing Wallace's chart on article usage and semantics, the use of the article in Matt 1:24 is best understood as anaphoric—referring back to the preceding mention (where there is no article) of this same angel in Matt 1:20. There is nothing to suggest that the article is monadic, pointing to a unique angel. See Wallace, *Greek Grammar Beyond the Basics*, 230. Further, it is fascinating to note that when New Testament writers unambiguously cite or allude to Old Testament passages whose focus is the angel of Yahweh, they do not use the phrase "angel of the Lord" (Acts 7:30, 35, 38 [Exod 3:1–3]). In this writer's judgment, the only instance where the New Testament writer may have the angel of Yahweh (who was Yahweh) in view is Rev 1. If this is the case, then John identifies the risen Christ with the angel. This would be expected, given the identification of the angel of Yahweh with Yahweh in the Old Testament and the use of that identification by New Testament writers to link Jesus and Yahweh (see Heiser, *The Unseen Realm*, 127–48, 267–69). Given the heavenly post-resurrection context, there would be no conflict with the Second Person of the Trinity coming in human form as the angel of Yahweh prior to that person's incarnation as Jesus. The point of Rev 1 would be to identify this angel (Rev 1:1, "his [God's] angel") with the later human Jesus. The phrase "who is and who was and who is to come" in Rev 1:4 is derived from the LXX of Exod 3:14, the revelation of the divine name from the burning bush, in which the angel of Yahweh appeared (Exod 3:1–3; cf. Rev 1:8; 4:8; Heb 13:8), and is closely related to the description of Jesus as the alpha and omega (Rev 1:8; 21:6; 22:13). The problem with this identification is Rev 22:16, where it is apparently Jesus (vs. God the Father) who sent the angel to John. However, this verse could merely be another way to co-identify Jesus and God. In any event, an explicit reference to "the angel of the Lord" does not occur in Revelation. For a lengthy discussion of Rev 1 and this issue, see Sean M. McDonough, *YHWH at Patmos: Rev. 1:4 in Its Hellenistic and Early Jewish Setting* (Tübingen: Mohr Siebeck, 1999).

15. Alan F. Segal, "'Two Powers in Heaven' and Early Christian Trinitarian Thinking," *The Trinity: An Interdisciplinary Symposium on the Trinity* (Oxford: Oxford University Press, 1999): 73–95; Daniel Boyarin, "The Gospel of the Memra: Jewish Binitarianism and the Prologue to John," *HTR* 94.3 (2001), 243–84.

found only twice. The instance in 1 Thessalonians 4:16 makes reference to the role of at least one archangel in the proclamation of the return of Christ. No specific archangel is mentioned.

Michael receives the title once in Jude 9, where the archangel "contends" with the devil about the body of Moses. This puzzling passage is most often thought to hearken back to passages such as Zechariah 3, where *hasśāṭān* (the "adversary") accuses Joshua the high priest. Bauckham's thoughts are representative: "The devil in his ancient role as accuser tried to establish Moses' guilt, in order to prove him unworthy of honorable burial and to claim the body for himself."[16] Bauckham's discussion of Jude 9 (especially pp. 65–76) has much to commend it, especially its assemblage of Second Temple literature that might contribute to the strange episode, but it is ultimately untenable because associating Zechariah 3 with the devil depends on violating Hebrew grammar.[17]

There is another possible point of reference for the content of Jude 9 that potentially redeems Bauckham's conclusion. According to Deuteronomy 34:6, God buried Moses "in the valley in the land of Moab opposite Beth-Peor; but no one knows the place of his burial to this day." The location has significance for Israelite cosmology and religion. This location is part of the geographical area that includes Oboth and Abarim (Num 21:10–11; 33:43–48). Mount Nebo, the mountain atop which Moses viewed the promised land before God laid him to rest (Deut 34:1), is in fact explicitly linked to Abarim in Deuteronomy 32:49. These locations were associated with the underworld and ancient cults of the dead. Consequently, the "valley" mentioned in Deuteronomy 34:6 may well be the valley of the *ʿōbĕrîm* mentioned in Ezekiel 39:11. Spronk discusses the place names:

> The participle Qal plural *ʿōbĕrîm* of the verb *ʿbr*, 'to pass from one side to the other' seems to have a special meaning in the context of the cult of the dead, denoting the spirits of the dead crossing the border between the land of the living and the world of the dead. It can be interpreted as a divine name in Ezek 39:11, 14, which may have

---

16. Richard J. Bauckham, *2 Peter, Jude*, WBC 50 (Dallas: Word, Inc., 1998), 59, 65–76.

17. As noted in chapter 2, the adversary in passages like Job 1–2 and Zech 3 is not the devil. Recall that Hebrew does not tolerate the definite article before a personal proper name. As was the case throughout Job 1–2, the definite article is present with *śāṭān* in Zech 3.

also been preserved in the geographical name Abarim (Num 21:10–11; 27:12; 33:44, 47–48; Deut 32:49; and Jer 22:20). Its Ugaritic cognate, then, would be 'brm in *KTU²* 1.22 i:15.

In the Ugaritic text *KTU²* 1.22 describing a necromantic session, the king invokes the spirits of the dead (Rephaim) and celebrates a feast, probably the New Year Festival, with them. It is told that they came over traveling by horse-drawn chariots. As they are taking part in the meal served for them they are explicitly called 'those who came over'.

The valley of the 'ōbĕrîm is located 'east of the sea' (v 11), which is probably the Dead Sea. So it was part of Transjordan. This is a region which shows many traces of ancient cults of the dead, such as the megalithic monuments called dolmens and place names referring to the dead and the netherworld, viz. Obot, Peor, and Abarim.[18]

In view of this data, it seems reasonable to conclude that Moses would have been buried in the place associated with the realm of the dead. It is in turn quite understandable if a Second Temple Jewish tradition arose about the body of Moses—arguably the central figure in Israelite history—being contested by the lord of the dead, Satan, by the time of that period. Michael was Israel's prince, the guardian of Yahweh's portion according to Daniel 10 and 12, so he would be the logical candidate to claim the body of Moses for the eschatological land of promise, or the domain of Yahweh in the afterlife.

New Testament writers utilize other functional terms, some of which, as noted earlier, also describe fallen supernatural beings. Paul referred to the supernatural beings appointed by God over the nations (Deut 32:8) as "rulers," "thrones," "dominions," and "authorities" hostile to God (Col 2:15; Eph 1:21).[19] He also used these terms more neutrally. In Colossians 1:16, God is credited with creating all things "in heaven and on earth, visible and invisible, whether thrones or dominions or rulers or authorities." The verse's use of these terms to refer to spiritual, disembodied ("invisible")

---

18. K. Spronk, "Travellers," *DDD* 876–77.

19. I take Eph 1:21 as referring to the defeat of supernatural hostile powers due to its link to the resurrection. The New Testament links the triumph of the resurrection with the de-legitimization of the powers of darkness put over the nations at the Babel judgment in several passages (Col 2:13–15; Eph 4:7–12; 1 Cor 15:20–28; 1 Pet 3:18–22). These thoughts in tandem call the gentiles to leave the spiritual rulers whose authority originated with Yahweh and turn back to Yahweh once more in response to the work of Christ, the seed of Abraham through whom the nations would be blessed (Gen 12:3).

beings *as they were created* informs us that they were intended by God to be overseers and administrators on his behalf. In Ephesians 3:10 we cannot presume that only the fallen rulers and authorities learned the fullness of the wisdom of God's salvation plan.[20] The spiritual authority (*kuriotēs*) of 2 Peter 2:10 and Jude 8 ("reject authority and blaspheme the glorious ones") is arguably God, though, as discussed below, it could refer to the heavenly council with God (Luke 12:8–9). If the latter option is coherent, the spiritual authorities referred to are obviously loyal members of the heavenly host.

## NEW TESTAMENT ANGELOLOGY:
## Nature, Abilities, Status

The nature and abilities of God's loyal heavenly host extend from, the ontological language we noted above. Angels are disembodied supernatural spirits. Hebrews 1:7 quotes Psalm 104:4 in this regard, characterizing angels as "winds" and "flames of fire."[21] Whereas the psalmist utilized the term *rûḥôt*, which often speaks of a supernatural entity, so the writer of Hebrews employs *pneumata*, which is often used in the same way (Acts 23:8; 1 Cor 3:16; Heb 12:9). Seven verses later (Heb 1:14) the writer refers to these entities as "ministering spirits" (*pneumata*).

As disembodied beings, angels have no need of physical procreation (Matt 22:30; Mark 12:25), though they can assume physical form and appear as men (Acts 12:7, 13–14).[22] Their disembodied spiritual nature is

---

20. It is interesting that "rulers" (*archai*) is juxtaposed with "angels" in Rom 8:38. Since the other pairings in Rom 8:38–39 are oppositional, "rulers" here is negative, being paired contrastively with "angels," the stock term for loyal members of the heavenly host. The "powers of the age to come" in Heb 6:5, aligned with "the goodness of the word of God" in the writer's thought, is likely a reference to spiritual gifts or the experience of God's inaugurated kingdom, not supernatural beings. See William L. Lane, *Hebrews 1–8*, WBC 47A (Dallas: Word, 1991), 141; Donald Guthrie, *Hebrews: An Introduction and Commentary*, TNTC 15 (Downers Grove, IL: InterVarsity Press, 1983), 146.

21. As we noted in chapter 1, Ps 104:4 is understood rightly in light of Ps 103:19–21.

22. Matthew 22:30 and Mark 12:25 do not undermine interpreting (with Peter and Jude, for example) the sons of God of Gen 6:1–4 as supernatural beings. As I noted in *The Unseen Realm* (p. 186): "The text does not say angels *cannot* have sexual intercourse; it says they *don't*. The reason ought to be obvious. The context for the statement is the resurrection, which refers either broadly to the afterlife or, more precisely, to the final, renewed global Eden. The point is clear in either option. In the spiritual world, the realm of divine beings, there is no need for procreation. Procreation is part of the embodied world and is necessary to maintain the physical population. In like manner, life in the perfected Edenic world also does not require maintaining the human species by having children—*everyone has an immortal resurrection body*. Consequently, there is no need for sex in the

apparently what makes them "greater in might and power" than humans (2 Pet 2:11).[23] That a spirit existence was considered superior to embodiment is indicated by certain statements about the incarnation of the Second Person of the Godhead as Jesus of Nazareth. Philippians 2:5–8 describes the incarnation as an act of humility and condescension. The writer of Hebrews informs us that the incarnation resulted in the son of God being made "a little lower than the angels" (Heb 2:7).[24] This secondary status was temporary. After his resurrection and subsequent ascension, Christ became "as much superior to angels as the name he has inherited is more excellent than theirs" (Heb 1:4), with "angels, authorities, and powers having been subjected to him" (1 Pet 3:22).

Despite having this exceptional nature, angels do not know everything; they are not omniscient. They do not know at what time Jesus will return (Matt 24:36; Mark 13:32) and didn't know precisely how God's salvation plan would work out (1 Pet 1:10–12).

As was the case in the Old Testament, angels are not considered infallible. Paul's comments in 1 Corinthians 11:10 indicate that Paul feared angels could be tempted. In discussing why women should have their head covered and the fact that a woman's hair was given to her as a "covering," Paul advises that women should heed his words "because of the angels." Recent scholarship has shown that in the Greco-Roman worldview, of which Corinth was obviously a part, Paul's discussion of these items is inherently sexual in nature, ultimately having to do with conceiving children.[25]

---

resurrection, just as there is no need for it in the nonhuman spiritual realm." For a discussion of Gen 6:1–4, see Heiser, *The Unseen Realm*, 92–109, 186–91. For the original context of Gen 6:1–4 that requires a supernatural reading of that passage, see Heiser, *Reversing Hermon*, 37–54.

23. The objects of this comparative statement in 2 Pet 2:11 are human false teachers.

24. The writer of Hebrews is quoting Ps 8:5 (8:6 in LXX, the source of the quotation). The Hebrew text reads *'elōhîm*, which the LXX translator took as a plural. As noted in chapter 1, *'elōhîm* is a general term that is broadly used in the Hebrew Bible to describe a disembodied resident of the spirit world.

25. See Troy W. Martin, "Paul's Argument from Nature for the Veil in 1 Cor 11:13–15: A Testicle instead of a Head Covering," *JBL* 123.1 (2004): 75–84 (see 75–76). Martin's thesis was contested by a subsequent essay: Mark Goodacre, "Does περιβολαιον Mean 'Testicle' in 1 Cor 11:15?" *JBL* 130.2 (2011): 391–96. Martin then produced a thorough response to Goodacre in defense of his original essay: Troy W. Martin, "Περιβολαιον as 'Testicle' in 1 Cor 11:15: A Response to Mark Goodacre," *JBL* 132.2 (2013): 453–65. The word for "covering" in 1 Cor 11:15b (*peribolaion*) is frequently used for male testicles. Troy Martin, whose specialty is Greco-Roman medical literature, marshals numerous examples in his research toward arguing that Paul's discussion in 1 Cor 11 was a plea for modesty and sexual fidelity, themes that were certainly needed in the Corinthian church (cf. 1 Cor 5–6). In his first article Martin

As Stuckenbruck has observed, the sexual nature of Paul's teaching in 1 Corinthians 11:2–16 is an echo of the sin of the watchers in 1 Enoch, the well-known Second Temple Jewish retelling of the violation of the cosmic order in Genesis 6:1–4.[26] Stuckenbruck has analyzed and critiqued the three primary scholarly proposals for understanding 1 Corinthians 11:2–16 in considerable detail. After demonstrating the deficiencies of these approaches, Stuckenbruck marshals a number of primary sources in his defense of a connection between the passage and Genesis 6:1–4 and 1 Enoch's watcher story. He writes:

> Although the wearing of head coverings among men in antiquity was not uncommon, the practice among women carried with it strong sexual connotations. Apparel was, of course, one way of marking the differences—or, better, boundaries—between the sexes, that is, to keep gender categories distinct. ... The notion in Graeco-Roman

---

explained: "Ancient medical conceptions confirm this association. Hippocratic authors hold that hair is hollow and grows primarily from either male or female reproductive fluid or semen flowing into it and congealing (Hippocrates, *Nat. puer.* 20). Since hollow body parts create a vacuum and attract fluid, hair attracts semen. ... Hair grows most prolifically from the head because the brain is the place where the semen is (78) produced or at least stored (Hippocrates, *Genit.* I). Hair grows only on the head of prepubescent humans because semen is stored in the brain and the channels of the body have not yet become large enough for reproductive fluid to travel throughout the body (Hippocrates, *Nat. puer.* 20; *Genit.* 2). At puberty, secondary hair growth in the pubic area marks the movement of reproductive fluid from the brain to the rest of the body (Hippocrates, *Nat. puer.* 20; *Genit.* I). Women have less body hair not only because they have less semen but also because their colder bodies do not froth the semen throughout their bodies but reduce semen evaporation at the ends of their hair (Hippocrates, *Nat. puer.* 20). ... According to these medical authors, men have more hair because they have more semen and their hotter bodies froth this semen more readily throughout their whole bodies (Hippocrates, *Nat. puer.* 20). The nature (Greek: *phusis*) of men is to release or eject the semen. ... . A man with long hair retains much or all of his semen, and his long hollow hair draws the semen toward his head area but away from his genital area, where it should be ejected. Therefore, 1 Cor 11:14 correctly states that it is a shame for a man to have long hair since the male nature (*phusis*) is to eject rather than retain semen. In contrast, the nature (*phusis*) of women is to draw up the semen and congeal (79) it into a fetus (Hippocrates, *Genit.* 5; *Nat. puer.* 12). ... This conception of hair as part of the female genitalia explains the favorite Hippocratic test for sterility in women. A doctor places a scented suppository in a woman's uterus and examines her mouth the next day to see if he can smell the scent of the suppository. If he smells the scent, he diagnoses her as fertile. If he does not smell the scent, he concludes she is sterile because the channels connecting her uterus to her head are blocked. The suction power of her hair cannot draw up the semen through the appropriate channels in her body. The male seed is therefore discharged rather than retained, and the woman cannot conceive" (pp. 78–80).

26. Loren T. Stuckenbruck, "Why Should Women Cover Their Heads Because of Angels?" *Stone-Campbell Journal* 4 (2001): 205–34 (esp. 228–34). Tertullian is an example of an early church leader who made this same connection: "It is on account of the angels, he says, that the woman's head is to be covered, because the angels revolted from God on account of the daughters of men" (*On Prayer* 22.5).

antiquity of female vulnerability and inferiority, assumed in many Jewish sources, and the attendant practice of prophylactic head covering fit well with the early Jewish mythological interpretations of Gen 6:1–4. With regard to this, NT scholars have customarily focused on the essentially evil character of the angels who "fell" because they were attracted by the beauty of the "human daughters." This would be much in line with the *Book of Watchers* of *1 Enoch* (see chapters 7–8) and the *Book of Giants*. ... [Paul's] reasons for commending head coverings are unable to break away from the deep-seated assumption that women constitute the locus where boundaries between different parts of the cosmos are most likely to be violated. ... Paul's reference to the angels betrays a subtle warning that more than just social relationships between men and women are at stake; ultimately, wearing veils is a matter of maintaining the cosmic order. The head coverings are prophylactic in the sense that they protect this order by helping to draw boundaries between distinct, yet sometimes socially overlapping, spheres more clearly. These boundaries, which have structured the universe since creation, are to be respected. ... The head coverings also function to keep women distinct from the angels who, for the sake of this argument, are considered an essentially different order of creation.[27]

What this means for our purposes is that Paul was worried that angels could fall again. The incident in Genesis 6:1–4 was considered by Second Temple Jewish writers to be the main catalyst to human depravity, and so Paul's concern would be understandable.[28]

---

27. Stuckenbruck, "Why Should Women Cover," 228–30.

28. The main problem stemming from Gen 6:1–4 was not the *Nephilim* for Second Temple Jews. While demons were considered the watcher-spirits, disembodied at the death of *Nephilim*, the primary theological concern deriving from this pre-flood transgression was what the watchers taught humanity leading to human self-destruction and idolatry. The leading scholarship on the watcher story and Gen 6:1–4 as the origin of demons includes: Reed, *Fallen Angels and the History of Judaism and Christianity*; Wright, *The Origin of Evil Spirits*. For the watcher story and Gen 6:1–4 as the leading catalyst of human depravity, see: Amar Annus, "The Antediluvian Origin of Evil in the Mesopotamian and Jewish Traditions A Comparative Study," in *Ideas of Man in the Conceptions of the Religions*, eds. Tarmo Kulmar and Rüdiger Schmitt (Münster: Ugarit-Verlag, 2012); 1–43; Miryam Brand, *Evil Within and Without: The Source of Sin and Its Nature as Portrayed in Second Temple Literature* (Göttingen: Vandenhoeck & Ruprecht, 2013); Loren T. Stuckenbruck, "The Origins of Evil in Jewish Apocalyptic Tradition: The Interpretation of Genesis 6:1–4 in the Second and Third Centuries B.C.E.," in *The Fall of the Angels*, eds. Christoff Auffarth and Loren T. Stuckenbruck (Leiden: Brill, 2004), 86–118.

As fallible beings it is no surprise that angels were not the agents of salvation (Heb 1:4–5). Rather, angels are cast as curious observers of God's plan of salvation, not privy to all its details:

Concerning this salvation, the prophets who prophesied about the grace that was to be yours searched and inquired carefully, inquiring what person or time the Spirit of Christ in them was indicating when he predicted the sufferings of Christ and the subsequent glories. It was revealed to them that they were serving not themselves but you, in the things that have now been announced to you through those who preached the good news to you by the Holy Spirit sent from heaven, things into which angels long to look. (1 Pet 1:10–12)

The passage reminds us that a divine nature does not translate to omniscience. Like humans, angels are imagers of God and therefore share his attributes, but neither possess them fully or have God's perfect nature.[29] We can clearly discern that angels are intelligent beings, both in their obedient service and self-willed rebellion. They are also emotional beings, as they "rejoice when sinners believe" (Luke 15:10; Heb 12:22).

Loyal angels are aware of their lesser status in this regard, and so they refuse the worship of humans in the New Testament:

---

29. I discuss this at length in *The Unseen Realm*, 39–43. Based on several points of Hebrew grammar and syntax, the image of God should not be understood as a quality or attribute. Rather, it refers to representational status. We don't possess a thing called the image; we *are* the image of God. We are therefore imagers of God. The plural language in Gen 1:26–27 ("let *us* create humankind in/as *our* image") signifies that the members of the heavenly host are also created imagers of God, representing him in the spiritual world like humans do on earth. Sharing God's attributes enable that representation (imaging). As I wrote in *The Unseen Realm* (p. 39): "Many Bible readers note the *plural* pronouns (*us; our*) with curiosity. They might suggest that the plurals refer to the Trinity, but technical research in Hebrew grammar and exegesis has shown that the Trinity is not a coherent explanation. The solution is much more straightforward, one that an ancient Israelite would have readily discerned. What we have is a single person (God) addressing a group—the members of his divine council." Elsewhere in *The Unseen Realm* I establish the idea of a Godhead is indeed present in the Old Testament, but not in Gen 1:26. Theologically, if the three persons of the Godhead are co-eternal and co-omniscient, there would be no need for God to inform the other persons of his decision to create humankind. They would already know and would have been part of the decision. The most exhaustive scholarly treatment of the plural language in Gen 1:26 is W. Randall Garr, *In His Own Image and Likeness: Humanity, Divinity, and Monotheism* (Leiden: Brill, 2003). See especially pp. 17–94. The answer to the plurality language is also *not* the so-called "plural of majesty." Joüon and Muraoka note that for verbal forms, "The we of majesty does not exist in Hebrew" (see *GBH*, 347 [§114e]). The plural of majesty does exist for nouns (see *GBH* §136d), but Gen 1:26 is not about the nouns—the issue is the verbal forms. See also Beckman, "*Pluralis Majestatis*: Biblical Hebrew."

Then I fell down at his feet to worship him, but he said to me, "You must not do that! I am a fellow servant with you and your brothers who hold to the testimony of Jesus. Worship God." For the testimony of Jesus is the spirit of prophecy. (Rev 19:10)

I, John, am the one who heard and saw these things. And when I heard and saw them, I fell down to worship at the feet of the angel who showed them to me, but he said to me, "You must not do that! I am a fellow servant with you and your brothers the prophets, and with those who keep the words of this book. Worship God." (Rev 22:8–9)

Scholars have noted that this New Testament idea is not unique:

In addition to the passages in Revelation, the motif of an angel refusing worship by a seer in a visionary encounter is preserved in the Second Temple period, in a number of Jewish, Jewish-Christian, and Christian writings. These are presently listed (with the names of the angelic figures in parentheses):

Tobit 12:16–22 (Raphael)

Apocalypse of Zephaniah 6:11–15 (Eremiel)

Ascension of Isaiah 7:2 (a glorious angel); 7:18–23 (one seated on a throne?): 8:1–10, 15

2 Enoch 1:4–8 (two huge men)

3 Enoch 1:7 (princes of the chariot); 16:1–5 (Metatron)

Cairo Genizah fragment "T.-S. K21.95.C" (Zehobadyah/youth/Metatron)[30]

Apocryphal Gospel of Matthew 3:3 (an angel of God)[31]

Not only do angels refuse worship, but in concert with the greatest commandment (Exod 20:3), humans are not to worship them. Their divine status does not entitle them to worship due only to the Most High

---

30. Beale designates this text as *Cairo Genizah Hekhalot A/2*, 13–18 (G. K. Beale, *The Book of Revelation: A Commentary on the Greek Text*, NIGTC [Grand Rapids: Eerdmans, 1999], 946).

31. Loren T. Stuckenbruck, "An Angelic Refusal of Worship: The Tradition and Its Function in the Apocalypse of John," in *Society of Biblical Literature 1994 Seminar Papers*, ed. Eugene H. Lovering Jr. (Atlanta: Scholars Press, 1995), 679–96 (esp. 680–81). Some Christian traditions (Roman Catholicism and the Orthodox Church) distinguish worship from veneration (adoration) and permit the latter practice with respect to angels.

God. Paul encountered some sort of angelic worship at Colossae and addressed it in Colossians 2:18–23:

> Let no one disqualify you, insisting on asceticism and worship of angels, going on in detail about visions, puffed up without reason by his sensuous mind, and not holding fast to the Head, from whom the whole body, nourished and knit together through its joints and ligaments, grows with a growth that is from God. If with Christ you died to the elemental spirits of the world, why, as if you were still alive in the world, do you submit to regulations— "Do not handle, Do not taste, Do not touch" (referring to things that all perish as they are used)—according to human precepts and teachings? These have indeed an appearance of wisdom in promoting self-made religion and asceticism and severity to the body, but they are of no value in stopping the indulgence of the flesh.

The phrase translated "worship of angels" (*thrēskeia tōn angelōn*) has generated some disagreement among scholars. Does the phrase describe worship *given* to angels (i.e., they are the object) or *participation* with angels in their worship? One scholar summarizes the options this way:

> The phrase has normally been taken (with the genitive being regarded as objective) to denote "the worship directed to the angels. ... This statement concerning angel-worship seems to go beyond speculation about angels present in the Jewish schools and denotes an actual cult of angels. The principalities and powers might have been in view but Paul here refers to angels as a class. ... There is little evidence for the worship of angels among the Jews. ... [A]nd so it is argued that the expression is evidence of the syncretistic character of the "philosophy" at Colossae. It was Jewish mixed with pagan elements. The angels determined the course of the cosmos and with it man's circumstances. Men submitted to the angels in the cult by performing the prescribed acts and by fulfilling the regulations laid down. ...
>
> Francis, on the other hand, has argued that the phrase (taking the genitive as subjective) denotes "the worship which the angels perform." Using a wide range of sources representing what he terms ascetic-mystic piety Francis drew attention to the many descriptions of angelic worship. ... Participation in the angelic worship is detailed

in several sources: so Isaiah participates in the worship of the fifth, sixth and seventh heavens (*Asc Isa* 7:37; 8:17; 9:28, 31, 33), while the daughters of Job praise and glorify God in an angelic tongue (*Test Job* 48–50). Frequently the Qumran literature refers to the members of the community as priests who offered sacrifice (= the Qumran way of life) not only before Yahweh but also *in communion with the* angels (cf. 1QSb 4:25, 26; 1QH 3:20–22). … Accordingly, the false teachers claimed to have joined in the angelic worship of God as they entered into the heavenly realm and prepared to receive visions of divine mysteries.[32]

No matter the alternative, Paul's warning is comprehensible. Angels are neither the correct object of worship, nor is the worship of God defined by religious performance. Paul was clear that spiritual worship was about the heart—sacrificially presenting one's life to Christ, not being conformed to the world, but being transformed by a renewed mind or heart (Rom 12:1–2).

Angels will actually be in a subservient status to glorified believers in the eschaton. The writer of Hebrews notes, "it was not to angels that God subjected the world to come," a thought that is to be framed by Paul's exhortation declaring that believers will "judge angels" (1 Cor 6:3). Paul is referencing the fact that the fallen spiritual beings who presently rule the nations will be replaced by believers.[33] The point is made twice in the book of Revelation:

The one who conquers and who keeps my works until the end, to him I will give authority over the nations, and he will rule them with a rod of iron, as when earthen pots are broken in pieces, even as I myself have received authority from my Father. And I will give him the morning star. (Rev 2:26–28)

---

32. Peter T. O'Brien, *Colossians, Philemon*, WBC 44 (Dallas: Word, 1982), 142–43. See also A. L. Williams, "The Cult of Angels at Colossae," *JTS* 10 (1909): 413–38. Scholarship on the symbiosis of human and angelic worship in Second Temple Judaism includes: Carol A. Newsom, "He Has Established for Himself Priests," 101–20; Devorah Dimant, "Men as Angels: The Self-Image of the Qumran Community," in *Religion and Politics in the Ancient Near East*, ed. A. Berlin (Bethesda, MD: University of Maryland Press, 1996), 93–103; F. O. Francis, "Humility and Angelic Worship in Col 2:18," in *Conflict at Colossae*, eds. F. O. Francis and W. A. Meeks, 2nd ed. (Missoula, MT: Scholar's Press, 1975), 163–95.

33. See Heiser, *The Unseen Realm*, 309–13.

Behold, I stand at the door and knock. If anyone hears my voice and opens the door, I will come in to him and eat with him, and he with me. The one who conquers, I will grant him to sit with me on my throne, as I also conquered and sat down with my Father on his throne. (Rev 3:20–21)

The point of these passages is that we share the rule of the nations with Christ as his family members. Numbers 24:17 says, "a star shall come out of Jacob, and a scepter will rise out of Israel." That text was considered messianic in Second Temple Judaism. While its royal nature is obvious ("a scepter will rise") we need to remember that divine beings are referred to as stars (Job 38:7).

The morning star language in Revelation makes complete sense in conveying the rule of a divine messiah. The idea is even more explicit in Revelation 22:16: "I am the root and the descendant of David, the bright morning star" (Rev 22:16). Incredibly, John has Jesus refer to his followers the same way in Revelation 2:28: "I will give him [who overcomes] the morning star." Believers have the authority to rule with Christ.

## NEW TESTAMENT ANGELOLOGY:
## Service in Heaven and on Earth

As noted earlier, the term "angel" (*angelos*; "messenger") is nearly always reserved for God's loyal emissaries in the New Testament. The objects of their service are *both* God and human believers. Angels serve God in heaven in roles of praise, council judgment, and enacting God's decrees. On earth they assist believers (and, perhaps less obviously, Jesus), a role that takes various forms, and are God's agents of judgment upon unbelievers.

Scenes of angelic interaction with people are likely more familiar to us. Consequently, we'll begin with a human focus for angelic service.

### 1. Ministry on Behalf of Believers

Descriptions of angelic activity on earth are more numerous in the New Testament than scenes of heavenly service. An earthly focus occupies roughly three-quarters of the approximately 180 references to angels in the New Testament. This frequency should not be surprising, as it is God's will that his heavenly agents serve his human family.

Instead of being objects of worship or adoration, angels are cast in the New Testament as "ministering spirits sent out to serve for the sake of those who are to inherit salvation" (Heb 1:14). Angels are portrayed rendering their service in a variety of ways. They delivered apostles from prison (Acts 5:18–21; 12:7–11). One comforted Paul when his life was threatened (Acts 27:23). Angels brought messages to people in dreams (Joseph: Matt 1.20–24; 2:13, 19) and visions (Mary, the mother of Jesus: Luke 1:26–38; Zechariah: Luke 1:8–23; Cornelius: Acts 10:3–7, 22 [cf. Acts 11:13]; Mary Magdalene and "the other Mary" at the empty tomb: Matt 28:1–7 [cf. Luke 24:23]; John 20:12–13; cf. 1 Tim 3:16). Angels appeared in the heavens to the shepherds to announce the birth of Jesus (Luke 2:9, 10).

Angels could also encounter humans physically. An angel struck Peter on the side to awaken him in prison and supernaturally freed him from his shackles (Acts 12:7). The apostle nevertheless presumed he was experiencing a vision until he found himself outside the jail alone on the street (Acts 12:7–11). The circumstance of an angel of the Lord appearing to Philip (Acts 8:26) is not qualified as a vision, and so a physical appearance is a possible reading of that encounter. Angels ministered to Jesus after he resisted the devil in the wilderness (Matt 4:11; Mark 1:13). An angel rolled back the stone covering the tomb of Jesus and subsequently used it for a seat (Matt 28:2).

These instances are all consistent with portrayals of angels in the Old Testament. It is not surprising, in view of this earlier revelation, that the New Testament has Jewish characters expressing the belief that angels could appear and speak to people (John 12:29; Acts 23:9). As the writer of Hebrews notes, an angel's true identity in such an encounter could be completely imperceptible: "Do not neglect to show hospitality to strangers, for thereby some have entertained angels unawares" (Heb 13:2). The implication is that angels could not be distinguished from ordinary men. The writer is apparently thinking of Old Testament episodes such as Genesis 18–19.[34] However, explicit references to angels as men are rare in the

---

34. There is no indication that Lot knew the men he saw in Sodom were more than ordinary men, though the reader knows they are angels (Gen 19:1). Only when the two visitors blinded the threatening mob did it become apparent that the two were more than men (Gen 19:9–14).

New Testament (Luke 24:4 [cf. John 20:12]); Acts 1:10; 10:30), and when they do occur, the "men" wear dazzling, luminous robes, suggesting they were extraordinary.[35]

One of the more pronounced ministries to people in which angels engage is that of interpreting visions or divine decrees. We saw earlier that this thematic portrayal (the "interpreting angel" motif) occurred in Old Testament apocalyptic literature.[36] The same is true of apocalyptic literature in the New Testament, particularly the book of Revelation, where angels regularly interpret the visions seen by John (1:1; 4:1; 10:7–10; 17:1, 17; 21:9, 10; 22:1, 6, 8). As one specialist of this motif notes:

> The book of Revelation is the archetype of the apocalyptic genre, and as such it largely conforms to the norms of the type. It presents itself as a revelation (ἀποκαλυψη, *apokalypsē*) given through the mediation of heavenly beings.[37]

Angels are also described in an advocacy role, popularly referred to as "guardian angels."[38] Earlier we saw that the Old Testament referred to holy ones as "mediators," a role that involved explaining divine decisions and functioning as witness on behalf of the innocent in their suffering. The New Testament contains hints of this same idea, though it is clear that believers no longer need an advocate mediator, because Jesus himself now intercedes for us before God (1 Tim 2:5).

Matthew 18:10 reads, "See that you do not despise one of these little ones. For I tell you that in heaven their angels always see the face of my Father who is in heaven." This statement of course precedes the high

---

35. Luke 2:9, 13 deserve mention here, even though the angel (and later a host of angels) who appeared to the shepherds at the birth of Jesus are not referred to as men. The luminous appearance is present in Luke 2:9 (and presumably v. 13), alerting the shepherds to a divine presence. The dazzling white robe description is also applied to Jesus at the transfiguration (Mark 9:3). When accompanied with luminosity, the white robes apparently signify divine presence. On its own (John 20:12; Acts 1:10) white robes could conceivably be a striking enough contrast with the earthy, invariably soiled attire of humans to telegraph divinity, or perhaps it denotes purity.

36. See chapter 2. Other than explicit conversations where angels interpret divine messaging or visions, recall that the New Testament associates angels with the dispensing of the law at Sinai, which certainly qualifies as revelation from God (Acts 7:53; Gal 3:19; Heb 2:2).

37. David P. Melvin, "Revelation," *LBD*. Aune (*Revelation 1–5*, WBC 52A [Dallas: Word, 1997], 12) makes the matter more textually specific: "The term δείχνυναι [*deiknunai*; "to show"] occurs eight times in Revelation, and in all instances but this one the subject of the verb is the *angelus interpres*, "interpreting angel" (1:1; 4:1; 17:1; 21:9, 10; 22:1, 6, 8)." See also Rev 10:7–10; 17:7.

38. This role may be the point of Rev 1–3, where angels are seemingly assigned to churches. See chapter 7.

priestly work of Christ and draws on Old Testament concepts of angelic mediation. Barrett notes, "Judaism believed in protecting and guiding angels."[39] Pseudo-Philo (Liber antiquitatum biblicarum 59.4) and the Testament of Jacob (1:10) draw on Psalm 91:11–12 (cf. Luke 4:10) to express the guardianship of angels. In the book of Tobit, when Tobit and his wife send their son on a journey, he tells her:

> Do not worry; our child will leave in good health and return to us in good health. Your eyes will see him on the day when he returns to you in good health. Say no more! Do not fear for them, my sister. For a good angel will accompany him; his journey will be successful, and he will come back in good health. (Tobit 5:21–22 NRSV)

Acts 12 apparently has some aspect of angelic oversight in view. After an angel freed Peter from prison, Peter went "to the house of Mary, the mother of John whose other name was Mark, where many were gathered together and were praying" (Acts 12:12). A servant girl named Rhoda responded to his knock recognized his voice but, in her excitement at hearing Peter, ran to tell those gathered instead of letting him inside. Despite their prayers, they didn't believe her report, replying, "It is his angel!" Peter kept knocking and was finally welcome (12:15–16). The believers gathered that night believed that Peter had a personal angel.

The idea of guardian angels apparently includes protection, as angels did rescue people, but angelic "oversight" in the human sphere also includes keeping track of evil perpetrated on the innocent for later

---

39. C. K. Barrett, *A Critical and Exegetical Commentary on the Acts of the Apostles*, ICC (Edinburgh: T&T Clark, 2004), 585. Barrett also suggests that Jews also believed these guardian angels "were sometimes thought to resemble the human beings they protected." He cites Gen 48:16; Tobit 5:4–6, 21; Matt 18:10; and Hermas, *Vision* 5:7 as examples, along with Hermann L. Strack and Paul Billerbeck, *Kommentar zum Neuen Testament aus Talmud und Midrasch: Die Briefe des Neuen Testaments und die Offenbarung Johannis: erl. aus Talmud u. Midrasch/von Paul Billerbeck* (München: C. H Beck, 1922–1961), 1:781–83; 2:707. None of these passages say anything about the angel looking like the person being guarded. Tobit 5:4–6, 20–21 and Hermas 5:1–2 certainly do affirm the notion of guardian angels, but Hermas post-dates the New Testament. Strack and Paul Billerbeck also note the later rabbinic example (Genesis Rabbah 78 [50a] on Gen 33:10) where the personal angel looks like the person he protects. This is actually a more relevant example but also post-dates the biblical material. The notion that one's guardian angel looked like the person with whom they are charged by God might derive from Acts 12:12–16, though that passage doesn't actually affirm it. A careful reading of that passage reveals that Rhoda didn't actually see Peter before she rushed to tell the others that he was at the door. She bases her identification solely on the familiarity of his voice. Readers would have to presume that others gathered *assumed* that the girl had seen a face before proclaiming, "It is his angel!" But that reads details into the passage.

judgment or a record of those who will inherit eternal life. Recall that the "books in heaven" concept was associated with the divine council in the ancient Near East. Jesus says specifically of believers in Revelation 3:5 that "I will confess his name before my Father and before his angels." The reference to angels speaks of both "council validation" of those who belong to Christ (see below), but also of angelic witness to such a verdict. Elsewhere in the book of Revelation, this "confession" (or rejection) has to do with the "book of life" (Rev 13:8; 17:8; 20:12, 15; 21:27). In Luke 10:20 Jesus told the seventy disciples, "do not rejoice in this, that the spirits are subject to you, but rejoice that your names are written in heaven." Other believers are recorded in the "book of life" (Phil 4:3). This may be the context for a verse like Luke 16:22, where, upon death, the poor man was carried by angels to the afterlife comfort of "Abraham's side." Given that some of these passages in Revelation are naturally associated with the apocalyptic eschaton, it is relevant to note that angels are also tasked with gathering the elect—those found in the book of life—at such time (Matt 13:39; 24:31; Mark 13:27).

## 2. Judgment of Unbelievers

That the New Testament portrays angels as agents of divine judgment should be no surprise. As we have seen, both the Old Testament and Second Temple Judaism describe God as having angel armies to punish the wicked. We saw that most of these portrayals were eschatological, but not all. This is true of the New Testament as well. The only exception is the judgment of Herod, whose ignominious end is described in Acts 12:21–23:

> On an appointed day Herod put on his royal robes, took his seat upon the throne, and delivered an oration to them. And the people were shouting, "The voice of a god, and not of a man!" Immediately an angel of the Lord struck him down, because he did not give God the glory, and he was eaten by worms and breathed his last.

As implied above, the New Testament motif of angelic judgment is nearly always apocalyptic, situated at the time of the end of days, in concert with the day of the Lord or "day of Christ" at his second coming. For example, Jesus told the assembled crowd a parable about weeds in a wheat field (Matt 13:24–30) and then explained its meaning (Matt 13:36–43):

Then he left the crowds and went into the house. And his disciples came to him, saying, "Explain to us the parable of the weeds of the field." He answered, "The one who sows the good seed is the Son of Man. The field is the world, and the good seed is the sons of the kingdom. The weeds are the sons of the evil one, and the enemy who sowed them is the devil. The harvest is the end of the age, and the reapers are angels. Just as the weeds are gathered and burned with fire, so will it be at the end of the age. The Son of Man will send his angels, and they will gather out of his kingdom all causes of sin and all law-breakers, and throw them into the fiery furnace. In that place there will be weeping and gnashing of teeth. Then the righteous will shine like the sun in the kingdom of their Father. He who has ears, let him hear.

The parable of the net set forth the same point. Part of Jesus' explanation was, "The angels will come out and separate the evil from the righteous and throw them into the fiery furnace" (Matt 13:49b–50a). Angels function in the role of destroyers as part of this frightful apocalyptic vision, assaulting the earth and the wicked with plagues, war, famine, disease, and cosmic upheaval at the time of the end (Rev 7:1–2; 8:5–13; 9:1, 13–15; 10:1, 5, 7; 15:1, 6, 7, 8; 16:1, 5; 17:1; 18:1, 21). Amid the judgment angels at times warn the inhabitants of earth and encourage the righteous to endure (Rev 14:6–10).

The reverse situation—gathering the elect—is described in Matthew 13:27. Jesus taught that, at the time of the end, God "will send out the angels and gather his elect from the four winds, from the ends of the earth to the ends of heaven." The synoptic parallel to this passage in Matthew 24:31 adds an element: "And he will send out his angels with a loud trumpet call, and they will gather his elect from the four winds, from one end of heaven to the other." Here the angels gather the elect in conjunction with a loud trumpet call. This description links the motif of angels gathering the elect with other passages dealing with the return of the Lord (1 Thess 4:16–18; cf. 1 Cor 15:52).

Casting a wider net beyond the angelic role of gathering the elect reveals that angels are more generally described as accompanying the Lord at his return: "For the Son of Man is going to come with his angels in the glory of his Father" (Matt 16:27; cf. Matt 25:31; 26:53; Mark 8:38;

Luke 9:26; 2 Thess 1:7). In certain instances the entourage is overtly militaristic; Jesus returns with an angelic army (Matt 26:53; Rev 19:11–16). The portrayal by design draws the attention of the reader to Yahweh's angelic host accompanying him at the day of the Lord (Zech 14:5).

## 3. Service in Heaven

Though it seems obvious that angels would be engaged in praising God, specific references to that effect are not common in the New Testament. Earlier we noted the instance in Luke 2:13, where "a multitude of the heavenly host" praised God at the announcement of the birth of messianic child. Angelic worship is noted in passing in Revelation 4–5, a scene which many readers presume is focused on angelic worship of the Lamb. In reality, it is the twenty-four elders, the four living creatures, and glorified human worshippers who fall down before the Lamb.[40] Only in Revelation 5:11–12 (cf. Rev 7:11) do angels enter the picture—and then in a great multitude:

> Then I looked, and I heard around the throne and the living creatures and the elders the voice of many angels, numbering myriads of myriads and thousands of thousands, saying with a loud voice,

> "Worthy is the Lamb who was slain,
> to receive power and wealth and wisdom and might
> and honor and glory and blessing!"

Angels have other responsibilities in heaven besides praising God. The term "archangel" suggests hierarchical rule. That is, certain angels have

---

40. These elements are important given the Second Temple Jewish notion of believing communities imagining their worship being synchronized with the activities in heaven. Scholars refer to this practice and its associated belief as "*merkabah mysticism.*" The term *merkabah* means "throne chariot" and is drawn from visions of God on his throne like Ezekiel 1. The sect at Qumran, for example, separated from the Jerusalem temple over the matter of celestial worship and its associated solar calendar. Since Rev 4–5 draws elements from Ezek 1, scholars consider Rev 4–5 an instance of *merkabah mysticism*. See David J. Halperin, *Faces of the Chariot: Development of Rabbinic Exegesis of Ezekiel's Vision of the Divine Chariot* (Tübingen: Mohr Siebeck, 1988); Ithamar Gruenwald, *Apocalyptic and Merkabah Mysticism* (Leiden: Brill, 2014); Andrei Orlov, "Celestial Choirmaster: The Liturgical Role of Enoch-Metatron in 2 Enoch and the Merkabah Tradition," *JSP* 14.1 (2004): 3–29; Carol A. Newsom, "He Has Established for Himself Priests"; Cameron Afzal, "Wheels of Time: Merkavah Exegesis in Revelation 4," *Society of Biblical Literature Seminar Papers* (Atlanta: Society of Biblical Literature, 1998), 465–82; Rachel Elior, *The Three Temples: On the Emergence of Jewish Mysticism*, trans. David Louvish (Liverpool: Liverpool University Press, 2005).

oversight over other angels. But the two references to archangels we noted earlier (1 Thess 4:16; Jude 9) do not reveal much about that oversight.

More interesting are those passages that cast angels as approving divine decisions, a role akin to the divine council scenes of the Old Testament. Revelation 4–5 is commonly accepted by scholars as a divine council scene. As Aune notes:

> The focus of the throne vision is God enthroned in his heavenly court surrounded by a variety of angelic beings or lesser deities (angels, archangels, seraphim, cherubim) who function as courtiers. All such descriptions of God enthroned in the midst of his heavenly court are based on the ancient conception of the divine council or assembly found in Mesopotamia, Ugarit, and Phoenicia as well as in Israel.[41]

While we clearly have a meeting in heaven involving God and his host, the role of angels operates on the periphery. One angel asks loudly (Rev 5:2): "Who is worthy to open the scroll and break its seals?" and then the multitude joins in the praise (Rev 5:11).

Other passages reveal more of what we've come to expect as council input. Several stand out:

> The one who conquers will be clothed thus in white garments, and I will never blot his name out of the book of life. I will confess his name before my Father and before his angels. (Rev 3:5)

> And I tell you, everyone who acknowledges me before men, the Son of Man also will acknowledge before the angels of God, but the one who denies me before men will be denied before the angels of God. (Rev 12:8–9)

In both passages Jesus presents believers destined for heaven not only to God, but also to the heavenly host. It is not that Jesus or the believer whose name is in the book of life need an administrative stamp of approval from the divine assembly. Rather, the scene is one of introducing a new family member into their heavenly home. The council

---

41. Aune, *Revelation 1–5*, 277. See R. Dean Davis, *The Heavenly Court Scene of Revelation 4–5* (Lanham, MD: University Press of America, 1992); J. M. Baumgarten, "The Duodecimal Courts of Qumran, Revelation, and the Sanhedrin," *JBL* 95.1 (1976): 59–78.

validates or enthusiastically endorses those who are in Christ who have endured in faith to the end.

The most dramatic passage in this regard is Hebrews 2:10–15 (LEB):

> For it was fitting for him for whom are all things and through whom are all things in bringing many sons to glory to perfect the originator of their salvation through sufferings. For both the one who sanctifies and the ones who are sanctified are all from one, for which reason he [Jesus] is not ashamed to call them brothers, saying,

> "I will proclaim your name to my brothers;
> in the midst of the assembly I will sing in praise of you."
> And again,
> "I will trust in him."
> And again,
> "Behold, I and the children God has given me."

> Therefore, since the children share in blood and flesh, he also in like manner shared in these same things, in order that through death he could destroy the one who has the power of death, that is, the devil, and could set free these who through fear of death were subject to slavery throughout all their lives.

Note that Jesus calls believers his siblings "in the midst of the assembly." Because of his incarnation, work on the cross, resurrection and ascension, Jesus brings human believers into the divine family, and the supernatural sons of God of the heavenly host rejoice.

# CHAPTER 7

# Special Topics in
# New Testament Angelology

OUR SURVEY OF TERMINOLOGY FOR THE HEAVENLY HOST AND ANGELIC service provided a starting point for understanding what the New Testament says about angels, but a number of thorny issues in New Testament angelology still require attention.

## WHO ARE THE "ANGELS OF THE SEVEN CHURCHES" IN REVELATION 1–3?

The book of Revelation is the New Testament's most well-known example of apocalyptic literature.[1] A central element of apocalyptic literature is visions involving angels. Revelation opens with John's vision of the son of man (Rev 1:9–20). The awestruck John describes him with these words:

> The hairs of his head were white, like white wool, like snow. His eyes were like a flame of fire, his feet were like burnished bronze, refined in a furnace, and his voice was like the roar of many waters. In his right hand he held seven stars, from his mouth came a sharp two-edged sword, and his face was like the sun shining in full strength. (Rev 1:14–16)

The "son of man" in the vision is the risen, glorified Christ: "he laid his right hand on me, saying, 'Fear not, I am the first and the last, and

---

1. See Adela Yarbro Collins, "The Book of Revelation," in *The Continuum History of Apocalypticism*, eds. Bernard McGinn, John J. Collins, and Stephen Stein (New York: Continuum, 2003), 195–219.

the living one. I died, and behold I am alive forevermore, and I have the keys of Death and Hades'" (Rev 1:17b–18). The "seven stars" in the right hand of Jesus are significant for our discussion. The passage anticipates our question and goes on, "As for the mystery of the seven stars that you saw in my right hand, and the seven golden lampstands, the seven stars are the angels of the seven churches, and the seven lampstands are the seven churches" (Rev 1:20).

How are we to understand these angels? Are they supernatural beings? If so, why pair them with churches? Or perhaps they are human beings, since the term *angelos* simply means "messenger," and New Testament writers (Luke 7:24; 9:52) and the Septuagint (Hag 1:13; Mal 1:1; 3:1 [cf. Matt 11:10; Mark 1:2]; Josh 7:22 [cf. Jas 2:25]) employ the word to speak of mere mortals. Aune introduces the controversy this way:

> The term ἄγγελος [*angelos*] "angel, messenger," occurs seventy-seven times in Revelation in both singular and plural forms. Only eight of these references are problematic, those that refer to "the angels of the seven churches" (1:20) and the seven occurrences of the singular term ἄγγελος as the particular addressee of each of the seven proclamations to the churches (2:1, 8, 12, 18; 3:1, 7, 14). Since most of the sixty-nine occurrences of the term ἄγγελος or ἄγγελοι [*angeloi*] refer to benevolent supernatural beings who serve as mediators and messengers between God and his creation, … Most scholars presume that the eight problematic references must also refer to beneficent supernatural beings.[2]

## 1. Proposed Identifications

Aune does not presume to have answered the question of identity in this comment. The question is not answered so simply. Several interpretive options have emerged out of the vocabulary and grammar of Revelation 1–3. The rationale for each can be succinctly explained.[3]

The dominant approach to the angel terminology in Revelation 1–3 is to view them as supernatural beings. The primary argument for this view is based on Revelation 1:20, which calls the seven angels "the seven stars."

---

2. Aune, *Revelation 1–5*, 108–9.

3. See Aune, *Revelation 1–5*, 110–12, for additional nuancing of the first two viewpoints. Compare Beale, *The Book of Revelation*, 217.

Star language "is used in various texts (primarily Jewish apocalypses) to refer to heavenly representatives of earthly nations."[4] Beale adds:

> The formal interpretation of the "stars" as "angels" of the churches in v 20b would seem to confirm further the suggestion above that the "stars" are drawn from Dan. 12:3, since Michael is seen as the guardian "angel" of Israel in Dan. 12:1 (cf. Dan. 10:21) and is associated directly with the "stars" of 12:3. ... Indeed, Dan. 12:3 probably likens the heavenly status of resurrected Israelites to that of angels since "stars" in Dan. 8:10 refer to angels, as borne out by 8:11; 7:27; and 8:24. ... 1 Enoch 104:2–6 develops Daniel 12:3 in this manner by promising believers who endure tribulation that they "will shine like the lights of heaven ... will have great joy like the angels of heaven ... will become companions of the hosts of heaven."[5]

Some scholars cite the analogy of the sons of God, divine "princes" allotted to the nations (Deut 32:8; Dan 10:20–21; 12:1) in favor of the angels of the churches being heavenly beings. The reasoning goes thus: since "angels" are over nations, they can also be over churches in some supervisory role. The Ascension of Isaiah 3:15–16 is especially interesting in this regard. The passage reflects Christian reworking to make the prophet Isaiah refer specifically to the resurrection of Christ: "And the descent of the angel of the church which is in the heavens, whom he will summon in the last days; and that the angel of the Holy Spirit and Michael, the chief of the holy angels, will open his grave on the third day."[6]

The notable idea for our discussion is that the church ("the church which is in the heavens") is corporately represented by an angel. That an angel (Michael) could represent the human family of God in the Old Testament (Dan 12:1) seems to be the touch point for this unidentified angel representing the body of Christ, the church. The analogy is imprecise with regard to individual churches but provides an interpretive trajectory for viewing the angels of the churches as heavenly beings that represent those churches.

A second approach is to view the angels of the seven churches in Revelation 1–3 as speaking of the human leadership of those churches.

---

4. Aune, *Revelation 1–5*, 110.
5. Beale, *The Book of Revelation*, 218.
6. *OTP*, 2:160.

The specific title (bishop? elder?) is not provided, of course. In view of this omission, some scholars suggest that the "angels" are generic prophetic figures who preach the message given via John's apocalypse to the churches.

The main defense of this viewpoint is that *angelos* is used in both the New Testament and Septuagint for human emissaries.[7] Aune points out that some scholars assert that "since the ἄγγελοι [*angeloi*] of the seven churches are the recipients of letters, it is presupposed that they are on earth, and that they should be understood as humans rather than angels."[8] The weakness of this contention is that angels regularly brought messages to humans on earth—the "angel of a church" need not be "stationed" on earth prior to receiving a message.

A third opinion that has gained little traction in scholarship is to view the seven angels as celestial bodies—specifically, the sun, moon, and the five planets visible in naked-eye astronomy (Mercury, Venus, Mars, Saturn, Jupiter). The textual rationale for this equation is in 1 Enoch 18:13–16 and 21:1–6, which mention seven fallen stars that are actually angels, and 2 Enoch 30:2–3, which names the seven stars created by God in accord with the above listing.

This perspective operates on the assumptions that these passages are to be read alongside each other and that the seven stars in the Enochian material are the same seven stars referred to in Revelation 1:20. There seems to be no basis for this textual marriage other than the number seven. Additionally, the seven stars in 1–2 Enoch are fallen angels, and there is no indication that the angels of Revelation 1–3 are fallen divine beings.

In his defense of this perspective, Wojciechowski cites the same references in 1–2 Enoch and notes (correctly) that the Greek term translated "star" (*astēr*) can include planets. He writes, "It seems therefore probable that the seven stars held by the Son of Man are to be identified with the sun, the moon and the five planets. The whole image represents his full

---

7. See Luke 7:24; 9:52; Jas 2:25 [citing LXX Josh 7:22]; Matt 11:10; Mark 1:2; Luke 7:27 [citing LXX Mal 3:1]; LXX Hag 1:13. Aune (*Revelation 1–5*, 111) cites other examples that he or other scholars incorrectly presume reference humans. For example, he cites Josephus in regard to angels dispensing the law as pointing to humans. This has no Old Testament precedent.

8. Aune, *Revelation 1–5*, 112.

power over the univers [sic]."[9] Unfortunately, the connections Wojciech-owski tries to make between the astrological thought about these celestial bodies and the descriptions of the churches in Revelation 1–3 are strained. This thesis has consequently not garnered much approval.

## 2. Features of the Text as Clues to Identification

Ultimately, the grammar of Revelation 1–3 provides the greatest clarity in showing us how to consider the angels of the churches.[10]

In each of the seven directives given to the churches ("To the angel of the church of X write"), each *church* is addressed with second-person *singular* pronouns. For example, Revelation 2 begins with the directive to the church at Ephesus. The speaker then says, "I know *your* works, *your* toil and *your* patient endurance, and how *you* cannot bear with those who are evil" (Rev 2:2, emphasis mine). In each case of the second person (your, you), the pronoun or verb form is grammatically singular. The point is: while the angel of the church is addressed by the directive, the messages are not for the angel. They are instead for the collective church.[11]

This perspective makes sense; when John was first commanded to write, the intended audience was specifically said to be the seven churches, not the angels (Rev 1:11, "Write what you see in a book and send it to the seven churches"). As Aune notes:

> The message of each proclamation is clearly said to be spoken by the Spirit ταῖς ἐκκλησίαις [tais ekklēsiais], "to the churches" (2:7, 11, 17, 29; 3:6, 13, 22), the addressee of each of the proclamations is the ἄγγελος [angelos] to which that message is directed (2:1, 7, 12, 18; 3:1, 7, 14).[12]

Each directive to each church concludes with the formulaic "He who has an ear, let him hear what the Spirit says to the *churches*" indicates

---

9. Michal Wojciechowski, "Seven Churches and Seven Celestial Bodies (Rev 1:16; Rev 2–3)," *Biblische Notizen* 45 (1988): 48.

10. Aune has marshaled the textual data that must take center stage when thinking about the angels of the churches coherently (Aune, *Revelation 1–5*, 109–12). His comments are summarized in the discussion that follows.

11. Aune points out (*Revelation 1–5*, 110) that the pronoun and verb number usage occasionally shifts to the plural, indicating a specific group within the church is being targeted. See Rev 2:10, 13, 23–25.

12. Aune, *Revelation 1–5*, 109. The quotation continues with Aune opining that the language is "suggesting the equivalency of churches and angels." Elsewhere on the same page Aune uses the phrase "alter ego," and so he is angling for the sort of placeholder relationship described above.

clearly that each message was for the congregation. Though each directive is addressed *to* an angel, its content is *for* the church.[13] The angel of each church is therefore some sort of surrogate. The angels and the churches are not identical, but they are related.

Given the other textual merits of understanding the angels in Revelation 1–3 as supernatural beings, it seems best to understand them as members of the heavenly host assigned to the churches in a surrogacy role.[14] Angelic mediation of God's will and word to believers—which involved both praise and admonition, as we saw in the Old Testament—seems to be operative in this relationship.

## CAN "FALLEN ANGELS" BE REDEEMED?

This question does not receive much attention in scholarship. The reason is, as we shall see, largely because Hebrews 2:14–18 seems to make the answer obvious.

The argument for the notion that fallen angels can be redeemed is articulated along two trajectories: (1) language in Revelation 1–3 directed toward the angels of the churches that includes calls for repentance, and (2) Colossians 1:19–20 ("For in him all the fullness of God was pleased to dwell, and through him to reconcile to himself all things, whether on earth or in heaven, making peace by the blood of his cross"). We will consider and evaluate both in turn.

We must not overlook the intended audience of the messaging of the risen Christ: the human membership of each respective congregation. It

---

13. Aune adds (p. 109) several interesting details that solidify this perspective: "The fact that the first occurrence of ἄγγελοι in 1:20 is anarthrous indicates that the author did not assume that his audience was familiar with these figures (e.g., they cannot be identical with the seven archangels of 8:2 or the seven bowl angels of 15:6). ... There is no indication that these ἄγγελοι are present in heaven. ... The phenomenon of addressing a group as if it were an individual and using second person singular verb forms and pronouns is a widespread literary phenomenon (address to the daughter of Zion in Zeph 3:14–20; speech to Tyre in Ezek 27), though in Hos 9:16; 14:1–3, Israel is initially addressed in singular pronouns and verb forms, which then switch to plural forms. In early Christian epistolary literature, which is usually addressed to particular churches, the verbs and pronouns are always second person plural in form (this also occurs in prophetic speeches, e.g., Zeph 2:1–5)."

14. See also G. R. Beasley-Murray, *Revelation* (rev. ed.; New Century Bible; London: Marshall, Morgan & Scott, 1978), 68–70; W. J. Harrington, *Understanding the Apocalypse* (Washington, D.C.: Corpus Books, 1969), 80–81; Beale (*The Book of Revelation*, 217) adds that "angelic beings are corporately identified with Christians as their heavenly counterparts elsewhere in the book."

is significant for discussing the first argument for angelic redemption. By way of example, consider the following examples from Revelation 2:

> To the angel of the church in Ephesus write: "The words of him who holds the seven stars in his right hand, who walks among the seven golden lampstands. ... Remember therefore from where you have fallen; repent, and do the works you did at first. If not, I will come to you and remove your lampstand from its place, unless you repent." (Rev 2:1, 5)

> And to the angel of the church in Smyrna write: "The words of the first and the last, who died and came to life. ... Be faithful unto death, and I will give you the crown of life." (Rev 2:8, 10)

> And to the angel of the church in Pergamum write: "The words of him who has the sharp two-edged sword. ... Therefore repent. If not, I will come to you soon and war against them with the sword of my mouth." (Rev 2:12, 16)

It is noteworthy that each of these instances contains the same statement that makes it clear that the intended audience of these calls for repentance is the church, not the angel through whom the message is mediated. Each passage ends with the statement, "He who has an ear, let him hear what the Spirit says to the churches" (Rev 2:7, 11, 17).

The text makes it clear that the risen Christ is speaking to the congregations, composed as they are of human believers. The angel is not the church; the angel is a communicative surrogate for the church. Consequently, the angel is not the target audience for the calls to repent. Moreover, there is no indication that the angel surrogates are fallen and estranged from God. Rather, in concert with the model of Michael, Israel's patron angel, we have every reason to believe these angels are faithful members of the heavenly host. The language of Revelation 1–3 does not support the idea that fallen angels can be redeemed.

## ARE FALLEN ANGELS INCLUDED IN RECONCILING "ALL THINGS"?

While Revelation 1–3 does not confirm that fallen angels are offered redemption, Colossians 1:19–20 has been utilized to justify that idea:

For in him [Jesus] all the fullness of God was pleased to dwell, and through him to reconcile to himself (*eis auton*) all things, whether on earth or in heaven, making peace by the blood of his cross.

Most scholars would acknowledge that "all things, whether on earth or in heaven," includes the heavenly host.[15] In light of that assumption, the issue that requires consideration is the meaning of "reconcile" and "making peace" through the cross. Most readers presume that this language refers to the forgiveness of sins, but that is not the case. The idea of reconciliation is multifaceted. For example, the work of Christ is connected to the renewal of creation. That has nothing to do with forgiving sins. Creation did not sin—it committed no moral offense against God. Its "reconciliation" (creation is, of course, included in "all things") means something different than forgiveness of sins. O'Brien introduces his discussion of the passage with some salient observations:

> The unusual feature of this passage is that it refers to the reconciliation of "all things" (τὰ πάντα; *ta panta*) and that as a *past* event. Although 2 Corinthians 5:19 (cf. John 3:16 and similar passages) speaks of the reconciliation of the world (κόσμος; *kosmos*), it is clear that it is the world of men which is in view. Further, it is argued that the freeing of creation from its bondage to decay so that it obtains the glorious liberty of the children of God (Rom 8:19–21) is a *future* eschatological event. Three related questions, therefore, arise: (a) What is the meaning of the phrase "to reconcile all things to him" … (b) What is the relationship of this expression to the words which follow, "having made peace through the blood of his cross" … (c) Is it possible or even desirable to equate verse 20 with the notion of God's leading the evil powers in his triumphal procession at chapter 2:15?[16]

Two points are especially crucial for accurate parsing of this question about angelic redemption. First, the reconciliation of which Colossians 1:20 speaks is a *past* event. Many who presume the passage is about the offer of salvation now being open to angels fail to grasp this point, as it derives from Greek grammar and syntax. One scholar explains:

---

15. This assent is not universal. See the extended discussion of other perspectives in O'Brien, *Colossians, Philemon*, 53–57.

16. O'Brien, *Colossians, Philemon*, 53–54.

*Eis auton* (to him) here does not indicate the completion of "imminent" reconciliation, and thus does not indicate a futuristic occurrence. The expression, which is construed in the aorist tense, "all things are reconciled *with him*," is to be interpreted as a parallel construction to the expression in stanza 1 [Col 1:16], "all things were created in him," and its special significance derives from there. It signifies, as the use of the aorist shows, the fulfillment of the corresponding expression in 1:16. Accordingly, reconciliation has its foundation in the creation and is now arriving at its completion in the dominion of the Son over all things.[17]

The point is that the statements in Colossians 1:16 ("for by him all things were created, in heaven and on earth, visible and invisible") must be understood in tandem with Colossians 1:20 ("through him to reconcile to himself all things, whether on earth or in heaven"). Both statements are in the same paragraph unit, and both verbs are aorist tense, the Greek tense which focuses on completed action—not action in process, or action yet unaccomplished.[18] Therefore, the reconciliation of Colossians 1:20 (which still needs to be defined) is rooted in creation, and now, after the cross, it is moving toward its consummation, which itself is expressed as the dominion of the Son over all things.

The link connecting the reconciliation language of Colossians 1:20 (and the original creation order of Col 1:16) to the kingship of the Son derives from Colossians 2:15, as noted above by O'Brien. The basis for its relevance in understanding Colossians 1:20 is that it also references supernatural powers—spirit beings "in heaven" that were created by the Son (Col 1:16) and which now have been reconciled to him through the cross. We will include the wider context here:

And you, who were dead in your trespasses and the uncircumcision of your flesh, God made alive together with him, having forgiven us

---

17. Markus Barth and Helmut Blanke, *Colossians*, trans. Astrid B. Beck, AYB 34B (New Haven: Yale University Press, 1994), 215.

18. Citing Fanning's work on verbal aspect, Wallace describes the point of the aorist: "The aorist tense 'presents an occurrence in summary, viewed as a whole from the outside, without regard for the internal make-up of the occurrence.'" See Wallace, *Greek Grammar Beyond the Basics*, 554. Citing Porter (positively), Runge says of the aorist tense: "The aorist conveys 'perfective' aspect, portraying the action as 'a complete and undifferentiated process.'" See Steven E. Runge, *Discourse Grammar of the Greek New Testament: A Practical Introduction for Teaching and Exegesis* (Bellingham, WA: Lexham Press, 2010), 129.

all our trespasses, by canceling the record of debt that stood against us with its legal demands. This he set aside, nailing it to the cross. He disarmed the rulers and authorities and put them to open shame, by triumphing over them in him. (Col 2:13–15)

Note first that the cross does result in the offer of redemption *for humanity*. But for supernatural rulers and powers—the supernatural forces arrayed against God due to their rebellion—there is no resulting offer of redemption. Instead, the cross brings their defeat and shame.

Connecting Colossians 1:20 with 1:16 and 2:15 shows us that "reconciliation" does not mean an offer of forgiveness that is still on the table. It means something else. Like in Colossians 1:16, 20, all the verb forms in Colossians 2:15 are aorist and therefore describe a real condition that is completed. The "reconciliation" that is being described in Colossians 1:20 must be defined as an already-completed reality that is consistent with both original creation order and the kingship of the risen Christ.

Of the various suggestions made by scholars for understanding the meaning of reconciliation in Colossians 1:20, only one both acknowledges that supernatural beings must be included and remains true to the verse's relationship to Colossians 1:16; 2:15.[19] Eduard Lohse articulates the meaning of reconciliation in concert with these contexts:

Although there has been no previous mention of it, it is presupposed here that unity and harmony of the cosmos have suffered a considerable disturbance, even a rupture. In order to restore the cosmic order reconciliation became necessary and was accomplished by the Christ-event. Through Christ, God himself achieved this reconciling. The universe has been reconciled in that heaven and earth have been brought back into their divinely created and determined order through the resurrection and exaltation of Christ. Now the universe is again under its head and thereby cosmic peace has returned. This peace which God has established through Christ binds the whole universe together again into unity and underlines that the restored creation is reconciled with God. Contrary to apocalyptic expectations,

---

19. As O'Brien's survey of scholarship on the issue makes clear, many scholars try to make the passage speak only of humans or angels, but not both (O'Brien, *Colossians, Philemon*, 54–57). The clarity of "all things in heaven and earth" would seem to rule this out, but those efforts are nevertheless made.

peace is not something which will come only at the end of time; rather, it has already appeared in all things and the cosmic work of redemption has been done (cf. Phil. 2:10f.). As the one who reconciled the cosmos, Christ has entered his kingly rule. Because he is the mediator of reconciliation, he is therefore also praised as the mediator of creation, as Lord over the universe, over powers and principalities.[20]

The point is that reconciling "all things, whether on earth or in heaven" in Colossians 1:20 refers to the restoration of creation order and authority. As O'Brien observes:

Heaven and earth have been returned to their divinely created and determined order and this has occurred through the resurrection and exaltation of Christ. The universe is again under its head, and cosmic peace—a peace which according to some apocalyptic expectations would only occur at the end time—has returned. ... The principalities are stripped of their power (cf. 2:14, 15) and the reconciliation of all things has taken place. ... Victory over these powers, presumed to be hostile toward God or Christ, does not mean they are done away with or finally destroyed. It is evident that they continue to exist, inimical to man and his interests (cf. Rom 8:38, 39). Nevertheless they cannot finally harm the person who is in Christ, and their ultimate overthrow in the future is assured (1 Cor 15:24–28; see on Col 2:15).[21]

In Colossians 1:20, "reconciliation" means the return to creation order and the re-installment of Christ to his position of rulership at the right hand of God (Acts 7:55–56; Eph 1:20; Col 3:1; Heb 1:3, 13; 1 Pet 3:22; Rev 5:1) after his incarnation, death, resurrection, and ascension. An offer of salvation to angels is not in view. Instead, the aberration of their dominion over the affairs of men is corrected. Their authority is now illegitimate.[22] Of course, they will not willingly surrender power, and so that

---

20. Eduard Lohse, *Colossians and Philemon,* Hermeneia (Philadelphia: Fortress Press, 1971), 59–60.

21. O'Brien, *Colossians, Philemon,* 54, 56.

22. After the fall Satan had "legal" claim over the souls of humankind. Estranged from God, humans are captive to death and its lord, the devil (Heb 2:14). The gods of the nations had been appointed by Yahweh as a punishment (Deut 32:8–9; cf. Deut 4:19–20; 17:1–3; 29:23–26). Their authority was legitimate, though their abuse of it was not (Ps 82), nor was their seduction of Israel (Deut 32:17). The cross rectifies both situations. The penalty for sin is paid; death is overcome. Those who believe will have everlasting life. The nations under dominion are no longer to be kept at a distance. They are welcomed back to the family of God through the messiah-seed of Abraham (Gal

must be—and will be—taken from them. Humans still estranged from God are thus deceived and enslaved by powers unauthorized by the true king. That is the point of the Great Commission—setting captives free.

## ARE ANGELS DENIED REDEMPTION?

The supremacy of Christ over angels is the central theme in the first two chapters of the book of Hebrews. Hebrews 1:13–14 establishes that point: "And to which of the angels has he ever said, 'Sit at my right hand until I make your enemies a footstool for your feet'? Are they not all ministering spirits sent out to serve for the sake of those who are to inherit salvation?"

Note the wording of verse 14 carefully. Angels are ministering spirits sent to serve *those who will inherit salvation.* The passage distinguishes angels from those who inherit salvation, suggesting that angels do not.

Why this wording? Why would the writer focus on human beings when it comes to salvation and, apparently, exclude angels? Hebrews 2:5–18 answers those questions and in so doing shuts the door on redemption for fallen angels. Consider the first four of those verses (Heb 2:5–8a):

For it was not to angels that God subjected the world to come, of which we are speaking. It has been testified somewhere,

"What is man, that you are mindful of him,
  or the son of man, that you care for him?
You made him for a little while lower than the angels;
  you have crowned him with glory and honor,
  putting everything in subjection under his feet."

The writer makes reference to the world to come, the new earth described in Revelation 21–22. The new earth is cast as a global Eden, the climactic consummation of God's salvation plan. Eden is restored. Human beings inherit this salvation precisely because the original Eden and the world itself were created *for human beings.* God's original plan was to live among his human family on earth. We who were made lesser than the divine beings (Heb 2:6–7) were destined to become members of

---

3:7–9, 26–29). The authority of their gods is broken. They have been fired, de-legitimized by a greater authority, the Most High himself, incarnate in Christ.

God's household. At the fall, this goal was derailed. The rest of the Bible is about God's effort to restore what was lost—to dwell among his people, transforming the earth into his kingdom.

The point is straightforward: the plan of salvation is focused on human beings because human beings were the original object of eternal life in God's presence on earth. Angels were not the focus, because the fall disrupted *an earthly enterprise*. God's human imagers were corrupted, left estranged from God—left unfit to live in God's presence.[23] In the end, it will be human beings who will share authority with Christ in ruling the new earth, not angels. This is why passages in the book of Revelation about the same eschatological outcome focus on human believers, not angels:

> The one who conquers and who keeps my works until the end, to him I will give authority over the nations, and he will rule them with a rod of iron, as when earthen pots are broken in pieces, even as I myself have received authority from my Father. And I will give him the morning star. (Rev 2:26–28)[24]

> The one who conquers, I will grant him to sit with me on my throne, as I also conquered and sat down with my Father on his throne. (Rev 3:21)

---

23. The supernatural being responsible for the temptation in Eden that resulted in the fall was not in the same situation. That entity was already fit for God's presence but rejected that status by seeking to usurp the Most High. See Heiser, *The Unseen Realm*, for a discussion of the shared vocabulary and motifs between Gen 3, Isa 14:12–15, and Ezek 28:1–19. The latter two passages are not about the fall, but the respective writers drawn on an episode of divine rebellion known from ancient Canaanite (Ugaritic) literature.

24. As I explained in *The Unseen Realm* (pp. 312–13), the "morning star" language is about messianic rule: "The 'morning star' phrase takes us back once more to the Old Testament, which at times uses astral terminology to describe divine beings. Job 38:7 is the best example ('the morning stars were singing together and all the sons of God shouted for joy'). Stars were bright and, in the worldview of the ancients, living divine beings since they moved in the sky and were beyond the human realm. The morning star language in Revelation 2:28 is messianic—it refers to a divine being who would come from Judah. We know this by considering two other passages in tandem. In Numbers 24:17, we read the prophecy that 'a star will go out from Jacob, and a scepter will rise from Israel.' Numbers 24:17 was considered messianic in Judaism, completely apart from the New Testament writers. In other words, literate readers of John's writing would have known the morning star reference was not about literal brightness. It was about the dawning of the returned kingdom of God under its messiah. Later in the book of Revelation, Jesus himself refers to his messianic standing with the morning star language: 'I am the root and the descendant of David, the bright morning star' (Rev 22:16)."

The apostle Paul makes the point emphatic by reminding the Corinthian believers that they would one day judge angels (1 Cor 6:3). Human believers have a higher status in the new earth.

The writer of Hebrews continues describing the hope of the eschaton (Heb 2:8b–13):

> Now in putting everything in subjection to him, he left nothing outside his control. At present, we do not yet see everything in subjection to him. But we see him who for a little while was made lower than the angels, namely Jesus, crowned with glory and honor because of the suffering of death, so that by the grace of God he might taste death for everyone. For it was fitting that he, for whom and by whom all things exist, in bringing many sons to glory, should make the founder of their salvation perfect through suffering. For he who sanctifies and those who are sanctified all have one source. That is why he is not ashamed to call them *brothers*, saying,
>
> > "I will tell of your name to my brothers;
> > in the midst of the congregation I will sing your praise."
>
> And again,
>
> > "I will put my trust in him."
>
> And again,
>
> > "Behold, I and the children God has given me."

Who is the "everyone" in the beginning of this passage? If we care about reading in context, it's the human beings the writer referred to a few lines ago ("What is man …?"). The Greek term translated "everyone" is *pantos*. The grammatical form is masculine singular, a reference to the totality of humankind.[25]

In verse 9 Jesus is compared to these humans, inferior as they are, to angels, because Jesus was human. God became a man in the person of Jesus Christ. The incarnation links Jesus to us. Why was the incarnation important? Because atoning for the sins of the world of humankind (John 3:16) required an eternal sacrifice. But eternal beings cannot die, and so God had to become a man. The eternal Son cannot die for sin unless he is human and capable of dying. One cannot have a resurrection that defeats

---

25. In Col 1:20 the term is *panta* (neuter plural; "all things"), because more than humanity is in view. See the discussion on Col 1:19–20 for why this does not point to angelic *redemption* from sin.

death unless there is first a death. In other words, atonement for sin could not be accomplished without incarnation.

Do you see the connection? The Second Person of the Godhead became a man because the object of the atonement was fallen humanity (Luke 19:10; 2 Cor 5:21). Jesus became a human because he needed to save humans. Becoming human was necessary because its ultimate purpose was a death that atoned for humans. Becoming human had no necessary link to angels, who are not human. Christ's death for sin substituted for our death for sin (Gal 3:13; Rom 4:25).

The necessity of a human sacrificial death means the death of Christ did not have angels, who are not human, as its object. As such, the atoning death is not linked to angelic sins, but to human sins.

The remainder of Hebrews 2 confirms this interpretation:

> Since therefore the children share in flesh and blood, he himself likewise partook of the same things, that through death he might destroy the one who has the power of death, that is, the devil, and deliver all those who through fear of death were subject to lifelong slavery. For surely it is not angels that he helps, but he helps the offspring of Abraham. Therefore he had to be made like his brothers in every respect, so that he might become a merciful and faithful high priest in the service of God, to make propitiation for the sins of the people. For because he himself has suffered when tempted, he is able to help those who are being tempted. (Heb 2:14–18)

A few key lines deserve comment.

> Since therefore the children share in flesh and blood, he [Jesus] partook of the same things. (Heb 2:14a)

This language establishes the rationale of the incarnation. Jesus became a human because we, the object he intended to redeem, are human.

> … that through death he might destroy the one who has the power of death, that is, the devil, and deliver all those who through fear of death were subject to lifelong slavery. (Heb 2:14b–15)

The obvious point here is that human death had to be overcome. Less obvious is the related thought that the devil also had to be overcome because he had the power of death over humanity. The idea is that, without redemption, Satan's power over humans—his "legal" ownership of every human, estranged from God in the wake of what happened in Eden—would remain intact. But Scripture nowhere endorses the notion that angelic sin resulted in this sort of bondage to Satan. Humanity is under the curse because of Eden. Angels are nowhere said to be under the curse of Eden—which is what the atoning sacrifice of Jesus targets— nor under any other curses that gives Satan "legal" claim to their lives.

> For surely it is not angels that he helps, but he helps the offspring of Abraham. Therefore he had to be made like his brothers in every respect, so that he might become a merciful and faithful high priest in the service of God, to make propitiation for the sins of the people. (Heb 2:16–17)

These statements make explicit the answer to our question. The sacrifice of Jesus does not help angels. It helps believers—the children of Abraham by faith (Gal 3:26–29). Jesus had to become like his human siblings, lower than angels (Heb 2:9–11), to atone for the sins of those siblings.

In summary, the language of Hebrews 2:5–18 leaves no doubt that the object of Christ's redemptive work is humanity, not angels.

## WHO ARE THE "ELECT ANGELS" IN 1 TIMOTHY 5:21?

In Paul's admonition to Timothy to rebuke unrepentant sinners, the apostle seemingly wants to underscore the importance of his words: "In the presence of God and of Christ Jesus and of the elect angels I charge you to keep these rules without prejudging, doing nothing from partiality." As Mangum observes, the wording is uncommon:

> Paul intensifies his warning in 1 Tim 5:21 by invoking God, Christ Jesus, and "elect angels" as witnesses to his exhortation. Paul uses a similar invocation in 1 Tim 6:13 and 2 Tim 4:1, but there he calls on only the presence of God and Christ Jesus. The addition of "elect angels" to the formula here is unusual. Paul may have added a third witness to the formula because of the preceding OT allusion in 1 Tim 5:19 referring to the need for "two or three witnesses." ... Since he had just mentioned the need for two or three witnesses, Paul may have felt it necessary to expand the witness formula to include a third

witness. … What is more unusual about this reference to angels is that they are described as "elect angels." The term *eklektos* ("elect") is typically used in NT writings for God's elect—people who have believed in Christ (Matt 24:31; Mark 13:27; Rom 8:33; Col 3:12; 2 Tim 2:10; Titus 1:1; 1 Pet 1:1; 2:9; Rev 17:14).[26]

As we saw earlier, "angel" is a generic term in the New Testament for heavenly beings loyal to God.[27] Scholars are divided in their understanding of what "elect" signifies. It is probably reasonable to conclude that the designation is designed to contrast these angels with members of the heavenly host in rebellion against God (i.e., "fallen angels").[28] However, other scholars argue that "elect angels" is a stock epithet akin to "holy angels" and is not intended to convey a contrast with fallen angels.[29] More popular conceptions include the notion that "elect" angels cannot sin, an idea that certainly overstates the data, as the closest parallel to the phrase is found in 1 Enoch 39:1, a clear reference to the watchers who transgressed with human women (cf. Gen 6:1–4): "And it shall come to pass in those days that the children of the elect and the holy ones [will descend] from the high heaven and their seed will become one with the children of the people."[30]

Elsewhere in the New Testament when angels are mentioned in tandem with Christ, the context is eschatological judgment (Matt 13:39, 41, 42; 16:27; 24:31; 25:31; Mark 8:38; Luke 9:26; 2 Thess 1:7; Heb 12:22–24; Rev 14:10, 14–20). The context of 1 Timothy is not eschatological, however. It therefore seems best to take the description generically. "Elect angels" are good angels in service to the Father and the Son. That Paul is calling them to bear witness is consistent with the role of angels we have discussed already in several places.

---

26. Douglas Mangum, *Lexham Bible Guide: 1 Timothy*, with material contributed by E. Tod Twist, ed. Derek R. Brown (Bellingham, WA: Lexham Press, 2013), 1 Tim 5:21.

27. See chapter 6.

28. See, for example, Andreas Köstenberger, "1 Timothy," in *The Expositor's Bible Commentary, Revised Edition, Vol 12: Ephesians—Philemon*, eds. Tremper Longman III and David E. Garland (Grand Rapids: Zondervan, 2006), 547; J. N. D. Kelly, *The Pastoral Epistles*, BNTC (London: Continuum, 1963), 127.

29. Johann E. Huther, *Critical and Exegetical Handbook to the Epistles of St. Paul to Timothy and Titus*, trans. David Hunter (Edinburgh: T&T Clark, 1881), 211–13.

30. *OTP*, 1:30. See chapter 8 for the modern myth of how such passages justify the belief that the events of Gen 6:1–4 will be repeated in the end times. Isaac's translation in Charlesworth's volume is misleading in this regard as it sounds futuristic. As other scholars have noted, the grammatical forms can (and should) be translated as past tense.

## WHAT ARE "TONGUES OF ANGELS"?

First Corinthians 13 begin, "Though I speak with the tongues of men and of angels." Paul's introductory line to this famous and beloved passage has engendered much curiosity and controversy. What did the apostle mean by "tongues of angels"?

Scholarly consideration has vacillated between two alternative explanations, both of which have ancient roots.[31] As early as the Second Temple period, Jewish apocalyptic texts bear witness to the notion that angels have their own esoteric language. Before the fifth century AD, the rabbinic community was of a different mind—that angels spoke Hebrew, the language of God according to the rabbis. After the fifth century, Jewish writings reflected more openness to the older, esoteric language perspective.

The idea that angels spoke Hebrew—and that this is the notion upon which Paul draws in 1 Corinthians 13:1—is based almost entirely on two Second Temple texts.[32] The first of these texts is from the book of Jubilees, created in the mid-second century BC.[33] In Jubilees 12:25–27, the claim is put forth that Hebrew was the original language of creation and that when God called Abraham out of Ur he needed to be supernaturally enabled to understand it:

And the LORD God said to me, "Open his mouth and his ears so that he might hear and speak with his mouth in the language which is revealed because it ceased from the mouth of all of the sons of men from the day of the Fall." And I opened his mouth and his ears and his lips and I began to speak with him in Hebrew, in the tongue of creation. And he took his father's books—and they were written in Hebrew—and he copied them. And he began studying

---

31. The only exhaustive study on the problem of angelic tongues is John C. Poirier, *The Tongues of Angels: The Concept of Angelic Languages in Classical Jewish and Christian Texts* (Tübingen: Mohr Siebeck, 2010). This publication is based on Poirier's dissertation: "The Tongues of Angels: The Conceptual, Sociological, and Ideological Dimensions of Angelic Languages in Classical Jewish and Christian Texts," Doctor of Hebrew Literature dissertation, Jewish Theological Seminary of America, 2005. The references that follow in the footnotes refer to Poirier's dissertation.

32. As Poirier notes, this view is also supported by appeal to Rabbi Yochanan's teaching in b. Sotah 33a and b. Shabbat 12b. Poirier demonstrates that the rabbi's teaching was motivated to a desire to empower literate rabbis over religious activity outside the synagogue (the rabbi taught angels spoke Hebrew but could not understand the vernacular—Aramaic). See Poirier, "The Tongues of Angels," 24–37. Our own consideration of angelic tongues is restricted to Second Temple and early Christian texts as those are far more relevant to Pauline thought.

33. *OTP,* 2:44.

them thereafter. And I caused him to know everything which he was unable (to understand). And he studied them (in) the six months of rain.[34]

This passage along with other elements in Jubilees suggests that the original language in Eden was Hebrew. In fact, the author of this work apparently believed "God used Hebrew to call the universe into existence [and] every living creature originally spoke Hebrew."[35] This included animals: on the day God expelled Adam and Eve from Eden, "the mouth of all the beasts and cattle and birds and whatever walked or moved was stopped from speaking because all of them used to speak with one another with one speech and one language" (Jubilees 3:29). The implication is that angels, as created beings in service to God, therefore spoke Hebrew.

Along with the book of Jubilees, the notion that Hebrew was the language of angels is witnessed in the Dead Sea Scroll 4Q464. This incomplete text is considered to be related to Jubilees.[36] Fragment 3 (column 1) reads as follows:[37]

1 [...]

2 [...] ...

3 [...] servant

4 [...] in one

5 [...] confused

6 [...] to Abraha{ra}m

7 [...] for ever, for he

8 [...] ... the holy language

9 [... Zeph 3:9 I will make] the peoples pure of speech

10 [...]

11 [...] ... [...]

---

34. *OTP*, 2:82. The phrase "day of the Fall" (the "overthrow") refers to the judgment episode at the tower of Babel, not the events of Eden (see Jubilees 10:26).

35. Poirier, "Tongues of Angels," 19.

36. Poirier ("The Tongues of Angels," 23) believes it to be a *pesher* commentary on Jubilees. See John C. Poirier, "4Q464: Not Eschatological," *Revue de Qumran* 20 (2002): 583–87.

37. García Martínez and Tigchelaar, *The Dead Sea Scrolls Study Edition*, 943.

Though the text is quite fragmentary, it seems evident that, in concert with Jubilees, reference is made to Abraham acquiring Hebrew ("the holy language").

The esoteric language option has more precedent than the Hebrew explanation. The last eight chapters (46–53) of the Testament of Job, a pseudepigraphical text that scholars date as early as the first century BC, describes the daughters of Job singing with angelic tongues.[38] These chapters describe a gift from Job to his daughters of three golden boxes, inside each of which were shimmering, multicolored cords, which the patriarch referred to as "amulets" of the Father (Testament of Job 47:11). After the daughters complain about the apparent uselessness of the gift, Job tells them, "Not only shall you gain a living from these, but these cords will lead you into the better world, to live in the heavens" (Testament of Job 47:2b–3).[39] When one of Job's daughters decides to adorn her amulet, "she took on another heart—no longer minded toward earthly things—but she spoke ecstatically in the angelic dialect, sending up a hymn to God in accord with the hymnic style of the angels" (Testament of Job 48:2–3). The other two daughters have similar experiences, speaking "the dialect of the archons" (Testament of Job 49:2) and "the dialect of the cherubim" (Testament of Job 50:2).

As Poirier has observed, the passage has garnered a good deal of attention from New Testament scholars in regard to Paul's reference to angelic tongues. Interestingly, the three successive dialects appear to denote heavenly rank in ascending order toward the divine presence (angel → archon → cherubim).[40] This observation is in accord with *merkabah* mysticism, where angels of ascending class are encountered in ascents through levels of heaven.[41]

The fact that the amulets that were to be worn came in golden boxes (and were thus "connected" with them) is also significant. As Poirier comments:

---

38. As Poirier notes and demonstrates ("The Tongues of Angels," 66–69), the Testament of Job may be a very early Christian text, a point that does not mar its importance for Pauline thinking.

39. *OTP*, 1:864. Translations in this section come from this source.

40. Poirier, "The Tongues of Angels," 73.

41. Poirier, "The Tongues of Angels," 73. Poirier draws on the work of Altmann for this point: Alexander Altmann, "The Singing of the Qedushah in Early Hekhalot Literature," *Melilah* 2 (1946): 1–24 (Hebrew).

Golden girdles are standard angelic wear throughout apocalyptic literature. Gold symbolized the divine throughout the Mediterranean world. Moreover, golden girdles were also associated with inspired unintelligible speech.[42]

Poirier marshals a number of examples in this regard from a range of sources. For example, in Daniel 10:5, the divine man who speaks to Daniel wears a sash of gold, quite similar to the angel in the Apocalypse of Zephaniah 6:12 who speaks to the prophet. The twenty-four elders of Revelation wear golden crowns (Rev 4:4, 10), as does another divine man in Revelation 14:14.[43]

There are other allusions to angelic language (occasionally mentioning "angelic wear") in Second Temple and early Christian literature that is not human in nature.[44] In the Apocalypse of Zephaniah 8:2–4, we read:

Thousands of thousands and myriads of myriads of angels gave praise before me. I, myself, put on an angelic garment. I saw all of those angels praying. I, myself, prayed together with them, I knew their language, which they spoke with me.[45]

The Ascension of Isaiah 6–11 contains several instances of non-human angelic languages. In this pseudepigraphical text, the prophet is transported to the seventh heaven, where he is able to praise God with the angels ("my praise was like theirs") and read books they had composed regarding the deeds of the children of Jerusalem," books "not like the books of this world" (Ascension of Isaiah 7; 9:20–23, 27–32).[46] A similar scene occurs in the Apocalypse of Abraham 15:2–7, where Abraham is taken to the seventh heaven and angelic creatures—whose form was

---

42. Poirier, "The Tongues of Angels," 74, 76.

43. Poirier, "The Tongues of Angels," 75 (notes 77, 78). See Gregory M. Stevenson, "Conceptual Background to Golden Crown Imagery in the Apocalypse of John (4:4, 10; 14:14)," *JBL* 114 (1995): 257–72; A. Leo Oppenheim, "The Golden Garments of the Gods," *JNES* 8 (1949): 172–93.

44. Poirier ("The Tongues of Angels," 104–11) also includes rabbinic material (e.g., Genesis Rabbah 74:7; Leviticus Rabbah 1:13).

45. It is worth noting that the angelic language here is used for intercessory prayer and hymns. As we have seen in our study, angels regularly intercede on behalf of humans to God (see chapter 5): Tobit 12:12; 1 Enoch 39:5; 40:6; 47:1–4; 99:3; 104:1; Testament of Dan 6:1–2; Testament of Levi 3:5–6; 5:5–7.

46. Poirier ("The Tongues of Angels," 95) and others note that this section of the Ascension of Isaiah is likely an early Christian work (first or second century AD). See J. Flemming and H. Duensing, "The Ascension of Isaiah," in *New Testament Apocrypha, vol. 2*, ed. Wilhelm Schneemelcher, trans. and ed. R. McL. Wilson (Philadelphia: Westminster John Knox Press, 1965), 642–63.

in some respects human (though they changed shapes)—are crying out in a language he does not know. Like Isaiah, Abraham later is able to participate in the angelic praise.

In my opinion, the esoteric-language explanation carries more weight. The Jubilees material requires the assumption that angels are in view. Jubilees 12:25 actually speaks of the original language in regard to "the sons of men," not angels. This is not the case with the esoteric angelic language idea; several texts assign a non-human tongue explicitly to angels. 2 Corinthians 12:1–7 may also add weight to this determination, depending on how it is read. In Paul's description of being transported to the heavens, he writes:

> I know a man in Christ who fourteen years ago was caught up to the third heaven—whether in the body or out of the body I do not know, God knows. And I know that this man was caught up into paradise—whether in the body or out of the body I do not know, God knows—and he heard things that cannot be told, which man may not utter. (2 Cor 12:2–4)

Does the statement in verse 4 mean that Paul could not understand the language? If so, Hebrew as the language of heaven is decisively ruled out. Paul could mean, however, that he felt forbidden to relate what he heard—that it was inappropriate for humans to convey such conversations. This latter possibility would be odd, given the numerous angelic conversations in the Bible and other Second Temple literature Paul would have had access to, so his experience may be more coherently understood as his hearing an unintelligible angelic language. But if this is the case, then his statement in 1 Corinthians 13:1 (the same audience as in 2 Corinthians) is merely hypothetical. "If I speak with the tongues of men and angels" would not mean that Paul did speak in an esoteric angelic language. The idea would be that, even if he could and lacked love, that ability would mean nothing.[47]

---

47. This of course removes 1 Cor 13:1 as an appeal for believers to speak in unintelligible syllables as though they were a heavenly language. Rather, speaking in tongues would be about a supernatural enablement to speak in other human languages, an interpretation supported by the Old Testament context of 1 Cor 14:21–24 (cf. Isa 28:11–12). See G. K. Beale and D. A. Carson, eds., *Commentary on the New Testament Use of the Old Testament* (Grand Rapids: Baker Academic, 2007), 740–42.

# CHAPTER 8

# Myths and Questions
# about Angels

ANGELS HAVE BEEN OBJECTS OF FASCINATION FOR CHRISTIANS FOR centuries. It should be no surprise, then, that a good number of speculative myths have arisen about them. This is partly because most people interested in angels do not have access to the primary sources and ancient languages required for an academic study like this one. English translations fail to preserve nuances important in angelology, and popular studies depend on those translations. Little attention is paid to the wider ancient contexts of the biblical material, such as the ancient Near East and the Second Temple period. But pure imagination is also part of the equation.

In preparing for this book, I asked readers of my earlier books (*The Unseen Realm* and *Supernatural*) to share strange things they've heard or ask questions they have about angels. Some of the responses were truly bizarre. Others had a peripheral relationship to something Scripture actually teaches.

This chapter is based on those responses and seeks to separate fact from the fictions that many Christians hold about angels. Toward that end, this chapter draws on the preceding study. There is no attempt to reproduce the textual references found in earlier chapters that support the argumentation here. Where appropriate, I have combined common misconceptions and questions.

# "ANGELS HAVE WINGS ... AND THEY'RE WOMEN, TOO"

As we saw in our first chapter, the terms *mal'ākîm* ("angel"), *kerubîm* ("cherubim"), and *śerāpîm* ("seraphim") are not interchangeable. They are, in effect, job descriptions performed by different spirit beings. In biblical literature, cherubim and seraphim are never sent to people to deliver messages. That task belongs to angels. Cherubim and seraphim are heavenly throne guardians, a role that at times brings them into contact with humans, but they are not sent to earth to instruct people. Conversely, angels are found in the divine presence as well. Old and New Testament writers place them there. Rather, the terminology distinguishes roles.

We have also seen that whenever angels encounter humans in their messaging role, they appear in human form. In the Old Testament their appearance makes them indistinguishable from men. It is only when they do something unearthly that their transcendent nature becomes apparent. The only visible exceptions in to this pattern are found in the New Testament, where members of the heavenly host appear to people along with luminous glory (Luke 2:9, 13) or dazzlingly white clothing (Matt 28:3). Angels are never described as having inhuman features (wings, multiple faces) like cherubim and seraphim are. The reverse is actually the case. Cherubim and seraphim may share human traits, but angels do not have creaturely attributes. The conclusion can be drawn, then, that angels—those divine beings sent to earth to interact with people—look like people and do not have wings.

Zechariah 5:9 is often offered as an exception to both the human (and male) portrayal of angels:

> Then I lifted my eyes and saw, and behold, two women coming forward! The wind was in their wings. They had wings like the wings of a stork, and they lifted up the basket between earth and heaven.

Despite the fact that even some scholars speak about these women with wings as angels, there is no textual basis for identifying the women as angels. The "women" (Hebrew, *našîm*) are never described as angels. In the very next verse the prophet speaks to an angel (*mal'āk*), a figure distinct from the women (Zech 5:10). When the angel speaks (Zech 5:11), the writer used the masculine form of the verb (yō'mer), not the feminine form (tō'mer). The text is clear.

Zechariah 5:8–11 therefore provides no biblical evidence for the notion that angels have wings or come to humans in female appearance.[1] While it is clear that wings mark the women as being from heaven (as opposed to earth), the point is not "these are angels." Rather, the point is to highlight their contrast with the wicked woman in the basket a few verses earlier (Zech 5:5–8). Akin to the removal of the filthy garments of Joshua the high priest in Zechariah 3, the women represent God's removal of wickedness from his land and people to Shinar (Babylon), where evil belongs.[2]

One could actually make a more reasoned case for the women being cherubim. In addition to their creaturely attribute of wings, Zechariah 5:9 notes, "The wind [rûaḥ] was in their wings." The term rûaḥ is frequently translated "Spirit"/"spirit." This is the same "locomotion" of the winged cherubim in Ezekiel 1:12, 20; 10:17. Like Ezekiel 1, the context is oriented to Babylon, the source of cherubim iconography.

Since Zechariah 5:8–11 cannot validate that angels are winged creatures, the passage also fails as evidence that angels can appear as women (biblically speaking, at least). If the women are not angels, then Zechariah 5:9 cannot teach us that angels can appear as women.

The assumption presupposes the idea that angels have gender. They do not—indeed they *cannot* be gendered, since they are spirit beings and gender is a biological attribute. When angels assume visible form or flesh to interact with human beings, Scripture always has them male. The flesh they assume is gendered because it is flesh, not because that corporality is an intrinsic part of angelic nature.[3]

---

1. Appeals to external material do not change the textual circumstance (the women are never called angels, whereas the man in the passage is). Bird-like depictions of Egyptian deities are of course well known, and Ugaritic material also contains instances of deities cast as birds (Marjo C. A. Korpel, *A Rift in the Clouds: Ugaritic and Hebrew Descriptions of the Divine* [Münster: Ugarit-Verlag, 1990], 544–52).

2. Joyce G. Baldwin, *Haggai, Zechariah and Malachi: An Introduction and Commentary,* TOTC 28 (Downers Grove, IL: InterVarsity Press, 1972), 137.

3. The reader will recall that some Second Temple Jewish writers were curiously hesitant to have angels eating, with the idea that angels who assumed human flesh could copulate with women. It is difficult to comprehend why the less-dramatic exhibition of fleshly behavior was unacceptable. It is clear from Heb 1:13–14 that New Testament writers considered episodes like Gen 18–19, where Yahweh and two angels shared a meal with Abram, inoffensive. The same of course can be said for Peter and Jude's acceptance of Gen 6:1–4 involving supernatural beings and their sexual transgression

With respect to the New Testament, the primary appeal to angels having wings comes from Revelation 10:1:

> Then I saw another mighty angel coming down from heaven, wrapped in a cloud, with a rainbow over his head, and his face was like the sun, and his legs like pillars of fire.

The argument goes: the passage never mentions wings, but because the angel "comes down from heaven," he must have wings. The same argument (and omission of any reference to wings) is characteristic of Revelation 14:6, 17, where angels emerge from the heavenly temple and altar, respectively (cf. Matt 28:2).

The flaw in this argument is its dependence on descent language. It is not difficult to demonstrate its terminal weakness. Are we to conclude that Jesus has wings? After all, he descends from heaven (1 Thess 4:16). Does the Holy Spirit have wings? He descends on Jesus at his baptism (Matt 3:16; Mark 1:10; Luke 3:22). The point with both examples is that for supernatural beings, descent from heaven does not require wings. The point may be a floating descent, or an urgent one, depending on the context. It may also be figurative language designed purely to denote point of origin—God's abode.[4] For example, the same language is used of Jesus'

---

and Paul's concern that the disaster of Gen 6:1–4 might reoccur (1 Cor 11:10). On these passages, see Heiser, *The Unseen Realm*, 92–109; Heiser, *Reversing Hermon*, chs. 1–3, 8. There is nothing in Gen 18–19 to exegetically justify that the angelic eating was a pretense. Genesis 18:8 says simply, "They ate." This "pretense hermeneutic" is characteristic of Second Temple interaction with the episode. In Tobit 12, for example, Raphael actually says he pretended to eat food in the presence of humans. It is interesting to note that the Gospel writers appear to have been aware of this hermeneutic. They intentionally have Jesus eating after his resurrection to subvert the notion that his resurrection was not truly corporeal (Luke 24:36–43, esp. v. 43). For discussion, see Sullivan, *Wrestling with Angels*, 180–95; Fletcher-Louis, *Luke-Acts*, 69. Some New Testament manuscripts insert "and some honeycomb" with the fish Jesus ate (Luke 24:42–43), which is striking given that "heavenly honeycomb" was the sort of food angels in Second Temple literature that angels could (were permitted to?) eat (Jos. Asen. 15–16). This scribal insertion is likely innocent. It should not (intentionally or otherwise) be considered a denial of the physicality of Jesus' resurrection body. Even if it were original to the text, it cannot do away with Jesus eating the fish (the text literally reads: "They gave him a piece of broiled fish, and he took and ate before them").

4. Interestingly, Luke's description of the Spirit's descent "like a dove" includes the descriptor "bodily form" (*sōmatikō eidei*). Of this—and the imagery in general—Bock writes: "The Spirit's descent comes with the opening of the heavens. Luke alone emphasizes the concrete nature of the experience by speaking of a descent in bodily form. The unique reference to σωματικῷ εἴδει (*sōmatikō eidei*, in bodily form) shows that the coming of the Spirit was a visible experience. Depictions of this event tend to overplay the metaphor. ... What was visible was not a dove, but rather what was seen is compared to a dove, since ὡς (*hōs*, as) is an adverb of manner. The manner of the Spirit's

first coming, which we know was by virtue of being born of Mary, having nothing to do with wings: "No one has ascended into heaven except he who descended from heaven, the Son of Man" (John 3:13). It is quite evident that descent language for divine figures does not require wings and so provides no support for angels having wings.

## "IS THE ANGEL OF THE BOTTOMLESS PIT GOOD OR EVIL?"

This issue derives from Revelation 9:1–5, 11:

> And the fifth angel blew his trumpet, and I saw a star fallen from heaven to earth, and he was given the key to the shaft of the bottomless pit. He opened the shaft of the bottomless pit, and from the shaft rose smoke like the smoke of a great furnace, and the sun and the air were darkened with the smoke from the shaft. Then from the smoke came locusts on the earth, and they were given power like the power of scorpions of the earth. They were told not to harm the grass of the earth or any green plant or any tree, but only those people who do not have the seal of God on their foreheads. They were allowed to torment them for five months, but not to kill them, and their torment was like the torment of a scorpion when it stings someone. ... They have as king over them the angel of the bottomless pit. His name in Hebrew is Abaddon, and in Greek he is called Apollyon.

The potential confusion here involves presuming that "the angel of the bottomless pit" (Abaddon/Apollyon) is the same angel mentioned in verse 1, who "was given the key to the shaft of the bottomless pit." They are not the same figure.[5] Further, the angel with the key to the bottomless pit should not be considered an evil divine being.[6]

---

descent was like the way a dove floats gracefully through the air." See Darrell L. Bock, *Luke: 1:1–9:50,* BECNT (Grand Rapids: Baker Academic, 1994), 338.

5. The language of Rev 9:11 distinguishes the king of the bottomless pit (Abaddon/Apollyon) from the angel who releases Abaddon/Apollyon. If the writer wanted to identify the two, we would be reading "he [the angel of Rev 9:1–2] is the king" rather than "they have a king" (Rev 9:11). Reading Rev 9:1–2 with Rev 20:1 also eliminates an identification of the angel of Rev 9:11 with Abaddon/Apollyon, who is clearly not a holy figure.

6. Beale devotes a good deal of space commenting on Rev 9:1–2 to establish the evil nature of the angel in that passage. He is persuaded by the "fallen" language in that regard. But he seems to miss how his arguments for an evil angel in Rev 9:1–2 fail completely in Rev 20:1. He writes that "in 20:1–3

At first glance it might seem as though the angel of Revelation 9:1 is an evil being because of John's description, "I saw a star fallen from heaven to earth." The verb is perfect tense and so should be translated "had fallen," a translation that seems to affirm the idea that the angel is evil. Aune notes in this regard:

> Falling stars often represent evil angelic beings or demons (*1 Enoch* 86:3; 88:1; 90:24; *T. Sol.* 20.14–17; Jude 13), or even Satan (*1 Enoch* 86:1; *Apoc. El.* 4:11; Luke 10:18; Rev 12:9). Here the fallen star should be understood as an angelic messenger (see 20:1) and not be identified with the angel of the abyss named Abaddon or Apollyon in 9:11 or Satan in 12:9. In *1 Enoch* 86:1, Enoch sees a star falling from heaven, followed (v 3) by many stars, all obviously fallen angelic beings.[7]

The use of "fall" language for divine beings in rebellion against God is quite consistent but not entirely one sided in that regard. One need only look at Revelation 20:1–2, where we have the same language about an angel and the key to the bottomless pit to establish this point and to suggest that "fallen" can mean "descend" if the context does not speak of rebellion and judgment:

> Then I saw an angel coming down from heaven, holding in his hand the key to the bottomless pit and a great chain. And he seized the dragon, that ancient serpent, who is the devil and Satan, and bound him for a thousand years, and threw him into the pit.

I suggest that Revelation 9:1–2 ought to be interpreted in light of Revelation 20:1. This prevents several interpretive inconsistencies: First, it makes little sense for God to give a fallen being control over the pit. Second, the idea that a fallen angel functions as a servant of God runs contrary to the rest of Old and New Testament angelology. Third, suggesting that the angel of Revelation 9:1–2 is an unholy being armed with the key to the bottomless pit contradicts Revelation 20:1, where a clearly

---

the Satanic realm comes under Christ's authority, which is executed by a mediating angel, though now in 20:1 only the devil is under the angel's authority" (Beale, *The Book of Revelation*, 984). Beale clearly sees the angel who "comes down" and holds the key to the bottomless pit in Rev 20:1 as a good angel.

7. Aune, *Revelation 1–5*, 525.

good angel has the same status or job.[8] It is far simpler to have the angel of Revelation 9:1 sent from heaven to release Abaddon/Apollyon in obedience to carrying out a woe decreed by God.[9]

## "ANGELS CAN NO LONGER REBEL"

Though it is a common idea in Christian angelology, there is no specific evidence in Scripture that suggests unfallen heavenly beings cannot rebel against God. To the contrary, scriptural evidence leaves that possibility on the table.

In chapter 2 we briefly discussed two passages in Job regarding the imperfection of God's holy ones:

Can mortal man be in the right before God?
  Can a man be pure before his Maker?
Even in his servants he puts no trust,
  and his angels he charges with error. (Job 4:17–18)

Behold, God puts no trust in his holy ones,
  and the heavens are not pure in his sight. (Job 15:15)

These passages are post-fall in context. That is, they are statements made about heavenly beings well after the events of Eden. We discussed these passages earlier in relation to the role of the heavenly host as mediators (Job 33:23). We noted that the point of the unflattering language of Job 4:17–18; 15:15 is fallibility, not rebellion. However, fallibility involves the *possibility* of rebellion. The only guarantee against rebellion would be moral perfection—having God's very nature in totality. Imperfect beings can indeed fail, and nothing about imperfection suggests they are immune to rebellion.

---

8. The Greek term in both Rev 9 and 20 for "bottomless pit" is *abyssos*. My approach does not require Abaddon/Apollyon *be* Satan, though a case can be made for that identification. Aune (*Revelation 1–5*, 525) notes, "In Rev 9:1 a star (= angelic being) descends from *heaven* to *earth* and is given a key to the *abyss*, while in 20:1 an angel descends from *heaven* (to *earth* is implied) with a key to the *abyss*; both passages imply a three-level cosmos."

9. Note as well that the presumed evil angel of Rev 9:1 never participates in the chaos unleashed by the fifth trumpet. There is nothing in the context that suggests this angel is hostile to God.

## "ANGELS EXIST OUTSIDE TIME AND SPACE"

Though this is a popular axiom for the nature of angels, it is difficult to know precisely what someone who expresses the thought actually means by it.[10]

Angels are not "timeless" in the sense of being eternal beings. They had a beginning as created beings. They are immortal (Luke 20:36), but that immortality is ultimately contingent, based on God's authority and pleasure. As God wills, angels are not subject to time in terms of aging or having a necessary terminus point for their existence, but this says nothing, for instance, about whether they can travel back in time or forward into the future. The latter would be more relevant to being "outside of time."

By "space," we do not refer to outer space but to the matter of how a bodiless being can be said to occupy space (i.e., place). Philosophical theologians have, of course, thought a great deal about the question. Peter Williams, following Peter Kreeft, suggests that "angels may be in definite places or make things happen in definite places" not because they are materially present or occupy material space but because they are "spiritually present."[11] By "spiritual presence" Williams and others mean that the presence of angels is evidenced by *activity*, not substance. The idea is certainly biblical, as angels are described as affecting people that are materially present without being materially present (Gen 21:17; 22:11, 15; 31:11; Matt 1:20; 2:13, 19; Acts 8:26; 10:3).[12]

This approach does not require angels be spatially present in a material way. They can, however, be materially and spatially present. For example, two angels share a meal with Abraham (Gen 18:1–8; cf. 19:1) and physically seize Lot (Gen 19:10); an angel struck Peter to awaken him (Acts 12:7).

---

10. The same expression is used to describe God as well. The subject of God's relationship to time and eternity is much more problematic than most suppose. It is not, for example, a foregone "orthodox" theology to say God is "outside of time." See William Lane Craig, *Time and Eternity: Exploring God's Relationship to Time* (Wheaton, IL: Crossway, 2001); Gregory Ganssle, ed., *God and Time: Four Views* (Downers Grove, IL: InterVarsity Press, 2001).

11. Peter Williams, *The Case for Angels* (Milton Keynes, UK: Paternoster Press, 2002), 86.

12. The Old Testament examples may not be appropriate because they feature the angel of Yahweh who, as I have argued in the present study and elsewhere, is the visible (or corporeal) Yahweh himself, whose nature transcends that of other spiritual beings. See chapter 3 and Heiser, *The Unseen Realm*, 127–48. The New Testament dream and visionary examples are therefore more germane.

Rather than existing "outside space," we might say that angels exist without regard to space. Space and spatiality are not necessary to angelic existence or presence.

## "ANGELS CAN READ MINDS AND MANIPULATE THE MATERIAL WORLD"

Though there is no scriptural evidence that members of the heavenly host knows a person's mind or thoughts the way God does, the question of whether angels can read minds is not as silly as it sounds. The question becomes reasonable in the context of angelic appearances in the mind or consciousness of people via dreams of visions. Such instances, which are obviously scriptural, can be parsed as angels having access to the consciousness of human beings. If they have such access, then (some would argue) they by definition have access to the thoughts already in a person's mind.

The absence of any scriptural explanation for how angels appear in dreams leaves us only with speculation. On one hand, we could presume that angels have access to information stored in a person's brain or consciousness. There is no way to demonstrate that idea is valid. On the other hand, we are on the same footing if we speculate that dreams are nothing more than transmissions of information into a person's consciousness. Information transmission is not information retrieval. To use a modern illustration, angels may be able to "write" to our CD or DVD, but not read from it. It is therefore just as reasonable to assume that angels cannot read minds. Both options are nothing more than speculation.[13]

When it comes to affecting the material world, we are on more scriptural footing. They can, as we have seen, assume material form and act upon material objects. The two angels that visited Lot, for instance, were able to strike the men of Sodom with blindness (Gen 19:10–11). No explanation is offered as to how this was done, but the two angels were the cause of that effect. An angel somehow freed Peter from his shackles (Acts 12:7),

---

13. Williams (*The Case for Angels,* 82) goes down the road of telepathic communication but fails to note the obvious competing speculation. The whole discussion assumes that "angel consciousness" is interactive with human consciousness, but until consciousness is really understood, we cannot know if such an assumption is reasonable.

opened an iron gate without touching it (Acts 12:10; cf. Acts 5:9), and struck Herod with a disease (Acts 12:23). An angel moved the stone from the tomb of Jesus (Matt 28:2).

The ability of spirit beings to assume human form, including material corporeality, becomes even more interesting when considering 2 Corinthians 11:14, where Paul wrote that "Satan disguises himself as an angel of light." The verb translated "disguises," *metaschēmatizō*, is rendered "masquerades" by other translators and scholars. Guthrie notes:

> The verb [*metaschēmatizō*] means "to disguise oneself" or "to pretend to be what one is not," thus "to masquerade." In the pseudepigraphical work Testament of Job, Satan disguises himself as a beggar (6.4), the king of the Persians (17.2), and later as a baker (23.1), and this same verb is used. A number of Jewish traditions also present Satan as transforming himself into an angel or an angel of light in order to get the better of those he tempts. For instance, Paul may have been aware of a passage in Life of Adam and Eve (9.1) in which Satan tempts Eve again after the fall: "Then Satan was angry and transformed himself into the brightness of angels and went away to the Tigris River to Eve and found her weeping."[14]

There are other Second Temple period texts that provide some context for Paul's words. In the Life of Adam and Eve 17:1–2, Eve saw Satan (the serpent?) in the form of an angel:

> Then Satan came in the form of an angel and sang hymns to God as the angels. And I saw him bending over the wall, like an angel. And he said to me, "Are you Eve?"[15]

The point is that Second Temple material shows us that the notion that spirit beings could change their appearance was alive and well in the first century. Some might suggest that the meaning is metaphorical, that Satan's "presentation" of himself as something he is not refers broadly to lies and deception, not visible appearance. Considered in isolation, that perspective is possible in 2 Corinthians 11:14, but some of the contemporary instances cited above go beyond such an abstraction. It may well be

---

14. George H. Guthrie, *2 Corinthians*, BECNT (Grand Rapids: Baker Academic, 2015), 528.
15. *OTP*, 2:277–79.

that Paul was thinking of visible manifestations in addition to deception. The possibility means that, along with assuming corporeal form, spirit beings might be able to alter that form—that is, changing appearance may be among their suite of abilities.

## "ANGELS TAKE PEOPLE TO HEAVEN"

In Luke 16:19–31, the parable of the rich man and Lazarus, we read this line: "The poor man died and was carried by the angels to Abraham's side" (Luke 16:22). Abraham's "side" (or "bosom") was figurative language referring to the blessed afterlife.[16]

Bock notes that "an angelic escort [to heaven] is a common Jewish image. In the Christian apocrypha, such imagery took on great detail, with pictures of angels doing battle over the souls of people who had passed away."[17] Two examples illustrate his point.

The Testament of Job ends with the death of Job. Prior to his passing, he tells his daughters:

> Now then, my children, since you have these objects you will not have to face the enemy at all, but neither will you have worries of him in your mind, since it is a protective amulet of the Father. Rise then, gird yourselves with them before I die in order that you may be able to see those who are coming for my soul, in order that you may marvel over the creatures of God. (Testament of Job 47:10–11)[18]

> After three days, as Job fell ill on his bed (without suffering or pain, however, since suffering could no longer touch him on account of the

---

16. Scholars disagree on whether the phrase is synonymous with terms like "heaven" or "paradise," though it is clear that the verse presumes Abraham is in heaven. Second Temple texts describe Abraham's ascent to heaven, and so there is no ambiguity on that point (Pseudo-Philo, Liber antiquitatum biblicarum 18.5; Testament of Abraham 10–14; Apocalypse of Abraham 15:4–30; 4 Ezra 3:14–15). Bock notes that "parable" may not be the right word for Luke 16:19–31 since it is never called a parable and lacks some expected features of parables (Darrell Bock, Luke: 9:51–24:53, BECNT [Grand Rapids: Baker Academic, 1996], 1362).

17. Bock, Luke: 9:51–24:53, 1368. In a footnote on the same page, Bock adds this observation: "For the reprobate, a satanic escort to hell is also a possibility T. Asher 6.4–6 (Marshall 1978: 636 notes that this text is textually disputed); SB 2:223–27; Tg. Song 4.12)." Fitzmyer is mistaken that Testament of Asher is the only source earlier than the second century for the idea of being escorted to heaven by angels. See Joseph A. Fitzmyer, The Gospel according to Luke X–XXIV, AYB 28A (New Haven: Yale University Press, 1985), 1132. The Testament of Job is possibly as old as the first century BC (OTP, 1:833–834). The Testament of Abraham is dated c. 100 AD.

18. OTP, 1:865.

omen of the sash he wore), after those three days he saw those who had come for his soul. And rising immediately he took a lyre and gave it to his daughter Hemera. To Kasia he gave a censer, and to Amaltheia's Horn he gave a kettle drum, so that they might bless those who had come for his soul. And when they took them, they saw the gleaming chariots which had come for his soul. And they blessed and glorified God each one in her own distinctive dialect. After these things the one who sat in the great chariot got off and greeted Job as the three daughters and their father himself looked on, though certain others did not see. And taking the soul he flew up, embracing it, and mounted the chariot and set off for the east. But his body, prepared for burial, was borne to the tomb as his three daughters went ahead girded about and singing hymns to God. (Testament of Job 52:1–12)[19]

The Testament of Abraham offers an account of the death of Abraham:

And immediately Michael the archangel stood beside him with multitudes of angels, and they bore his precious soul in their hands in divinely woven linen. And they tended the body of the righteous Abraham with divine ointments and perfumes until the third day after his death. And they buried him in the promised land at the oak of Mamre, while the angels escorted his precious soul and ascended into heaven singing the thrice-holy hymn to God, the master of all, and they set it (down) for the worship of the God and Father. (Testament of Abraham 20:10–12, Recension A)[20]

The Testament of Job is perhaps as old as the first century BC, providing evidence that Jewish traditions about angels escorting believers to the blissful afterlife had been put to writing. The idea was certainly part of Second Temple Jewish thought. The specific Abraham material is, at best, contemporary to the Gospel of Luke.

---

19. *OTP,* 1:867–68.
20. *OTP,* 1:895.

# "BELIEVERS HAVE THE AUTHORITY TO COMMAND ANGELS"

Hebrews 1:14 has at times been used to justify the notion that believers have authority over angels. The verse says of angels (emphasis mine): "Are they not all ministering spirits sent out to serve *for the sake of* those who are to inherit salvation?" In other words, God has tasked angels to perform tasks that will benefit believers on their faith journey. But some suggest that what is meant is that God has sent angels to minister *at the behest of* believers, suggesting that Christians can command angels to do their bidding.

There are two reasons why Hebrews 1:14 does not give Christians authority to command angels—one grammatical, the other contextual.

First, the preposition translated "for the sake of" (*dia*) has a limited semantic range. When it occurs before an article, noun, or pronoun in the genitive case, it has the meaning "through" or "by means of." This preposition can also occur before the accusative case, where it denotes cause or purpose ("because of"; "for the sake of"). In Hebrews 1:14, *dia* is followed by a plural article in the accusative case. The accusative marks the object of the service of angels, not the source of their service. The leading Greek reference grammars never speak of *dia* as meaning "at the behest of."[21]

The second reason that Hebrews 1:14 does not mean angels were sent to serve *at the behest of* Christians is the wider context of the New Testament—and really the entire Bible: there isn't a single instance in Scripture where a human being commands an angel. Human beings converse with angels. They ask questions. They do not give angels orders. This fact demonstrates that interpreting Hebrews 1:14 in such a way is idiosyncratic and creates incongruity with the rest of Scripture.

---

21. I speak here of Wallace, *Greek Grammar Beyond the Basics*; Friedrich Blass, Albert Debrunner, and Robert Walter Funk, *A Greek Grammar of the New Testament and Other Early Christian Literature* (Chicago: University of Chicago Press, 1961); A. T. Robertson, *A Grammar of the Greek New Testament in the Light of Historical Research* (Logos Bible Software, 2006); James Hope Moulton and Nigel Turner, *A Grammar of New Testament Greek: Syntax*, Vol. 3 (Edinburgh: T&T Clark, 1963–).

## "CHRISTIANS BECOME ANGELS WHEN THEY DIE"

Many who embrace the idea are not conscious of its biblical roots.[22] These roots are deep, though "becoming an angel" is precisely what's in view.

The idea that believers become angels after death draws on several scriptural threads. Two that might be familiar to most Christians are the doctrine of glorification (being made like Jesus; 1 John 3:1–3); statements that a believer's existence in the afterlife makes them "like the angels" (Matt 22:30; Mark 12:25); and Paul's teaching that the believer's resurrection body is "celestial flesh" (a "spiritual body"; 1 Cor 15:35–49). Less familiar is the fact that the family and inheritance vocabulary used of Christians in the New Testament is tied to vocabulary for the divine family (divine council) in the Old Testament, and Eden (including the new Eden) derives from "cosmic abode" motifs in the ancient Near East.

I devoted a good deal of attention to all of these trajectories in *The Unseen Realm*, and so readers are directed to that discussion for details and sources.[23] Briefly, these threads weave a tapestry of the believer's destiny that culminates in being made divine. Christian theologians use various terms for the doctrine: glorification, deification, *theosis* among them. The idea is not that we become the same as Yahweh or Jesus, but, as John wrote, "we shall be like him" (1 John 3:2). Believers are already "partakers of the divine nature" (2 Pet 1:4). We are destined to reconstitute the divine council of Yahweh alongside his spiritual children, the "sons of God," the members of his loyal heavenly host. The same language is used of believers (1 John 3:1–3). We are the "holy ones," the common term for angels in the Old Testament.[24] We have been "adopted" into God's heavenly family. Our "inheritance" is in heaven, and that heaven will come to earth as the new global Eden. We will be placed over the nations, currently under the dominion of the fallen sons of God, displacing them in that role, sharing messianic rule with Jesus, our brother (Heb 2:5–18;

---

22. This popular belief extends (for most Christians) also to the aborted, infants, and others who die unable to believe. This has a solid biblical basis if Rom 5:12 is not over-read. In most Christian contexts, that verse is indeed misunderstood and so the idea of infant salvation is based on theologizing and pastoral compassion (e.g., God makes exceptions for such unfortunates under the presumption of Adamic guilt, or he will make grieving parents forget their loss). These positions are void of exegetical merit. Fortunately, they are unnecessary if Rom 5:12 is read accurately.

23. Heiser, *The Unseen Realm*, 307–21, 377–81.

24. The English translation "saints" unfortunately obscures the terminological connection with Old Testament "holy ones."

Rev 2:26–28; Rev 3:21). In so doing, we will "judge angels," ruling over them in terms of Old Testament divine council hierarchical terminology (1 Cor 6:3; John 1:12).

The end result is not that glorified believers become angels. Rather, we are fully grafted into the glorious family council of God. Our "already" status in that regard becomes full reality at death. We join the heavenly children of God in a blended divine family and actually outrank angels in the new global Eden.

# Bibliography

Abegg, Martin G., Jr. *Qumran Sectarian Manuscripts*. Bellingham, WA: Logos Bible Software, 2003.

Afzal, Cameron. "Wheels of Time: Merkavah Exegesis in Revelation 4." Pages 465–82 in *Society of Biblical Literature Seminar Papers*. Atlanta: Society of Biblical Literature, 1998.

Albright, William Foxwell. "A Catalogue of Early Hebrew Lyric Poems (Psalm LXVIII)." *Hebrew Union College Annual* 23.1 (1950): 1–39.

Alden, Robert L. *Job*. The New American Commentary 11. Nashville: Broadman & Holman, 1993.

Altmann, Alexander. "The Singing of the Qedushah in Early Hekhalot Literature." *Melilah* 2 (1946): 1–24.

Angel, Joseph L. *Otherworldly and Eschatological Priesthood in the Dead Sea Scrolls*. Leiden: Brill, 2010.

Annus, Amar. "The Antediluvian Origin of Evil in the Mesopotamian and Jewish Traditions A Comparative Study." Pages 1–43 in *Ideas of Man in the Conceptions of the Religions*. Edited by Tarmo Kulmar and Rüdiger Schmitt. Münster: Ugarit-Verlag, 2012.

———. "On the Origin of Watchers: A Comparative Study of the Antediluvian Wisdom in Mesopotamian and Jewish Traditions." *Journal for the Study of the Pseudepigrapha* 19.4 (2010): 277–320.

Auffarth, Christoff, and Loren T. Stuckenbruck, eds. *The Fall of the Angels*. Leiden: Brill, 2004.

Aune, David E. *Revelation 1–5*. Word Biblical Commentary 52A. Dallas: Word, 1997.

Baldwin, Joyce G. *Haggai, Zechariah and Malachi: An Introduction and Commentary*. Tyndale Old Testament Commentaries 28. Downers Grove, IL: InterVarsity Press, 1972.

Bampfylde, Gillian. "The Prince of the Host in the Book of Daniel and the Dead Sea Scrolls." *Journal for the Study of Judaism in the Persian, Hellenistic, and Roman Period* 14 (1983): 129–34.

Barton, George A. "The Origin of the Names of Angels and Demons in the Extra-Canonical Apocalyptic Literature to 100 A.D." *Journal of Biblical Literature* 31.4 (1912): 156–67.

Barry, John D., ed. *The Lexham Bible Dictionary*. Bellingham, WA: Lexham Press, 2016.

Barrett, C. K. *A Critical and Exegetical Commentary on the Acts of the Apostles*. International Critical Commentary. Edinburgh: T&T Clark, 2004.

Barth, Markus, and Helmut Blanke. *Colossians*. Translated by Astrid B. Beck. Anchor Yale Bible 34A. New Haven: Yale University Press, 1994.

Bauckham, Richard J. *2 Peter, Jude*. Word Biblical Commentary 50. Dallas: Word, 1998.

Baumgarten, J. M. "The Duodecimal Courts of Qumran, Revelation, and the Sanhedrin." *Journal of Biblical Literature* 95.1 (1976): 59–78.

Beale, G. K. *The Book of Revelation: A Commentary on the Greek Text*. New International Greek Testament Commentary. Grand Rapids: Eerdmans, 1999.

Beale, G. K., and D. A. Carson, eds. *Commentary on the New Testament Use of the Old Testament*. Grand Rapids: Baker Academic, 2007.

Beasley-Murray, G. R. *Revelation*. Revised edition. New Century Bible. London: Marshall, Morgan & Scott, 1978.

Begg, Christopher. "Angels in Pseudo-Philo." Pages 537–54 in *Angels: The Concept of Celestial Beings: Origins, Development and Reception*. Edited by Friedrich V. Reiterer, Tobias Nicklas, and Karin Schöpflin. Berlin: De Gruyter, 2007.

———. "Angels in the Work of Flavius Josephus." Pages 525–36 in *Angels: The Concept of Celestial Beings: Origins, Development, and Reception*. Edited by Friedrich V. Reiterer, Tobias Nicklas, and Karin Schöpflin. Berlin: De Gruyter, 2007.

Berlin, Adele, ed. *Religion and Politics in the Ancient Near East*. Bethesda, MD: University of Maryland Press, 1996.

Blass, Friedrich, Albert Debrunner, and Robert Walter Funk. *A Greek Grammar of the New Testament and Other Early Christian Literature*. Chicago: University of Chicago Press, 1961.

Bock, Darrell L. *Luke: 1:1–9:50*. Baker Exegetical Commentary on the New Testament. Grand Rapids: Baker Academic, 1994.

———. *Luke: 9:51–24:53*. Baker Exegetical Commentary on the New Testament. Grand Rapids: Baker Academic, 1996.

Bokovoy, David E. "שמעו והעידו בבית יעקב: Invoking the Council as Witnesses in Amos 3:13." *Journal of Biblical Literature* 127.1 (2008): 37–51.

Boyarin, Daniel. "The Gospel of the Memra: Jewish Binitarianism and the Prologue to John." *Harvard Theological Review* 94.3 (2001): 243–84.

Boyle, Marjorie O'Rourke. "The Covenant Lawsuit of the Prophet Amos: III 1–IV 13." *Vetus Testamentum* 21 (1971): 338–62.

Brand, Miryam. *Evil Within and Without: The Source of Sin and Its Nature as Portrayed in Second Temple Literature*. Göttingen: Vandenhoeck & Ruprecht, 2013.

Burnett, David A. "Abraham's Star-Like Seed: Neglected Functional Elements in the Patriarchal Promise of Genesis 15." MA thesis, Criswell College, 2015.

Byrne, Brendan. *"Sons of God"—"Seed of Abraham": A Study of the Idea of the Sonship of God of All Christians in Paul Against the Jewish Background.* Rome: Pontifical Biblical Institute Press, 1979.

Byrne, Máire. "The Influence of Egyptian Throne Names on Isaiah 9:5: A Reassessment of the Debate in Light of the Divine." Pages 87–100 in *A Land Like Your Own: Traditions of Israel and Their Reception.* Edited by Jason M. Silverman. Eugene, OR: Pickwick, 2010.

Cairns, Alan. *Dictionary of Theological Terms.* Belfast; Greenville, SC: Ambassador Emerald International, 2002.

Callan, Terrance. "Pauline Midrash: The Exegetical Background of Gal. 3:19b." *Journal of Biblical Literature* 99.4 (1980): 549–67.

Charlesworth, James H., ed. *The Old Testament Pseudepigrapha.* 2 vols. New York: Doubleday, 1983, 1985.

Chisholm, Robert B., Jr. "Does God Deceive?" *Bibliotheca Sacra* 155.617 (1998): 11–28.

Cho, Sang Youl. *Lesser Deities in the Ugaritic Texts and the Hebrew Bible: A Comparative Study of Their Nature and Roles.* Piscataway, NJ: Gorgias Press, 2007.

Clifford, Richard J. *The Cosmic Mountain in Canaan and the Old Testament.* Cambridge, MA: Harvard University Press, 1972.

Clines, David J. A. *Job 1–20.* Word Biblical Commentary 17. Dallas: Word, 1989.

———. *Job 21–37.* Word Biblical Commentary 18A. Nashville: Thomas Nelson, 2006.

Collins, Adela Yarbro. "The Book of Revelation." Pages 195–218 in *The Continuum History of Apocalypticism.* Edited by Bernard McGinn, John J. Collins, and Stephen Stein. London: Continuum, 2003.

Collins, John J. "Powers in Heaven: God, Gods, and Angels in the Dead Sea Scrolls." Pages 9–20 in *Religion in the Dead Sea Scrolls,* edited by John J. Collins and Robert A. Kugler. Grand Rapids: Eerdmans, 2000.

Collins, John J., and Robert A. Kugler, eds. *Religion in the Dead Sea Scrolls.* Grand Rapids: Eerdmans, 2000.

Cooke, G. "The Sons of (the) God(s)." *Zeitschrift für die alttestamentliche Wissenschaft* 35 (1964): 22–47.

Craig, William Lane. *Time and Eternity: Exploring God's Relationship to Time.* Wheaton, IL: Crossway, 2001.

Craigie, Peter C. *The Book of Deuteronomy.* The New International Commentary on the Old Testament. Grand Rapids: Eerdmans, 1976.

———. "Ugarit and the Bible: Progress and Regress in 50 Years of Literary Study." Pages 99–111 in *Ugarit in Retrospect: Fifty Years of Ugarit and Ugaritic.* Edited by Gordon D. Young. Winona Lake, IN: Eisenbrauns, 1981.

Cross, Frank Moore. "The Council of Yahweh in Second Isaiah." *Journal of Near Eastern Studies* 12 (1953): 274–77

Curtis, A. H. W., and J. F. Healey. *Ugarit and the Bible.* Edited by George J. Brooke. Münster: Ugarit-Verlag, 1994.

Dahood, Mitchell, S.J. *Psalms I: 1–50*. Anchor Yale Bible 16. New Haven: Yale University Press, 1965.

Davidson, Maxwell. *Angels at Qumran: A Comparative Study of 1 Enoch 136; 72–108 and Sectarian Writings from Qumran*. Sheffield: Sheffield Academic Press, 1992.

Davidson, Richard M. "The Divine Covenant Lawsuit Motif in Canonical Perspective." *Journal of the Adventist Theological Society* 21/1–2 (2010): 45–84.

Davis, Carl Judson. *The Name and Way of the Lord: Old Testament Themes, New Testament Christology*. Sheffield: Sheffield Academic Press, 1996.

Davis, R. Dean. *The Heavenly Court Scene of Revelation 4–5*. Lanham, MD: University Press of America, 1992.

Day, Peggy. *An Adversary in Heaven: śāṭān in the Hebrew Bible*. Atlanta: Scholars Press, 1988.

Del Olmo Lete, Gregorio, and Joaquín Sanmartín. *A Dictionary of the Ugaritic Language in the Alphabetic Tradition*. 2 vols. Leiden: Brill, 2015.

Dequeker, L. "The 'Saints of the Most High' in Qumran and Daniel." *Old Testament Studies* 18 (1973): 108–87.

Dick, Michael P. *Born in Heaven, Made on Earth: The Making of the Cult Image in the Ancient Near East*. Winona Lake, IN: Eisenbrauns, 1999.

Dietrich, M., O. Loretz, and J. Sanmartin, eds. *KTU: The Cuneiform Alphabetic Texts from Ugarit, Ras Ibn Hani and Other Places*. 2nd ed. Münster: Ugarit-Verlag, 1995.

Dimant, Devorah. "Men as Angels: The Self-Image of the Qumran Community." Pages 93–103 in *Religion and Politics in the Ancient Near East*. Edited by Adele Berlin. Bethesda, MD: University of Maryland Press, 1996.

Donner, Herbert, and Wolfgang Röllig. *Kanaanäische und aramäische Inschriften*. 2nd ed. Wiesbaden: Harrassowitz, 1966–1969.

Duncan, Julie. "A Critical Edition of Deuteronomy Manuscripts from Qumran, Cave IV. 4QDt$^b$, 4QDt$^e$, 4QDt$^h$, 4QDt$^j$, 4QDt$^b$, 4QDt$^k$, 4QDt$^l$." PhD diss., Harvard University, 1989.

Elior, Rachel. *The Three Temples: On the Emergence of Jewish Mysticism*. Translated by David Louvish. Liverpool: Liverpool University Press, 2005.

Erickson, Millard J. *The Concise Dictionary of Christian Theology*. Wheaton, IL: Crossway, 2001.

Evans, Craig A., and Stanley E. Porter, eds. *Dictionary of New Testament Background*. Downers Grove, IL: InterVarsity Press, 2000.

Fitzmyer, Joseph A. *The Gospel according to Luke X–XXIV*. Anchor Yale Bible 28A. New Haven: Yale University Press, 1985.

Fleming, David Marron. "The Divine Council as Type Scene in the Hebrew Bible." PhD diss., Southern Baptist Theological Seminary, 1989.

Flemming, J., and H. Duensing. "The Ascension of Isaiah." Pages 642–63 in *New Testament Apocrypha*. Vol. 2. Edited by Wilhelm Schneemelcher. English translation edited by R. McL. Wilson. Philadelphia: Westminster John Knox Press, 1965.

Fletcher-Louis, Crispin H. T. *Luke-Acts: Angels, Christology, and Soteriology*. Tübingen: Mohr Siebeck, 1997.

Fossum, Jarl E. "Kyrios Jesus as the Angel of the Lord in Jude 5–7." *New Testament Studies* 33.2 (1987): 226–43.

———. *The Name of God and the Angel of the Lord: Samaritan and Jewish Concepts of Intermediation and the Origin of Gnosticism*. Tübingen: Mohr Siebeck, 1985.

Francis, F. O. "Humility and Angelic Worship in Col 2:18." Pages 163–95 in *Conflict at Colossae*. Edited by F. O. Francis and W. A. Meeks. 2nd ed. Missoula, MT: Scholar's Press, 1975.

Freedman, David Noel, ed. *Anchor Yale Bible Dictionary*. 6 vols. New York: Doubleday, 1992.

Fröhlich, Ida. "Mesopotamian Elements and the Watchers Traditions." Pages 11–24 in *The Watchers in Jewish and Christian Traditions*. Edited by Angela Kim Harkins, Kelley Coblentz Bautch, and John C. Endres. Minneapolis: Fortress, 2014.

———. "Theology and Demonology in Qumran Texts." *Henoch* 32.1 (2010): 101–28.

Gammie, John G. "The Angelology and Demonology in the Septuagint of the Book of Job." *Hebrew Union College Annual* 56 (1985): 1–19.

Ganssle, Gregory, ed. *God and Time: Four Views*. Downers Grove, IL: InterVarsity Press, 2001.

Garr, W. Randall. *In His Own Image and Likeness: Humanity, Divinity, and Monotheism*. Leiden: Brill, 2003.

George, Andrew R. "Sennacherib and the Tablet of Destinies." *Iraq* 48 (1986): 133–46.

Gesenius, F. Wilhelm. *Gesenius' Hebrew Grammar*. Edited by Emil Kautzsch. Translated and edited by Arthur E. Cowley. 2nd Eng. ed. Oxford: Clarendon Press, 1910.

Gieschen, Charles A. *Angelomorphic Christology: Antecedents and Early Evidence*. Leiden: Brill, 1998.

Goldingay, John E. *Daniel*. Word Biblical Commentary 30. Dallas: Word, 1989.

———. *Old Testament Theology, Volume One: Israel's Gospel*. Downers Grove, IL: InterVarsity Press, 2003.

———. *Psalms, Volume 2: Psalms 42–89*. Baker Commentary on the Old Testament. Grand Rapids: Baker Academic, 2006.

Goodacre, Mark. "Does περιβολαιον Mean 'Testicle' in 1 Cor 11:15?" *Journal of Biblical Literature* 130.2 (2011): 391–96.

Goodman, David. "Do Angels Eat?" *Journal of Jewish Studies* 37.2 (1986): 160–75.

Gray, G. B. "The Meaning of the Hebrew Word דגל." *Jewish Quarterly Review* 11 (1899): 92–101.

Gruenwald, Ithamar. *Apocalyptic and Merkabah Mysticism*. Leiden: Brill, 2014.

Guthrie, Donald. *Hebrews: An Introduction and Commentary*. Tyndale New Testament Commentaries 15. Downers Grove, IL: InterVarsity Press, 1983.

Guthrie, George H. *2 Corinthians*. Baker Exegetical Commentary on the New Testament. Grand Rapids: Baker Academic, 2015.

Halperin, David J. *Faces of the Chariot: Development of Rabbinic Exegesis of Ezekiel's Vision of the Divine Chariot*. Tübingen: Mohr Siebeck, 1988.

Hamori, Esther J. *"When Gods Were Men": The Embodied God in Biblical and Near Eastern Literature*. Berlin: De Gruyter, 2008.

Handy, Lowell K. *Among the Host of Heaven: The Syro-Palestinian Pantheon as Bureaucracy*. Winona Lake, IN: Eisenbrauns, 1994.

Harrington, W. J. *Understanding the Apocalypse*. Washington, D.C.: Corpus Books, 1969.

Hartenstein, Friedhelm. "Cherubim and Seraphim in the Bible and in the Light of Ancient Near Eastern Sources." Pages 154–88 in *Angels: The Concept of Celestial Beings—Origins, Development and Reception*. Edited by Friedrich V. Reiterer, Tobias Nicklas, and Karin Schöpflin. Berlin: De Gruyter, 2007.

Hayman, Peter. "Monotheism—A Misused Word in Jewish Studies?" *Journal of Jewish Studies* 42.1 (1991): 1–15.

Hawthorne, Gerald F., and Ralph P. Martin, eds. *Dictionary of Paul and His Letters*. Downers Grove, IL: InterVarsity Press, 1993.

Heiser, Michael S. "Are Yahweh and El Distinct Deities in Deut. 32:8–9 and Psalm 82?" *HIPHIL* 3 [http://see-j.net/] (2006). Posted October 3, 2006. http://see-j.net/index.php/hiphil/article/view/29.

———. "Co-Regency in Ancient Israel's Divine Council as the Conceptual Backdrop to Ancient Jewish Binitarian Monotheism." *Bulletin for Biblical Research* 26.2 (2015): 195–225.

———. "Deuteronomy 32:8 and the Sons of God." *Bibliotheca Sacra* 158 (2001): 52–74.

———. "The Divine Council in Late Canonical and Non-Canonical Second Temple Jewish Literature." PhD diss., University of Wisconsin–Madison, 2004.

———. "Does Deuteronomy 32:17 Assume or Deny the Reality of Other Gods?" *Bible Translator* 59.3 (2008): 137–45.

———. "Does Divine Plurality in the Hebrew Bible Demonstrate an Evolution from Polytheism to Monotheism in Israelite Religion?" *Journal for the Evangelical Study of the Old Testament* 1.1 (2012): 1–24.

———. "Monotheism and the Language of Divine Plurality in the Hebrew Bible and the Dead Sea Scrolls." *Tyndale Bulletin* 65.1 (2014): 85–100

———. "Monotheism, Polytheism, Monolatry, or Henotheism? Toward an Assessment of Divine Plurality in the Hebrew Bible." *Bulletin of Biblical Research* 18.1 (2008): 1–30.

———. "The Mythological Provenance of Isaiah 14:12–15: A Reconsideration of the Ugaritic Material." *Vetus Testamentum* 51.3 (2001): 354–59.

———. *Reversing Hermon: Enoch, the Watchers and the Forgotten Mission of Jesus Christ*. Crane, MO: Defender, 2017.

———. "Should *elohim* with Plural Predication Be Translated 'Gods'?" *Bible Translator* 61.3 (2010): 123–36.

———. *Supernatural: What the Bible Teaches about the Unseen World—And Why It Matters*. Bellingham, WA: Lexham Press, 2015.

———. *The Unseen Realm: Recovering the Supernatural Worldview of the Bible*. Bellingham, WA: Lexham Press, 2015.

———. "You've Seen One *Elohim*, You've Seen Them All? A Critique of Mormonism's Use of Psalm 82." *Foundation for Ancient Research and Mormon Studies Review* 19.1 (2007): 221–66.

Hinson, David Francis. *Theology of the Old Testament*. London: SPCK, 2001.

Hoftijzer, Jacob, and Karel Jongeling, eds. *Dictionary of the North-West Semitic Inscriptions*. 2 vols. Leiden: Brill, 2003.

Houtman, C. "What Did Jacob See in His Dream at Bethel? Some Remarks on Gen 28:10–22." *Vetus Testamentum* 27 (1977): 337–51.

Huffmon, Herbert B. "The Covenant Lawsuit in the Prophets." *Journal of Biblical Literature* 78 (1959): 285–95.

Hundley, Michael. "To Be or Not to Be: A Reexamination of Name Language in Deuteronomy and the Deuteronomistic History." *Vetus Testamentum* 59 (2009): 533–55.

Huther, Johann E. *Critical and Exegetical Handbook to the Epistles of St. Paul to Timothy and Titus*. Translated by David Hunter. Edinburgh: T&T Clark, 1881.

Jacobsen, Thorkild. "Primitive Democracy in Ancient Mesopotamia." *Journal of Near Eastern Studies* 2 (1943): 159–72.

Jenni, Ernst, ed. *Theological Lexicon of the Old Testament*. With assistance from Claus Westermann. Translated by Mark E. Biddle. 3 vols. Peabody, MA: Hendrickson, 1997.

Jobes, Karen H., and Moises Silva. *Invitation to the Septuagint*. Grand Rapids: Baker, 2000.

Johnson, Norman B. *Prayer in the Apocrypha and Pseudepigrapha: A Study of the Jewish Concept of God*. Philadelphia: Society of Biblical Literature and Exegesis, 1948.

Johnson, Ronn. "The Old Testament Background for Paul's Principalities and Powers." PhD diss., Dallas Theological Seminary, 2004.

Joines, Karen R. "Winged Serpents in Isaiah's Inaugural Vision." *Journal of Biblical Literature* 86.4 (1967): 410–15.

Joosten, Jan. "A Note on the Text of Deuteronomy xxxii 8." *Vetus Testamentum* 57.4 (2007): 548–55.

Joüon, Paul, and Takamitsu Muraoka. *A Grammar of Biblical Hebrew*. Revised English ed. Roma: Pontificio istituto biblico, 2006.

Kaiser, Walter C., Jr. *Toward Old Testament Ethics*. Grand Rapids: Zondervan, 1983.

Kaufman, Stephen A. *The Akkadian Influences on Aramaic*. Chicago: University of Chicago Press, 1974.

Kee, Min Suc. "The Heavenly Council and Its Type-Scene." *Journal for the Study of the Old Testament* 31.3 (2007): 259–73.

Keel, Othmar, and Adolphe Gutbug. *Jahwe-Visionen und Siegelkunst: eine neue Deutung der Majestätsschilderungen in Jes 6, Ez 1 und 10 und Sach 4*. Stuttgart: Verlag Katholisches Bibelwerk, 1977.

Keel, Othmar, and C. Uehlinger. *Göttinnen, Götter und Gottessymbole. Neue Erkentnisse zur Religionsgeschichte Kanaans und Israels aufgrund bislang unerschlossener ikonographischen Quellen*. Freiburg: Herder, 1992.

Kelly, J. N. D. *The Pastoral Epistles*. Black's New Testament Commentary. London: Continuum, 1963.

Khan, Geoffrey, ed. *Encyclopedia of Hebrew Language and Linguistics*. 4 vols. Leiden: Brill, 2013.

Kingsbury, Edwin C. "The Prophets and the Council of Yahweh." *Journal of Biblical Literature* 83.3 (1964): 279–86.

———. "The Theophany Topos and the Mountain of God." *Journal of Biblical Literature* 86.2 (1967): 205–10.

Knafl, Anne K. *Forming God: Divine Anthropomorphism in the Pentateuch*. Winona Lake, IN: Eisenbrauns, 2014.

Koehler, Ludwig, Walter Baumgartner, and Johann J. Stamm. *The Hebrew and Aramaic Lexicon of the Old Testament*. Translated and edited under the supervision of Mervyn E. J. Richardson. 5 vols. Leiden: Brill, 1994–2000.

Korpel, Marjo C. A. *A Rift in the Clouds: Ugaritic and Hebrew Descriptions of the Divine*. Münster: Ugarit-Verlag, 1990.

Köstenberger, Andreas. "1 Timothy." Pages 487–561 in *Ephesians—Philemon*. Vol. 12 of *The Expositor's Bible Commentary, Revised Edition*. Edited by Tremper Longman III and David E. Garland. Grand Rapids: Zondervan, 2006.

Kramer, Samuel Noah. "Sumerian Theology and Ethics." *Harvard Theological Review* 49 (1956): 45–62.

Kraus, Hans-Joachim. *Theology of the Psalms*. Translated by Keith Crim. Minneapolis: Fortress, 1992.

Kuhn, Harold B. "The Angelology of the Non-Canonical Jewish Apocalypses." *Journal of Biblical Literature* 67.3 (1948): 217–32.

Lane, William L. *Hebrews 1–8*. Word Biblical Commentary 47A. Dallas: Word, 1991.

Leiffer, Dorothy. "Development of Angelology in the Apocrypha and Pesudepigrapha." Masters thesis, Northwestern University, 1926.

Lichtenberger, Hermann. "Spirits and Demons in the Dead Sea Scrolls." Pages 22–40 in *The Holy Spirit and Christian Origins: Essays in Honor of James D. G. Dunn*, edited by James D. G. Dunn, Graham Stanton, Bruce W. Longenecker, and Stephen C. Barton. Grand Rapids: Eerdmans, 2004.

Lohse, Eduard. *Colossians and Philemon*. Hermeneia. Philadelphia: Fortress Press, 1971.

Longman, Tremper, III, and Peter Enns, eds. *Dictionary of the Old Testament: Wisdom, Poetry & Writings*. Downers Grove, IL: InterVarsity Press, 2008.

Lopez, Kathryn Muller. "The Divine Council Scene in Second Temple Literature." PhD diss., Emory University, 2002.

Lubetski, Meir. "King Hezekiah's Seal Revisited." *Biblical Archaeology Review* 27.4 (2001): 24–36.

Mangum, Douglas. *Lexham Bible Guide: 1 Timothy*. With material contributed by E. Tod Twist. Edited by Derek R. Brown. Bellingham, WA: Lexham Press, 2013.

Martin, Troy W. "Paul's Argument from Nature for the Veil in 1 Cor 11:13–15: A Testicle instead of a Head Covering." *Journal of Biblical Literature* 123.1 (2004): 75–84.

———. "Περιβολαιον as 'Testicle' in 1 Cor 11:15: A Response to Mark Goodacre." *Journal of Biblical Literature* 132.2 (2013): 453–65.

Martínez, Florentino García, and Eibert J. C. Tigchelaar. *The Dead Sea Scrolls Study Edition*. 2 vols. Leiden: Brill, 1997–1998.

McCarter, P. Kyle, Jr. *II Samuel*. Anchor Yale Bible 9. New Haven: Yale University Press, 1984.

McDonough, Sean M. *YHWH at Patmos: Rev.1:4 in its Hellenistic and Early Jewish Setting*. Tübingen: Mohr Siebeck, 1999.

Melvin, David P. "In Heaven as It Is on Earth: The Development of the Interpreting Angel Motif in Biblical Literature of the Neo-Babylonian, Persian, and Early Hellenistic Periods." PhD diss., Baylor University, Waco, TX, 2012.

Michalak, Aleksander R. *Angels as Warriors in Late Second Temple Jewish Literature*. Tübingen: Mohr Siebeck, 2012.

Millard, Alan R. "The Celestial Ladder and the Gate of Heaven (Gen 28:12, 17)." *Expository Times* 78 (1966/1967): 86–87.

Miller, Geoffrey David. "The Wiles of the Lord: Divine Deception, Subtlety, and Mercy in I Reg 22." *Zeitschrift für die alttestamentliche Wissenschaft* 126.1 (2014): 45–58.

Miller, Patrick D. *Genesis 1–11: Studies in Structure and Theme*. Sheffield: University of Sheffield, 1978.

Miller, Patrick D. *Israelite Religion and Biblical Theology: Collected Essays*. Sheffield: Sheffield Academic Press, 2000.

Miller, Stephen R. *Daniel*. New American Commentary 18. Nashville: Broadman & Holman, 1994.

Mosca, Paul G. "Once Again the Heavenly Witness of Ps 89: 38." *Journal of Biblical Literature* 105.1 (1986): 27–37.

Moulton, James Hope, and Nigel Turner. *Syntax*. Vol. 3 of *A Grammar of New Testament Greek*. Edinburgh: T&T Clark, 1963.

Muilenburg, James. "The Book of Isaiah, Chapters 40–66: Introduction and Exegesis." *Interpreter's Bible*, vol. 5. Nashville: Abingdon Press, 1956.

Mullen, E. Theodore, Jr. *The Divine Council in Canaanite and Early Hebrew Literature*. Chico, CA: Scholars Press, 1980.

Mullen, E. Theodore, Jr. "The Divine Witness and the Davidic Royal Grant: Ps 89: 37–38." *Journal of Biblical Literature* 102.2 (1983): 207–18.

Muñoa, Philip. "Raphael, Azariah, and Jesus of Nazareth: Tobit's Significance for Early Christology." *Journal for the Study of the Pseudepigrapha* 22.1 (2012): 3–39

Murray, Robert. "The Origin of Aramaic *'îr*, Angel." *Orientalia* 53.2 (1984): 306.

Newsom, Carol. "He Has Established for Himself Priests: Human and Angelic Priesthood in the Qumran Sabbath Shirot." Pages 101–20 in *Archaeology and History in the Dead Sea Scrolls: The New York University Conference in Memory of Yigael Yadin*. Edited by Lawrence H. Schiffmann. Sheffield: Sheffield Academic Press, 1990.

Newsom, Carol. *Songs of the Sabbath Sacrifice: A Critical Edition*. Atlanta: Scholars Press, 1985.

Nickelsburg, George W. E. *1 Enoch 1: A Commentary on the Book of 1 Enoch, Chapters 1–26; 81–108*. Hermeneia. Minneapolis: Fortress, 2001.

Nielsen, Kirsten. *Yahweh as Prosecutor and Judge: An Investigation of the Prophetic Lawsuit (Rîb-Pattern)*. Sheffield: University of Sheffield, 1978.

Noll, Stephen F. "Angelology in the Qumran Texts." PhD diss., University of Manchester, 1979.

———. *Angels of Light, Powers of Darkness*. Downers Grove, IL: InterVarsity Press, 1998.

O'Brien, Peter T. *Colossians, Philemon*. Word Biblical Commentary 44. Dallas: Word, 1982.

Oldenburg, Ulf. "Above the Stars of El." *Zeitschrift für die alttestamentliche Wissenschaft* 82.2 (1970): 187–208.

Olyan, Saul M. *A Thousand Thousands Served Him: Exegesis and Naming of Angels in Ancient Judaism*. Tübingen: Mohr Siebeck, 1993.

Oppenheim, A. Leo. "The Golden Garments of the Gods." *Journal of Near Eastern Studies* 8 (1949): 172–93.

Orlov, Andrei. "Celestial Choirmaster: The Liturgical Role of Enoch-Metatron in 2 Enoch and the Merkabah Tradition." *Journal for the Study of the Pseudepigrapha* 14.1 (2004): 3–29.

Paul, Shalom. "Heavenly Tablets and the Book of Life." In *Columbia University Ancient Near Eastern Studies*. New York: Columbia University, 1973.

Penner, Ken, and Michael S. Heiser. *Old Testament Greek Pseudepigrapha with Morphology*. Bellingham, WA: Lexham Press, 2008.

Poirier, John C. "4Q464: Not Eschatological," *Revue de Qumran* 20 (2002): 583–87

———. *The Tongues of Angels: The Concept of Angelic Languages in Classical Jewish and Christian Texts*. Wissenschaftliche Untersuchungen Zum Neuen Testament 287. Tübingen: Mohr Siebeck, 2010.

———. "The Tongues of Angels: The Conceptual, Sociological, and Ideological Dimensions of Angelic Languages in Classical Jewish and Christian Texts." Doctor of Hebrew Literature diss., Jewish Theological Seminary of America, 2005.

Provençal, Philippe. "Regarding the Noun שרף [śārāp] in the Hebrew Bible." *Journal for the Study of the Old Testament* 29.3 (2005): 371–79.

Rahlfs, A. *Septuaginta: With Morphology.* Electronic edition. Stuttgart: Deutsche Bibelgesellschaft, 1979.

Reed, Annette Yoshiko. *Fallen Angels and the History of Judaism and Christianity: The Reception of Enochic Literature.* Cambridge: Cambridge University Press, 2005.

Reemstma, Joel A. "Punishment of the Powers: Deuteronomy 32 and Psalm 82 as the Backdrop to Isaiah 34." Paper presented at the Annual Meeting of the Evangelical Theological Society, San Diego, CA, 2014.

Rexine, J. E. "*Daimōn* in Classical Greek Literature." *Greek Orthodox Theological Review* 30.3 (1985): 335–61.

Ringgren, H. *Israelite Religion.* Minneapolis: Augsburg Fortress, 1966.

Roberts, J. J. M. "Whose Child Is This? Reflections on the Speaking Voice in Isaiah 9:5." *Harvard Theological Review* 90.2 (1997): 115–29.

Robertson, A. T. *A Grammar of the Greek New Testament in the Light of Historical Research.* Reprint, Bellingham, WA: Logos Bible Software, 2006.

Robins, Gay. "Cult Statues in Ancient Egypt." In *Cult Image and Divine Representation in the Ancient Near East.* Edited by Neal H. Walls. Boston: American Schools of Oriental Research, 2005.

Robinson, H. W. "The Council of Yahweh." *Journal of Theological Studies* 45 (1944): 151–57.

Rowland, Christopher. "A Man Clothed in Linen, Dan 10.6ff. and Jewish Angelology." *Journal for the Study of the New Testament* 24 (1985): 99–110.

———. *The Open Heaven: A Study of Apocalyptic in Judaism and Early Christianity.* Eugene, OR: Wipf & Stock, 1982.

Runge, Steven E. *Discourse Grammar of the Greek New Testament: A Practical Introduction for Teaching and Exegesis.* Bellingham, WA: Lexham Press, 2010.

Salters, R. B. "Psalm 82:1 and the Septuagint." *Zeitschrift für die alttestamentliche Wissenschaft* 103.2 (1991): 225–39.

Schöpflin, Karin. "God's Interpreter: The Interpreting Angel in Post-Exilic Prophetic Visions of the Old Testament." Pages 189–203 in *Angels: The Concept of Celestial Beings—Origins, Development and Reception.* Edited by Friedrich V. Reiterer, Tobias Nicklas, and Karin Schöpflin. Berlin: De Gruyter, 2007.

Scott, James M. *Adoption as Sons of God: An Exegetical Investigation into the Background of Yiothesia in the Pauline Corpus.* Tübingen: Mohr Siebeck, 1992.

Segal, Alan. *Two Powers in Heaven: Early Rabbinic Reports about Christianity and Gnosticism.* 1977. Reprint, Waco, TX: Baylor University Press, 2012.

Segal, Alan F. "'Two Powers in Heaven' and Early Christian Trinitarian Thinking." Pages 73–95 in *The Trinity: An Interdisciplinary Symposium on the Trinity.* Edited by Stephen T. Davis, Daniel Kendall, and Gerald O'Collins. Oxford: Oxford University Press, 1999.

Seitz, Christopher R. "The Divine Council: Temporal Transition and New Prophecy in the Book of Isaiah," *Journal of Biblical Literature* 109.2 (1990): 229–47.

Silva, Moisés, ed. *New International Dictionary of New Testament Theology and Exegesis.* 5 vols. Grand Rapids: Zondervan, 2014.

Skehan, P. W. "A Fragment of the 'Song of Moses' (Deut 32) from Qumran." *Bulletin of the American Schools of Oriental Research* 136 (1954): 12–15.

Smith, Mark S. *The Origins of Biblical Monotheism: Israel's Polytheistic Background and the Ugaritic Texts.* Oxford: Oxford University Press, 2001.

———. "When the Heavens Darkened: Yahweh, El, and the Divine Astral Family in Iron Age II Judah." Pages 265–77 in *Symbiosis, Symbolism, and the Power of the Past: Canaan, Ancient Israel, and Their Neighbors from the Late Bronze Age Through Roman Palaestina.* Edited by William G. Dever and Seymour Gitin. Winona Lake, IN: Eisenbrauns, 2003.

Sommer, Benjamin D. *The Bodies of God and the World of Ancient Israel.* Cambridge: Cambridge University Press, 2009.

Stevenson, Gregory M. "Conceptual Background to Golden Crown Imagery in the Apocalypse of John (4:4, 10; 14:14)." *Journal of Biblical Literature* 114 (1995): 257–72.

Stuckenbruck, Loren T. "An Angelic Refusal of Worship: The Tradition and Its Function in the Apocalypse of John." Pages 679–96 in *Society of Biblical Literature 1994 Seminar Papers.* Edited by Eugene H. Lovering Jr. Atlanta: Scholars Press, 1995.

———. "The 'Angels' and 'Giants' of Genesis 6:1–4 in Second and Third Century BCE Jewish Interpretation: Reflections on the Posture of Early Apocalyptic Traditions." *Dead Sea Discoveries* 7.3 (2000): 354–77.

———. *The Book of Giants from Qumran: Text, Translation, and Commentary.* Tübingen: Mohr Siebeck, 1997.

———. "Giant Mythology and Demonology: From Ancient Near East to the Dead Sea Scrolls." Pages 31–38 in *Demons: The Demonology of Israelite-Jewish and Early Christian Literature in Context of Their Environment.* Edited by Armin Lange, Hermann Lichtnberger, and K. F. Diethard Römheld. Tübingen: Mohr Siebeck, 2003.

———. "The Origins of Evil in Jewish Apocalyptic Tradition: The Interpretation of Genesis 6:1–4 in the Second and Third Centuries B.C.E." Pages 86–118 in *The Fall of the Angels.* Edited by Christoff Auffarth and Loren T. Stuckenbruck. Leiden: Brill, 2004.

———. "Why Should Women Cover Their Heads Because of Angels?" *Stone-Campbell Journal* 4 (2001): 205–34.

Sullivan, Kevin P. *Wrestling with Angels: A Study of the Relationship between Angels and Humans in Ancient Jewish Literature and the New Testament.* Leiden: Brill, 2004.

Tabor, James. "Firstborn of Many Brothers: A Pauline Notion of Apotheosis." Pages 295–303 in *Society of Biblical Literature Seminar Papers 21.* Chico, CA: Scholars Press, 1984.

Tigay, Jeffrey H. *Deuteronomy.* The JPS Torah Commentary. Philadelphia: Jewish Publication Society, 1996.

Van der Toorn, Karel, Bob Becking, and Pieter W. van der Horst, eds. *Dictionary of Deities and Demons in the Bible*. 2nd rev. ed. Grand Rapids: Eerdmans, 1999.

VanGemeren, Willem A., ed. *New International Dictionary of Old Testament Theology and Exegesis*. 5 vols. Grand Rapids: Zondervan, 1997.

Vaux, Roland de. *Ancient Israel: Its Life and Institutions*. Grand Rapids: Eerdmans, 1997.

Veijola, Timo. "The Witness in the Clouds: Ps 89:38." *Journal of Biblical Literature* 107.3 (1988): 413–17.

Vellanichal, Matthew. *The Divine Sonship of Christians in the Johannine Writings*. Rome: Pontifical Biblical Institute Press, 1977.

Vermes, Geza. "The Archangel Sariel: A Targumic Parallel to the Dead Sea Scrolls." Pages 159–66 in *Christianity, Judaism, and Other Greco-Roman Cults: Studies for Morton Smith at Sixty*. Edited by Jacob Neusner. Leiden: Brill, 1975.

Wallace, Daniel B. *Greek Grammar Beyond the Basics: Exegetical Syntax of the New Testament*. Grand Rapids: Zondervan, 1996.

Walton, John. "Demons in Mesopotamia and Israel: Exploring the Category of Non-Divine but Supernatural Entities." Pages 229–46 in *Windows to the Ancient World of the Hebrew Bible: Essays in Honor of Samuel Greengus*. Edited by Bill T. Arnold, Nancy L. Erickson, and John H. Walton. Winona Lake, IN: Eisenbrauns, 2014.

White, Ellen. *Yahweh's Council: Its Structure and Membership*. Tübingen: Mohr Siebeck, 2014.

Williams, A. L. "The Cult of Angels at Colossae." *Journal of Theological Studies* 10 (1909): 413–38.

Williams, Peter. *The Case for Angels*. Milton Keynes, UK: Paternoster Press, 2002.

Willis, Timothy M. "Yahweh's Elders (Isa 24,23): Senior Officials of the Divine Court." *Zeitschrift für die alttestamentliche Wissenschaft* 103.3 (1991): 375–85.

Wise, Michael O. "מי כמוני באלים: A Study of 4Q491c, 4Q471b, 4Q427 7, and 1QHa 25:25–26:10." *Dead Sea Discoveries* 7.2 (2000): 173–219.

Wojciechowski, Michal. "Seven Churches and Seven Celestial Bodies (Rev 1:16; Rev 2–3)." *Biblische Notizen* 45 (1988): 48–50.

Wood, Alice. *Of Wings and Wheels: A Synthetic Study of the Biblical Cherubim*. Berlin: De Gruyter, 2008.

Wright, Archie T. *The Origin of Evil Spirits: The Reception of Genesis 6:1–4 in Early Jewish Literature*. Tübingen: Mohr Siebeck, 2013.

Wyatt, N. *Space and Time in the Religious Life of the Near East*. Sheffield: Sheffield Academic Press, 2001.

Zatelli, Ida. "Astrology and the Worship of the Stars in the Bible." *Zeitschrift für die alttestamentliche Wissenschaft* 103.1 (1991): 86–99.

# Index of Subjects
# and Modern Authors

# Index of Scripture and Other Ancient Literature

## Malachi

## New Testament

### Matthew

### Mark

### Luke

## Deuterocanonical Works

### Tobit

## Wisdom of Solomon

## 2 Maccabees

## Old Testament Pseudepigrapha

### Apocalypse of Abraham

### Apocalypse of Elijah

### Apocalypse of Moses

### Apocalypse of Zephaniah

### Ascension of Isaiah

### Assumption of Moses

### 2 Baruch

### 3 Baruch

### 4 Baruch

### 1 Enoch

# Take your studies further into the Bible's supernatural worldview

Supernatural has piqued the interest of many readers, encouraging them to study the ancient worldview of the Bible. But there's much more to learn. In *The Unseen Realm*, Dr. Michael S. Heiser provides a full scholarly treatment of the same content, examining the subject in detail. It's perfect for expanding your studies into this vital area of biblical understanding.

Visit **TheUnseenRealm.com** to learn more.

LEXHAM PRESS

# *The Unseen Realm* made accessible for everyone

What the Bible teaches
about the unseen world —
and why it matters

## SUPER NATURAL

Michael S. Heiser

*The Unseen Realm* has opened the eyes of many readers to the supernatural worldview of the Bible. But not everyone is up to reading such a thorough academic book. In *Supernatural*, Dr. Michael S. Heiser presents the same content in a condensed format, making it easier to understand and digest. It's perfect for sharing with friends, family members, or congregants.

Visit **LexhamPress.com/Supernatural** to learn more.

LEXHAM PRESS